Advance

"In our fast-changing, volatile, and unpredictable world, we need leaders who embody a mindset of abundance and lead with compassion and purpose. Ashish's book Hardwired for Happiness presents a highly accessible and practical set of frameworks that we can all use to become more joyful, kinder, compassionate, and purposeful."

—Sundaram Nagarajan, President and CEO at Nordson Corporation

"Into our third year of the pandemic and an ever uncertain and complex world, Hardwired for Happiness brilliantly brings us back to the fundamentals. This book beautifully weaves in the latest breakthroughs from science, philosophy, and ancient spiritual wisdom to help leaders thrive and overcome their personal and professional challenges."

—Patrick Criteser, President and CEO at Tillamook

"Beautifully combining storytelling and research, Ashish Kothari provides a map that can help you find the path to your best self. A powerful and accessible guide."

—Tal Ben-Shahar, Co-founder of Happiness Studies Academy

"Through his life, Ashish achieved many summits of excellence. He has done it again. Ashish distilled the essence from hundreds of books and talks from great masters in the fields of psychology, neuroscience, and ancient wisdom, and from the book of his own life, to gift us an elegant guide to support us in taking a journey inward to living our best life. It is filled with simple yet powerful practices, supported by a wealth of references, research nuggets, and heartfelt stories. A book to keep by our bedside and return to frequently, using it as a life compass."

—Johanne Lavoie, Partner at McKinsey & Company, coauthor of
Centered Leadership: Leading with Purpose, Clarity, and Impact

"Hardwired for Happiness is a fascinating journey in which Ashish offers a well-carved path to help you move from living outside in to inside out. The book is also an excellent collection of some of the most impactful insights from contemplative thought leaders. Written in a simple, conversational language, the book will as much appeal to your brain as it will touch your heart."

—Amit Sood, MD, Executive Director and CEO at the Global Center for Resiliency and Wellbeing

"With Hardwired for Happiness, Ashish Kothari has given us a foundational and sweeping description of the embodied path to awakening and joy. His offering is at one moment intimate, raw, and a deeply truthful portrayal of his own journey as a seeker and student of truth, and at another moment the output of his years of scholarship and study of the disciplines of well-being from sleep to diet to movement to prayer. This beautiful book is a companion on the journey that can guide one through the cultivation of mature emotional and spiritual intelligence and the development of a truly generous and open heart. The fruits of this inner work are well captured throughout the book in chapters on compassion, kindness, and the path of living with intention. In a truly timely way Ashish will help meet those of us turning afresh to the profound questions of meaning, purpose, community, and service. I urge you not to miss this gem."

—Amy Elizabeth Fox, Chief Executive Officer at Mobius Executive Leadership

"Rich and compelling from page one! Forget about the typical self-help tutorial—this is a life-changing read. Ashish literally unlocks the secrets to living a fuller and freer life! Grounded in solid research, it offers a practical and easy-to-follow roadmap to help anyone become the best version of themselves."

—Rob McCutcheon, President at Husqvarna North America

"Authentic, compassionate, practical. In this timely book, Ashish shares his own journey with vulnerability and offers a highly accessible approach that everyone can use to become better versions of ourselves and achieve our full potential."

—Carl-Martin Lindahl, CEO and
Board Director at SVP Worldwide

"Today, organizations win by providing personalized and meaningful professional experiences for their workforce. Hardwired for Happiness is a master class for progressive leaders who aspire to align culture and values with people to create a supportive workplace—and business—that thrives."

—Shannon Sisler, Executive Vice President,
Chief People Officer at Crocs

"Kothari masterfully provides an insightful and probing method of self-discovery that encourages one to delve into practices that foster a greater sense of inner fulfillment and joy. This book is truly impactful in bringing transformative awareness in how we approach situations and relationships. Hardwired for Happiness is a must-read that easily becomes a trusted resource for continuing to grow meaningful and inspirational connections with others."

—Christy Bradley Orazi,
Chief Procurement officer at MUFG

"Hardwired for Happiness offers a blueprint for living a rich and intentional life. The nine-step practice that Ashish has laid out allows you to live from within and let go of fear, anxiety, anger, and resentment. For me, it established a strong framework for happiness, making better decisions, and, more importantly, allowing me to self-reflect and be more self-aware. It's a must-read for a mindful leader!"

—Amish Patel, Vice President—Technology Platforms, Cloud,
and Exponential Engineering at Anthem

"Insightful, well researched, engaging! So many insights that are practical and easily applicable to everyday life. Ashish combines research and personal stories to make a book that is easy to read and understand all the concepts. I highly recommend it to all the people who are interested in becoming their best self."

—Soma Somasundaram, President and CEO at Champion X

"In a firm of exceptional problem-solvers, Ashish Kothari has cracked the code on how to solve virtually any problem. His nine-part approach draws on the disciplines of neuroscience, psychology, philosophy, and leadership to provide a path through the darkness created by our fear-based mindsets. It has been a joy to see Ashish apply his nine practices in his own life and I am so glad he is now sharing his wisdom with the rest of the world."

—Victoria Bough, Partner at McKinsey & Company

"What an honest capture of the inner turmoil we feel every day of our lives, though we have everything: the emptiness, the 'rat race,' and above all, the fear of losing it all. With this book, Hardwired for Happiness, Ashish has truly provided simple and impactful tools to challenge ourselves and break out of the cycle or 'perceived scarcity,' and his own life journey makes it so honest. This is a courageous approach that reignites the joy of living, enjoying every moment, and above all, feeling free!"

—Sumit Dangi, CFO and Treasurer at Jewelers Mutual Insurance

"Simple, straightforward, and from the heart! Hardwired for Happiness is a must-read for leaders looking to navigate the future filled with lots of unaddressed complexity and uncertainty. This book demystifies the science behind our fears, and will allow us to face and master our fears rather than ignore them to thrive and be more effective. Ashish's journey, his story, his perspectives, and the nine practices that he espouses will help create work–life harmony so that you can work well by living well."

—Dhiraj Rajaram, CEO at Mu Sigma

"A great read on self-reflection and leader development and on life in general! I warmly recommend this book to anyone who wants to reorient themselves on a path to deeper meaning, mindfulness, well-being, contentment, and gratitude."

—Rasmus Hougaard, Managing Partner at Potential Project and author of *Compassionate Leadership: How to Do Hard Things in a Human Way*

"Meeting Ashish in early 2021 was like a ray of sunshine in the midst of the global pandemic. He would join our calls from his home in Colorado, full of energy despite it often being very early in the morning for him. We immediately connected over a shared mission—helping people live a better life. We shared personal stories, discussed the latest research in health and well-being, and put our heads together to come up with concrete ways to help our colleagues. This book, I believe, is a great reflection of the Ashish I came to know: his intellectual curiosity, deep personal reflections, and a quest to give individuals some concrete tools to help them in their journey. An inward journey from fear to freedom, and towards a better life."

—Annastiina Hintsa, CEO at Hintsa Performance

"Hardwired for Happiness provides valuable tools to get in touch and truly (re)discover yourself. Ashish lays out nine simple yet powerful practices and beautifully describes each practice in detail while providing users with practical ways to put that into daily use (i.e., journaling, meditation, community practice, etc.). The book addresses delicate and complex subjects, yet is written so well that it's an easy read. This is not just another book, it should serve as your life's reference manual."

—Gautam Jha, Director at American Securities

HARDWIRED FOR HAPPINESS

9 Proven Practices to Overcome Stress and Live Your Best Life

ASHISH KOTHARI

HOUNDSTOOTH
PRESS

Hardwired for Happiness

9 Proven Practices to Overcome Stress and Live Your Best Life

ISBN 978-1-5445-3466-4 Hardcover
     978-1-5445-3465-7 Paperback
     978-1-5445-3464-0 Ebook

A Poem from Your Future Self

My own path now has been repaved, a sense of
renewal and courage holds me tall

As I step forth, each stone below a jewel gleaming
with ever brighter color and brilliance

For I have rediscovered my happiness and the
ease from whence it came

The sun's warmth touches my back, propelling me
forward on the path of my true calling

As the wind stirs me, I feel joyous in anticipation
of all those I can help

My eyes soften with acceptance and gratitude from
where I've come to where I am going

A journey like no other, to cherish, to behold,
with peace and wisdom inside…

—LIZZIE KOTHARI

Thank you for purchasing my book, *Hardwired for Happiness: 9 Proven Practices to Overcome Stress and Live Your Best Life.*

Please use this QR code to reach the Happiness Squad website, learn more about us and get access to the following:

- Digital wallpaper for your desktop, laptop and phone of the 9 practices
- Weekly blog highlighting some tips and tricks to rewire your brain for happiness
- Joining the exclusive Happiness Squad community getting you connected with others like yourself on their journey inwards
- Latest news on new initiatives we are launching to support you on your journey
- Our full range of services to support individuals and organizations in Hardwiring for happiness

About Happiness Squad

Our Purpose: *Catalyzing human flourishing to unlock full potential (at individual, team, company and community level)*

Our Mission: *Launch a happiness revolution touching a billion+ lives over the next 20 years and help them live with more joy, health, love and meaning*

How to reach us:

Website: www.happinesssquad.com

Email: info@happinesssquad.com

Contents

Introduction

We live in a world of four major paradoxes. First, we exist in a time of abundance and are more prosperous than ever, with most people in middle class enjoying more comforts and conveniences than kings and queens of the past. However, we are not necessarily more joyful or satisfied. Studies show that happiness among adults has been on a slow decline over the past twenty years. Americans who consider themselves in "excellent" mental health fell from 43 percent to just 34 percent in 2019, according to a Gallup poll.[1] We experience heaviness, meaninglessness, and even the smallest things can trigger and upset us.

Second, we are living longer than ever but not necessarily in better health. Breakthroughs in medicine have extended our life span as we have found cures and eliminated most of the diseases caused by external organisms (microbes and viruses) that used to kill us one hundred years ago, like influenza, tuberculosis, and diphtheria.[2] Today, the top three causes of death are heart disease, cancer, and stroke, which are primarily lifestyle related. Approximately 85 percent of older adults have at least one chronic health condition, and 60 percent have at least two chronic conditions, according to the Centers for Disease Control and Prevention.[3]

Third, major advances in technology have connected us globally, significantly increased our pace of communication, and allowed us to collaborate over long distances. A century ago, it took two weeks for a post to arrive from England to the United States. Today with email or text messages, we can communicate across the world within seconds. Not only that, with Google translate, it is possible today for me to talk to someone in China even if I don't understand Mandarin, and they don't understand English. This speed and ease of communication should allow us to better understand other perspectives, resolve differences, and come closer. But global tension and distrust has never been higher. Across the world, we are seeing a rise of nationalist sentiment and anti-globalization movements. We are also lonelier as individuals than ever, with a 2018 report from Cigna and Edelman highlighting that 61 percent of Americans reported feeling lonely, up from 54 percent the previous year.[4]

Fourth, technology has made everyday tasks much more efficient. Think about how complicated it was to book a trip to another city twenty years ago: you would have to call a travel agent, who would look up the available options, share them with you, and then you'd wait two weeks for paper tickets to arrive in the mail. Today you can go on a travel-booking website like Kayak or Travelocity and complete the whole process in less than five minutes. The same is true for things like banking, ordering food, hailing taxis, and the list goes on. Yet despite these conveniences, we are busier than ever. Our modern, fast-paced world comes at a steep price: each day feels like a race against the clock, executing a long list of "to dos" and collapsing every night, exhausted, in front of a screen with more bad news. We often feel like boats lost at sea, at the mercy of the winds and waves, without a North Star to guide us. When we come face-to-face with obstacles, we are reactive and defensive. Our anxiety has manifested into a perennial state of stress, exhaustion, and fatigue.

So what explains these four paradoxes that are a core part of modern existence? I believe these paradoxes are a direct result of our brains being maladapted to the world we are living in. The very intelligence that allowed the human species to climb to the top of the food chain—despite not being the strongest or the largest—has turned against us. You see, neurobiologically, we are wired to look for danger. Our brains evolved to keep our bodies safe and alive, not necessarily to keep us content and joyful. Up until around 20,000 years ago, before we as humans settled down, our ability to sense a saber-toothed tiger hiding in the shadows and react with lightning speed made all the difference between life and death. We *had* to choose fight or flight to survive.

Today, dangerous wild predators have been replaced by an increasingly complex modern existence: balancing a demanding career with equally busy family life, absorbing the 24/7 news and social media cycle that is filled with bad news (because bad news sells!). We see (on continuous replay) reports of volatile and uncertain wars breaking out, climate change driving fires or floods, and weekly if not daily reports of shootings and violence. Feeling the world is spinning out of our control, we are constantly triggered multiple times in a day. Our brains have a hard time separating physical threats from those to our fragile egos and still react in the same way: fight or flight. We find ourselves constantly trying to make sense of it all and desperate to stay safe. The truth is, despite all our resources, we are living in a heightened state of psychological scarcity and fear—a fear of not being smart or successful enough, a fear of being left behind, a fear of not being loved. As a result of this scarcity and fear mindset, we may experience some joy when things go our way, but the *mood* of joyfulness is not accessible to us.

■ ■ ■

I grew up in a middle-class family in India and was blessed to have wonderful parents who prioritized my care, education, and stability. From an early age, they instilled in my younger sister and me the core values of family, hard work, and academic excellence. Mathematics came easily to me, and I remember conversations with my parents about my report cards that mixed congratulations for my high marks with gentle encouragement to do better. From the age of eleven my singular focus was to earn an engineering degree after high school. I studied relentlessly and felt only as good as my next test score.

Despite growing up in the birthplace of Yoga and Buddhism, I became hardwired to follow a traditional path of "success" that measured my grades, where I went to school, and the prestige of the companies that hired me. My passport to a better life was the opportunity to escape to the United States, which I did after university when I applied for a computer science job at IBM. At age twenty-three, I walked out of Chicago's O'Hare International Airport with $5,000 and the name of another Indian programmer I had never met. I spent the next twenty years seeking happiness through professional and financial success. I worked sixty to one hundred hours each week, traveling extensively across two to three cities. I had unconsciously normalized an unhealthy level of work to climb the ladder and was afraid of slipping down if I stopped moving.

At forty-two, I had checked all the items that were supposed to bring me happiness: I met my wife, Lizzie and had our son, Ashwin. I had built a wonderful network of friends, mentors, and colleagues. I worked for the most prestigious consulting firm in the world, which also brought great pride to my parents. My work was highly impactful: generating significant return on investment on fees that clients paid for our services. And I had moved to Boulder, Colorado, which some described as "a town nestled within mountains and reality." I should have been blissfully happy and satisfied, yet I continued to hustle faster, harder, and longer.

In truth, I lived in a state of high anxiety and stress. I had built a deep expertise with over 20,000 hours of consulting work in a field that no longer brought me happiness and in fact was incoherent with my own views. I had gained weight over the years and no longer slept well. Each day left me feeling emptier, but I was frozen in place by fear. I wanted to change my area of expertise but wasn't sure what would bring me joy. Then there were all the doubts and fears that arise when one contemplates a change: What if I did something different and failed at it? Would I disappoint those who had supported me? Would I maintain the same lifestyle for my family?

Then opportunity knocked. I was invited to a leadership program at McKinsey & Company that was designed to create space for introspection and self-awareness, foster connection, and increase effectiveness. The program was held at a site that housed one of the oldest monasteries in Europe. Over the next five days, leveraging the techniques I learned and supported by the mystical, spiritual energy that surrounded me, I discovered three key insights which would change the trajectory of my life.

First, I realized I was happiest and most energetic when I was building and maintaining connections and making a positive impact in people's lives. Second, I saw that I sought safety and success in the external world at the cost of driving emptiness within. I was also exposed to techniques like mindfulness and journaling that had a dramatic effect on my overall effectiveness and how I experienced life. I understood that if I could break away from my fears and shed the layers of armor I had donned to hide them, I could unlock more joy and lightness in my life. Third, I was not alone. Everyone in the class came alive. I realized how quickly relationships develop and love flourishes when we release our deep fears and let others see us as the beautiful, imperfect humans we all are.

Together, these insights helped me discover my personal *Ikigai*, or reason for being. A Japanese word dating back to the Heian period (794 to 1185), *Ikigai* is the intersection of what you love, what you are good at, what the world needs, and is willing to pay for. I was going to dedicate the rest of my life to helping others flourish and find happiness to unlock their human potential and live their best lives, too.

The fields of psychology, neurosciences, and ancient wisdom traditions were completely new to me. Luckily, I was grateful to be at a wonderful company that allowed me to go part time (70 percent) to pursue my passion. The next five years were a tremendous period of personal growth and learning. I read over 500 books and listened to more than 2,000 hours of lectures from thought leaders. I took courses in ontological coaching, neurosciences, and psychology, as well as studying with mystical teachers from the East, and I formally trained to become a coach myself. I turned myself into a living laboratory, continuously experimenting with new techniques and practices. I didn't accept anything unless it worked and made a difference in my life.

Two decades in consulting meant I was really well-versed in the art and science of helping organizations and people make sustainable shifts in their behaviors and habits to achieve their goals. I had used this to help my clients make substantial and long-lasting improvements in performance, whether it was driving revenue improvements, reducing costs, or increasing the speed of execution. I was going to turn that expertise into helping people integrate what I was learning from these new fields to transform their lives, too. I began helping my clients and colleagues using these techniques through one-on-one coaching sessions. Eventually, at my company, I helped create a brand-new leadership program to support leaders and organizations build adaptability and resilience capabilities to combat rising stress, fatigue, and burnout (specifically from the raging pandemic). On this journey of personal growth, we could help design organizations where people could operate without fear, show up fully, and deliver high performance not at the expense of wellbeing, but because of it.

An ancient Cherokee tale describes a grandfather and his grandson having a conversation about life. "I have a fight going on inside me," the old man says. "It's taking place between two wolves. One is evil—he is anger, envy, sorrow, regret, greed, arrogance, self-pity, guilt, resentment, inferiority, lies, false pride, superiority, and ego."

The grandfather looks at his grandson and continues. "The other wolf embodies positive emotions. He is joy, peace, love, hope, serenity, humility, kindness, benevolence, empathy, generosity, truth, compassion, and faith. Both wolves are fighting to the death. The same fight is going on inside you, too."

The grandson takes a moment to reflect on this. At last, he looks up at his grandfather and asks, "Which wolf will win?"

The old Cherokee says, simply, "The one you feed."

Over the course of this book, I will introduce you to nine practices that will enable you to feed the good wolf on your own journey toward connection, fulfillment, and happiness. As I learned the hard way, trying to fit into an external model of success only keeps you in a place of fear, always afraid of not being enough. If you can tune inward and use your internal compass, you can rewire your brain to seek joy, health, love, and meaning.

Introduction to the Nine Key Practices
That Help Us Become Happier

Each of the nine practices are supported through both scientific research in the fields of psychology and neurosciences, as well as through teachings from ancient wisdom traditions like Buddhism and the Yoga Sutras. Furthermore, I will share evidence of the positive impact of these on the lives of 1,000+ leaders across different fields whom I have supported/ coached over my career. Throughout the book I will share examples from my own life as well as stories from others to demonstrate the great benefits of these practices and to inspire you to forge ahead on your own journey.

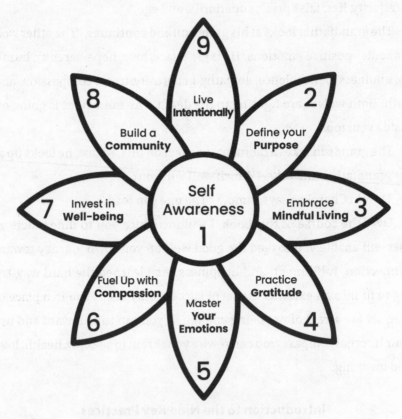

Figure 0.1: Hardwired for happiness practices

Practice 1: Cultivate Self-Awareness to Know Who You Really Are

We are all unique observers who are shaped by the broader cultural contexts in which we grew up: what we learned from our parents, teachers, and role models; and schooled by our own life experiences. In this practice, you will understand who you really are and develop strategies to move past the fears that hold you back. You will deepen your awareness of your starting point as well as habitual responses to stressors; pause to create space; and choose a more conscious response driven not from fear but freedom to evolve into what life is asking from you.

Practice 2: Define Your Purpose

Viktor Frankl, an Auschwitz survivor and the father of logotherapy, which describes a search for a life meaning as the central human motivational force, said, "Ever more people today have the means to live, but no meaning to live for." Discovering your personal purpose is critical and will become your North Star to guide you when you are lost in the ever-increasing complexity of the world. In this practice you will discover your personal "why" to reveal your core values and beliefs. These are the guiding lights to illuminate the path ahead of you.

Practice 3: Embrace Mindful Living

We are blessed with the highest developed brains of any species on Earth. Unfortunately, for most of us, our minds are crowded with too many thoughts all running in different directions. We are unable to focus on any given thought as it is happening, and therefore miss out on the enjoyment at that moment. According to Harvard University research, 47 percent of study participants had a wandering mind, which directly related to their unhappiness. The good news is that all of us are born with the ability to refocus using mindfulness and use this superpower to transform any experience, day to day, moment to moment.

Practice 4: Practice Gratitude

In our haste to accumulate more, be more, and do more, we lose track of all the good that we already have and what truly matters to us. By consciously developing a gratitude practice, you will redirect your energies toward more "being" and less "doing," and break free from the golden shackles that bind you to goals and belongings that no longer nourish you. In the words of Willie Nelson, "When I started counting my blessings, my whole life turned around."

Practice 5: Master Your Moods and Emotions

We are blessed with a rich memory and a vivid imagination, but these gifts can also cause suffering and high levels of anxiety. Too often we remain stuck in the past, reliving negative events, or obsess over controlling our future, imagining all that can go wrong. At its worst, those experiences can become rooted in our bodies and harden our hearts, closing us off from growth and joy. This practice introduces radical acceptance to open your heart and create lightness and new possibilities in your future life.

Practice 6: Fuel Up with Compassion and Kindness

Practicing self-compassion is of utmost importance, especially at the beginning of your journey of self-discovery. You must give yourself permission to make mistakes. This practice begins with you, introducing simple techniques that allow you to stoke the flame of love and compassion that is universal in us all, from the moment you wake up to the very end of your day. Only through compassion for yourself are you able to offer kindness and generosity to others, which in turn fills your life with satisfaction, trust, and optimism. As the Dalai Lama said, "Love and compassion are necessities, not luxuries. Without them humanity cannot survive."

Practice 7: Invest in Your Wellbeing

In this practice you will learn to invest in your physical, mental, and spiritual wellbeing to thrive and perform at your very best. You'll consider how much daily movement your body needs, what and how you eat, and minimize the effects of aging. You will refocus and break your dopamine addictions, recharging your brain every night through better quality and quantity of sleep, and make learning a lifelong habit. You will integrate play into your daily life, create space to spend time with loved ones, and deepen your personal connection to the universe.

Practice 8: Strengthen Your Community

We are social beings biologically wired for connection. When we are young, we depend on our family relationships and thrive on friendships and joy that come from play. As we grow up, there just does not seem to be enough time to keep up with those social connections, and in the blink of an eye, decades pass by and our relationships atrophy. This practice will help you build and strengthen a vibrant group of friends and connections, whether it's three or 300, who will share in your successes and support you when you need to get back on your feet.

Practice 9: Live with Intention

In the hustle and bustle of our daily lives, we lose track of what truly matters to us. We make an unconscious over-investment in our careers and the pursuit of "more," and we get used to making regular withdrawals from the areas that offer tangible returns in the short term. Keeping what truly matters to us front and center and allocating our time and energy accordingly to live in coherence and harmony with our dreams is critical. Learning to live intentionally allows you to practice setting intentions and to form new habits that will enable you to live into those commitments, in service of making the shift you want to make.

. . .

Overcoming our deeply rooted fears of not having enough, doing enough, or *being* enough is a lifelong journey, with many challenges along the way. It is common to feel anger, anxiety, uncertainty, lethargy, shame, guilt, and frustration as you bump up against each hurdle. As you start to stretch into new possibilities, it's human nature to pull back to the comfort zone you know (even if it doesn't actually bring you much "comfort").

However, if you are willing to commit to taking the journey inward, the benefits and rewards are life changing. The fear and anxiety melt away, and you begin flowing smoothly like water through any obstacle or resistance. Professionally, you will achieve higher successes with lower levels of effort, as you tap into the power of your teams by creating a higher level of psychological safety. When you are not leading from a place of fear but have a deeper inner compass guiding you toward what matters, you will be able to help others in a similar journey. In turn, together you will be able to harness the collective wisdom of your team to truly drive a step change in performance. You will be able to become joyful and happy regardless of the external environment around you.

A life free of fear is hard won, but all the richer for it.

My Journey

"Ever more people today have the means to live,
but no meaning to live for."
—Viktor Frankl

S ix years ago, I had the good fortune of discovering my purpose for being, my *Ikigai*, something that was worth doing even if I failed: supporting and empowering others in hardwiring for happiness so they could fill their lives with more joy, health, meaning, and love. Living my life from the inside out guided by my passions, values, and strengths versus outside in has had a profound effect on my life. It is my hope that as you read about my experiences you will see glimpses of yourself, glean the courage and conviction to make similar changes in your life, and self-author your own story. My journey is far from complete—in fact, it is not at the beginning of the end; it is at the end of the beginning.

Growing up, as young as age seven, I remember conversations with my mother and father going over my annual report cards. It was a mix of congratulations for the scores I got (which were usually in the 90-plus percent), my class rank (usually number two to four), gentle encourage-ment, and a push that I could do better. My parents never said outright that I had to be number one, but I felt a huge responsibility to make them proud. They had made many sacrifices to support my education. All the parents I knew would regularly ask about our grades and how well we were doing at school.

During the late seventies and eighties, India was still a closed economy experiencing slow growth. There were few opportunities for the younger generation, and competition was fierce. The best and brightest pursued a science path with a focus on engineering or medicine. Mathematics came easy to me, thanks to my parents—my mother was a state gold medalist with a PhD in mathematics, and my father placed first in his state in engineering college. From the age of eleven, my singular focus became getting an engineering degree after high school.

Despite having grown up in a country known for its rich spiritual history, I knew nothing of those wise teachings. For 2,000 years, ancient wisdom held true that the "best way out of suffering was IN." To me, the best way out of suffering was "IIT," or the Indian Institute of Technology. It was one of the most prestigious engineering colleges, and getting in was no easy task. Every year, 200,000 students competed for only 2,000 spots.

During high school, I studied for two to twelve hours every day. After school I would come home, rest, do my homework, go to a coaching class, eat dinner, study a bit more, and then go to bed. There was almost no time for games, hobbies, or other extracurricular activities. I read college-level books on calculus, solid mechanics, and other advanced subjects. Even my weekends included at least one day of coaching classes. Normalizing an intense work week had only just begun for me.

My hard work paid off though, and I secured a placement at IIT Bombay in 1991. I could write a whole book on my experiences at IIT, the fun times we had, the troubles we got into, and the friends I made, but there are three key ways in which I began to self-identify. Until college, I had been in the top three in my class, consistently scoring 90 percent or more on all my exams. Now, in the company of some of the brightest people in my country,

I realized I was nothing special. In my first year at IIT, where grading was on a curve, I secured just 60 percent. My fears of not being good enough and disappointing my parents overwhelmed me, and I doubled down on my efforts to compete against the raw brilliance surrounding me. Slowly but surely I climbed my way back to the top, eventually finishing second in my class. This solidified my resolve to work harder than anyone else to excel and be worthy. I would regularly put in sixty-plus hours of studying in order to complete my assignments and get high marks. To escape the stress and loneliness of this grueling academic life, I turned to alcohol, cigarettes, and food. Booze-fueled dinners on weekends at local bars and restaurants were the norm on campus, and I fell right into it. Some of my closest friendships were formed over drinks, and it allowed me to finally relax and enjoy the company of those around me.

The end goal of college was to get a job in the land of opportunity—the United States. I was studying chemical engineering but had no interest in pursuing a doctorate, as many of my classmates did. I had recently discovered the world of computer programming, and I knew there was a rising demand for this role in the United States. In my final year, I applied for and landed a job with IBM. Six months later, they put me on a flight to Chicago with $5,000 and the name of another Indian programmer living in the United States. Just like that, not knowing a soul other than my paternal aunt who lived in New Jersey, I walked out of Chicago's O'Hare airport in 1997.

Between 1997–2005, I climbed the corporate ladder in steadfast pursuit of the American Dream. I poured my blood, sweat, and tears into work to chase promotions and pay raises so I could buy myself all the comforts, luxuries, and accolades to be happy. I had become so "Americanized" that my mother used to joke that the only thing Indian about me was my looks, and my love for Indian food and Indian movies. I moved from IBM to

Keane, KPMG, Deloitte, and Charter Consulting, and along the way, I also completed my MBA part time at the University of Chicago. But my fears were always just below the surface: that I wasn't good enough, or that I'd be discovered as an impostor. I could only prevent others from ever finding out the "truth" if I outworked them. I regularly worked 100–120 hours per week between my job and pursuing my MBA. I climbed and climbed to be the best, to feel worthy.

I had normalized a new, unhealthy level of working, but I also discovered a deep joy from building relationships and helping others in any way I could. I don't know what initiated the shift, or maybe there was always something in me that just needed to come to the forefront. My circle of friends exploded from about ten to one hundred during business school. Twenty years later, I am still in touch with most of them. Today, among my MBA friends, work colleagues, clients, neighbors, and others in my personal and professional circles, my connections have grown to over 1,000 people. I feel so privileged to stay in touch with this amazing set of people along my life's journey. I believe this is how the seed for my deeper purpose in life, my *Ikigai,* was sown.

In 2005, I had the good fortune of joining McKinsey & Company, the leading consulting firm in the world. What followed was a terrific period of personal and professional growth, working with some of the best and brightest minds in a highly values-driven culture that promoted high collaboration, drive for excellence, team spirit over individualism, and servant leadership. In seven years, I rose from associate to partner. I had arrived.

It was at McKinsey where I met and fell in love with Lizzie, who was a talented recruiter and an amazing human being. We were married in 2008 and had our son, Ashwin, in 2010. Life was great. I had built a wonderful network of friends, mentors, and colleagues. I had built a reputation and expertise in procurement, a field that allowed me to have high-impact opportunities to serve clients. I worked for the most prestigious consulting firm in the world, which brought great pride to my parents. I lived very comfortably. In 2014, my family and I moved to Boulder, Colorado, which has rightly been described as "a town nestled within mountains and reality." I had even gotten my US citizenship.

By the time I turned forty, I had achieved the American Dream and then some. According to my own definition of success, I should have been blissfully happy.

At McKinsey, I built a deep functional expertise with over 20,000 hours in the field of procurement and driving sustainable change by building capabilities and transforming culture. My group was typically able to deliver results that were measurable in reduced operating costs generating high return on investment on our fees, often within the budget period. I enjoyed the tight-knit group and deep, caring culture at the firm. I also appreciated building trust-based relationships with clients and supporting them in executing bold strategies that they might not have implemented on their own. I was proud of the impact we were driving, but I was getting bored from the sameness of the actions needed to extract the most savings from suppliers for my clients. It was not coherent with how I lived my personal life. Here I was trying to encourage the clients to go for every penny they could capture from negotiations, when in my personal life, I didn't even negotiate when buying a car, something almost everyone does. Spending so much time doing something that didn't carry personal value started to feel like a chore. It lost more appeal when compared to the time I was spending away from my wife and fast-growing son.

The long hours, high amount of travel, and unhealthy lifestyle were also starting to take a toll on my body. I was on the road four days a week, often traveling across two to three cities. Eating and drinking with my team once again became my reward for my hard work. In my thirties and forties, I didn't handle the excess as well as I had in college. My weight crept up over 200 pounds, and I started to get aches and pains. I developed sleep apnea and needed a CPAP machine to get a good night's sleep. I often woke up curled in a ball, unable to shake a pervasive mood of anxiety and high stress.

On paper my life looked perfect, but inside I was a mess. Going into work each day felt like diving into an abyss. I just couldn't see myself doing that for the next twenty-plus years. I knew I wanted to shift my work away from procurement, but I didn't really feel strongly about what I wanted to shift it *to*. Yes, other departments could be exciting, but I'd be coming in with zero experience. I could just leave McKinsey and take a corporate role with lesser hours and travel, but I would miss the amazing culture. I'd also be starting from scratch.

I was kept frozen in place by fear: fear of disappointing others who had supported me in making partner; fear of not being able to develop an expertise in a new area and failing; fear of not being able to take care of my family; or having to move us to a less desirable city. So I remained stuck in place, day after day, week after week, month after month. My fears pulled me back, and I hadn't yet developed a strong enough force to move me elsewhere.

There is a saying attributed to the Buddha that when "the student is ready, the teacher will appear." For me, those teachers were Johanne Lavoie and Amy Fox. Johanne was a partner at McKinsey and an expert in leadership development, focused on helping executives develop human-centered organizations. Amy was the founder and CEO of Mobius Executive Leadership, a premier coaching, training, and leadership development company. Together they ran a leadership program at McKinsey called Mastering Leadership Development, and I was lucky to be accepted into the program. The program was held at a site that housed one of the oldest monasteries in Europe and was designed to create space for introspection and self-awareness, to foster connection, and to teach several techniques—including mindfulness—to increase leadership effectiveness.

Over five days, in that mystical, spiritual place, I discovered my personal *Ikigai*, or reason for being. I decided I would spend the rest of my life helping others thrive, live with more joy, health, meaning, and love, and unlock their full human potential.

Finally, realizing my own deeper purpose brought forth a tremendous surge of energy that propelled me forward. Now that I knew what I wanted to do, I had to figure out how I would get there. The first thing I had to do was create time and space in my busy life so I could upskill myself in this new domain. I connected with some of the leaders at McKinsey and got permission to go part time (70 percent) and pursue my passion.

The fields of psychology, neurosciences, and ancient wisdom traditions were completely new to me, and I wanted to learn from the best. I enrolled in the ontological coaching program taught by Julio Olalla and his daughter, Veronica Love, at the Newfield Network. I undertook a ten-day silent meditation Vipassana training, and completed two programs with a well-renowned Indian mystic, Sadhguru. In addition, I completed courses through organizations like Coaches Rising, including the neuroscience of change and the art of development coaching. Over the next four years, I read more than 500 books and listened to over 2,000 hours of lectures from thought leaders in the field of growing human flourishing.

I turned myself into a living laboratory, continuously experimenting with new techniques and practices that I learned from my training. I didn't want to accept anything on face value, only if it worked and made a difference in my life. I also started to notice common patterns and underlying beliefs across the works of different leaders, from ancient spirituality to modern psychology. The words may have been different, but the insight and results were the same. In parallel, I also started coaching clients and colleagues to help them overcome their own obstacles and struggles. Many of them felt the same: worried about not being enough, struggling to balance work and life, searching for meaning, struggling with resentment, anger, and anxiety. I shared the knowledge I'd gleaned and worked with them to test the different interventions and tools that I had experimented with myself. Over time, it became the framework for *Hardwired for Happiness,* which I have filled with the tools and practices to generate maximum impact for readers.

I also connected with my mentors and sponsors in procurement. I explained the shift I wanted to make and gained their support. I handed off initiatives to other leaders so I could singularly focus on scaling our leadership programs across clients to create human-centered organizations. I wanted to help design organizations where people could operate without fear, show up fully, and deliver high performance not at the expense of their wellbeing, but *because* of it. The fears that had always held me back earlier did not fully go away, but I found the courage to move forward and answer Brené Brown's question, "What is worth doing even if you fail?"

With their support, I joined the Leadership service line within McKinsey and found a family of lovely colleagues who shared my passion for human development and self-growth. Together we created a brand-new leadership program to help leaders and organizations build adaptability and resilience capabilities to combat rising stress, fatigue, and burnout resulting from the raging pandemic. I integrated many of the practices I had experimented with to test the impact of bringing more awareness, purpose, love, connectivity, and wellbeing into the lives of individuals and the organizations they were leading.

Over the following years, I supported over 1,000 clients through a mix of facilitated workshop-based learning journeys and one-on-one coaching. I experimented with different modalities of instruction including live and virtual workshops, completely digital participant-led journeys, digital interventions through nudges, and creating learning communities. I also got involved with our Center for Societal Benefit (now part of McKinsey Health Institute), where I got to learn and contribute to creating the first-ever "mental health in the workplace" survey, and a playbook of interventions to help employers assess the state of wellbeing for their employees and take actions to improve it.

As the COVID-19 pandemic raged on, I was moved by the high degree of human suffering I witnessed. Our own surveys as well as other industry leaders showed high degrees of stress and anxiety, with up to 60 percent of employees in many cases reporting burnout. I felt called by the universe to take all my learnings on human thriving and bring them to the world to help as many people and organizations as I could. It was this drive and call to service that inspired me to write this book in 2021, and it's behind the launch of my new company "Happiness Squad," which aims to help individual leaders and organizations unleash the power of happiness and human thriving to achieve their fullest potential.

Even though I am still early in my journey, I already feel a dramatic shift in how I experience life. The heaviness, emptiness, fatigue, anxiety, and stress have been replaced with calm, focused energy, happiness, and joy. My practice of writing a gratitude journal every night has transformed my state of being so I am no longer triggered when things don't go well. My mindfulness practice has allowed me to be more effective through holding my focus on the task at hand. In addition, when I find my mind wandering to the past or future, I can consciously bring it back to the present moment. By changing my diet and integrating exercise, I have lost thirty pounds and gained huge stores of energy.

In the chapters that follow, I am excited to share the nine practices that have made the biggest difference for me, my colleagues, and my clients. I will share practical tips on how you can integrate these into your day-to-day lives. It is my sincere hope that just like me, these practices will help you rewire your brain to seek happiness, not fear. My invitation for you is to join me as we walk together on a path of self-discovery, happiness, and limitless potential.

Foreword

Getting the Most Out of This Book

In his book *Man's Search for Meaning*, Viktor Frankl wrote that success cannot be pursued; it must ensue. Happiness works the same way; it must *ensue*. Research conducted by Sonja Lyubomirsky, one of the prominent thought leaders in the field, reports that while just 10 percent of happiness is circumstantially driven (what is happening to us), 40 percent is driven by our conscious choices, and 50 percent of happiness is driven by our set point, or our outlook on life (is the glass half full or half empty?). I fundamentally believe that happiness is a mindset—an inner game that everyone has the ability to develop and master if they put in the effort. No matter what genetics you inherited, where you grew up, or what has happened to you thus far, you can feel happier and get more out of life by transforming your mindset using the nine specific practices in this book.

Now you might feel overwhelmed at the thought of adding *nine* new habits to your already busy life. Don't worry! First, I am a big proponent of integration versus addition. As you read these practices, you'll find tips to how you can integrate each practice into "what you already do" versus "doing something completely different." Second, each practice is broken down into micropractices—something you can do in five minutes or less. If you are willing to commit to five minutes daily as a start, over time these micropractices will become habits and get hardwired into your brain. Finally, to maximize your success, choose only one or two practices at a time, starting with the ones you feel fit your personality and interests. Commit to the practices and be deliberate, consistent, and persistent in their execution to make them into habits. To keep the practices fresh and interesting, I've included three different types of exercises for each practice: journaling (writing and processing), meditation (creating a silent space within for the wisdom to emerge), and community (engaging with others and talking things through).

Establishing Your Starting Point

There are several widely accepted scales for measuring happiness and lots of debate on which is the most accurate one. No scale is perfect, and we should not let perfection be the enemy of progress. The actual number matters less—what matters more is the overall direction in which your life is going and whether you feel more or less happy over time.

I have chosen the Oxford Happiness Questionnaire for the purposes of this book because I found it easy to understand, comprehensive, and just the right length—not too long and not too short. I encourage you to take it now in order to establish a baseline for your current state of happiness. This will be your starting point.

The Oxford
Happiness Questionnaire

INSTRUCTIONS: On the next page are a number of statements about happiness.

INSTRUCTIONS: Please indicate how much you agree or disagree with each statement by entering a number alongside it according to the scale below.

1—strongly disagree / **2**—moderately disagree /
3—slightly disagree /**4**—slightly agree /
5—moderately agree / **6**—strongly agree

_____ 1. I don't feel particularly pleased with the way I am. (X)

_____ 2. I am intensely interested in other people.

_____ 3. I feel that life is very rewarding.

_____ 4. I have very warm feelings toward almost everyone.

_____ 5. I rarely wake up feeling rested. (X)

_____ 6. I'm not particularly optimistic about the future. (X)

_____ 7. I find most things amusing.

_____ 8. I am always committed and involved.

_____ 9. Life is good.

_____ 10. I don't think the world is a good place. (X)

_____ 11. I laugh a lot.

_____ 12. I am well satisfied with everything in my life.

_____ 13. I don't think I look attractive. (X)

_____ 14. There's a gap between what I would like to do and what I have done. (X)

_____ 15. I am very happy.

_____ 16. I find beauty in some things.

_____ 17. I always have a cheerful effect on others.

_____ 18. I can find some time for everything I want to do.

_____ 19. I feel that I'm not especially in control of my life. (X)

INSTRUCTIONS: Below are a number of statements about happiness. Please indicate how much you agree or disagree with each statement by entering a number alongside according to the scale above.

_____ 20. I feel able to take anything on.

_____ 21. I feel fully mentally alert.

_____ 22. I often experience joy and elation.

_____ 23. I don't find it easy to make decisions. (X)

_____ 24. I don't have a particular sense of meaning and purpose in my life. (X)

_____ 25. I feel I have a great deal of energy.

_____ 26. I usually have a positive influence on events.

_____ 27. I don't have fun with other people. (X)

_____ 28. I don't feel particularly healthy. (X)

_____ 29. I don't have particularly happy memories of the past. (X)

How to Calculate Your Score:

STEP 1: Your scores on the twelve items marked with an X should be "reverse-scored"—that is, if you gave yourself a 1, cross it out and change it to a 6. If you gave yourself a 2, change that to a 5. Change a 3 to a 4; change a 4 to a 3; change a 5 to a 2; and change a 6 to a 1.

STEP 2: Using the changed scores for those twelve items, now add your scores for *all* the twenty-nine items.

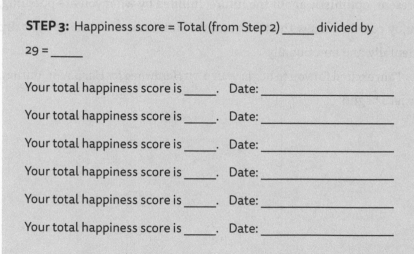

STEP 3: Happiness score = Total (from Step 2) _____ divided by 29 = _____

Your total happiness score is _____. Date: _____

Your total happiness score is _____. Date: _____

Your total happiness score is _____. Date: _____

Your total happiness score is _____. Date: _____

Your total happiness score is _____. Date: _____

Your total happiness score is _____. Date: _____

The lowest possible score on the Oxford Happiness Questionnaire is 1 (if you gave yourself a 1 for all twenty-nine items), and the highest possible score is 6 (if you gave yourself a 6 for all twenty-nine items). The average is around 4.30.

Reprinted/adapted with permission from Springer Nature E-book: Oxford Happiness Questionnaire by Leslie J Francis, COPYRIGHT 2014

Keep a record of your score and the date you completed the scale. As you read through the chapters and engage in the practices and exercises, retake the questionnaire at least once a month or after a particular goal has been met to continue assessing your progress. You will be able to observe how your happiness changes and increases.

The scientific term for happiness is "subjective wellbeing," meaning that the only person who can determine your level of happiness is YOU! No matter what is going on in your life or what propelled you to pick up this book, you will soon learn how to feel satisfied with the past and present, optimistic about the future, fulfilled by what you are pursuing, enjoy connections with others and the universe, and thrive physically, mentally, and emotionally.

I am excited for you to begin your own *Hardwired for Happiness* journey, so let's begin!

Cultivate Self-Awareness

"We see the world not as it is but as we are."

—Anaïs Nin

Self-awareness is the ability to step back and observe yourself and the world around you objectively, thus separating your perceptions of yourself, others, and the world from the true reality of how things are. At its core, self-awareness is the ability to observe the observer. It is the foundational practice that supports the other eight practices. If you only believe in your own truth, it narrows your vision and limits your ability to observe both yourself and the world around you. Self-awareness allows you to shift toward a more objective viewpoint about how you experience the world by creating a separation between your consciousness and the thoughts, emotions, and sensations that you experience in any given moment.

Self-awareness unlocks almost all the other practices in your journey by rewiring your brain from seeking fear to seeking happiness. You will shift from an external worldview of what it takes to be successful, happy, and fulfilled to an internal view of who you are, what your values are, and what matters to you. No one else can answer these questions for you!

By creating space between your consciousness and the thoughts, emotions, and bodily sensations that you might be experiencing, you can gain higher agency to do something about that experience. For example: saying "I am angry" offers limited options to help yourself move through a difficult moment. Saying "I feel angry" now offers a choice: anger is the feeling and can be changed if you choose to do something about it.

If you are not able to look inward, it is hard to discover your purpose, feel grateful for how much you already have, and be able to discover your fears, and overcome them. Similarly, self-awareness is critical toward developing kindness and compassion for others, building authentic relationships, and setting intentions.

Consider this parable: A group of six blind men heard that a strange animal called an elephant had been brought to their village. Curious, they decided to investigate and see what it looked like—using their sense of touch, since they couldn't see. The first blind man touched the elephant's leg and reported that it "looked" like a tree trunk. The second blind man touched the elephant's stomach and said that the elephant was a wall. The third blind man touched the elephant's ear and said that it was a fan. The fourth blind man touched the elephant's tail and described the elephant as a piece of rope. The fifth blind man felt the elephant's tusks and described it as a spear. The sixth blind man rubbed the elephant's snout and got very scared because he thought it was a snake. All of them got into a big argument about what the elephant actually looked like. Every one of them was correct and yet collectively they were all wrong because they hadn't accepted themselves as unique observers (they were blind) and only considered their own perspective of the elephant.

Over the course of this chapter, I will share several best practices and actions that can help you develop a deeper understanding of your own self, how you make sense of the world around you, and how the world makes sense of you. These practices will invite you to look deeper into the nature of obstacles that you might face in your journey, your own role in creating them, and design strategies to overcome them.

The Science-Based Benefits of Self-Awareness

Extensive research has been done on the multiple benefits of self-awareness both personally and professionally. Daniel Goleman, bestselling author of the groundbreaking book *Emotional Intelligence*, considered self-awareness as the foundational skill that enables the rest: self-regulation, motivation, empathy, and social skills. Individuals with a higher level of self-awareness demonstrate an increased ability to take perspectives, self-regulate, and be more creative and self-confident.[5] By being more self-aware of your own biases and assumptions, you can create the space to begin to understand and consider others' perspectives. This will help you not only make better decisions but also be more empathetic and build deeper connections with others. By increasing self-awareness, you will also be able to better regulate your emotions.

Self-awareness is also proven to reduce stress and to improve wellbeing,[6] resilience,[7] and our ability to meet goals.[8] When you understand your own strengths and weaknesses, you can anticipate the obstacles you might encounter. With that knowledge you can adapt to any situation, acquire extra knowledge when necessary, and make positive decisions that move you forward. By being more connected to what matters to you individually—your own *dharma*, or purpose—you will be able to dig deep and find the energy to get back on your feet and bounce back every time you fall.[9] Accurately naming the emotions that you feel enables you to better manage them, increasing your psychological wellbeing. Like other highly self-aware individuals, you will be happier, feel a higher degree of personal and social control, a higher job satisfaction, and be a better leader.

Professionally, lack of self-awareness can be a significant handicap in leadership. A study conducted by Adam D. Galinsky and colleagues at Northwestern University's Kellogg School of Management found that often, as executives climb the corporate ladder, they become more self-assured and confident. On the downside, they tend to become more self-absorbed and less likely to consider the perspectives of others.[10] By becoming more aware of how others see you, you will increase your empathy, which will help you to better understand their perspectives. This will enable you to empower, include, and recognize others, which increases the effectiveness of their teams and their ability to drive results.

Understanding the True Nature of Self

Asking ourselves the question, *"Who am I?"* is not new. Its importance was realized as early as 3,000 years ago, as demonstrated by the inscription of the ancient Greek words "know thyself" on the Temple of Apollo. It is one of the most powerful questions you can ask yourself but probably rarely do. It is powerful because knowing who you are helps to establish your unique vantage point from which you observe the world and yourself. We are all unique observers, even twins who might share the same DNA.

As I started my journey, I immersed myself in spiritual learning to better understand the power of asking this question, *"Who am I?"* I read the Bible, the Koran, Gita, Yoga sutras, and the book of *Tao Te Ching*. I studied books, documentaries, and *dharma* talks given by renowned teachers including Sadhguru, His Holiness the Dalai Lama, Thich Nhat Hanh, and Eckhart Tolle.

I've distilled five key learnings here from my spiritual studies that have had a transformative effect on my view of myself and my worldview. They have helped me answer the question, "Who am I?" and I hope they will also resonate with you. As you contemplate these key learnings, I would strongly encourage you to also build a regular practice of daily spiritual reading to support your own growth toward becoming more self-aware. You will find a list of my favorite books in the Appendix.

1. You are not your body or your mind. You are the ever-pervading consciousness that observes the sensations, emotions, and thoughts that run through them.

What is the first thing you think of when answering the question, "Who am I?" Your first response might be: "I am Sam, or I am Samantha." But that is a name that was given to you. You might say, "I am a man," or, "I am a woman," but that is the gender/sex associated with your body. Other answers could be, "I am a consultant" (your profession), or "I am a father/mother" (your relationship to others). Anything that can be an object of your perception cannot be you. Because you can witness your body and your mind, they are not the real "you." Similarly, your memories and intellect cannot be the real "you," either. So who is the real "you?"

Almost all religions, spiritual texts, and philosophies across Hinduism, Christianity, Buddhism, Islam, Yoga sutras, Zen, and Stoicism offer their perspectives on this nature of consciousness and our true self. The Yogic traditions that resonate with me point toward the existence of individual consciousness sometimes called "soul," "spirit," or "Atman" as well as universal consciousness called "Paramatman" or "Brahman" or "holy spirit." In the Bhagavad Gita, which is one of the primary scriptures of the Hindu religion, it is written about the universal, indestructible, and timeless nature of the soul:

No weapon can pierce the soul; no fire can burn it; no water can moisten it; nor can any wind wither it. The soul is uncleavable [indivisible]; it cannot be burnt or wetted or dried. The soul is immutable, all-permeating, ever calm, and immovable—eternally the same. The soul is said to be imponderable, unmanifested, and unchangeable.

—The Bhagavad Gita II: 23–25[11]

2. You experience the entire world within you. Only you are the creator of your own joy and suffering. The external world provides the stimulus, but you create the experience.

The following is based on a line of inquiry I learned from Sadhguru at the Isha foundation: shift your attention right now to any object in front of you, for example, a tree. If I asked where you see the tree, what would you say? *It is right in front of me.* But I didn't ask you where the tree was, I asked where do you *see* it? In a technical sense, light rays bounce off the tree, entering your eyes, forming an image on your retina. The electrical sensations then carry through the optic nerve that your brain interprets as a tree. So you actually see the tree within you. Similarly, listening and hearing are senses that take place within your body. Sadhguru asked me, "Have you ever experienced anything outside you?" and I realized the answer was no. Everything we ever experience is created by you based on what you see, hear, and feel.

I invite you to consider the possibility that the whole experience of the external world is created within you and hence by you. By that reasoning, if you are the creator of your experience, you are the One who is behind the pleasant emotions like joy, happiness, and bliss, as well as the unpleasant ones like anger, fear, and resentment. And if you are the creator, shouldn't you be able to create your own experience, regardless of what happens externally?

3. Your fundamental nature of existence is one of interbeing— in constant connection with other people and nature.

Bring your attention to something in your home or on your body and examine how it came into your possession. Let's take the shirt you are wearing. Think about the multitude of people whose endeavors made that shirt possible: designers and material buyers, laborers, advertisers, retail workers. The list can go on and on. Every object around us is possible through an interwoven web of human connections.

Now consider the food you eat. Let's take an apple and think about all the things in nature that conspired to make it possible: sunlight, water, nutrients from the Earth, the clouds that produced the rain, the rivers and lakes that held the water which evaporated to create the cloud, the bees and other insects that pollinated the tree, the wind that carried the seed from which the tree sprung up. It is simply impossible to exist in isolation from the world around us. As you expand your view of "self" and what we consider "yours" to include the whole universe, you will feel responsible and motivated to protect not just the smaller "me" but the bigger "we" and create conditions for both yourself and the world to thrive.

Consider the simple act of breathing—breath brings us into this world and it's the last thing to leave us when we die. Every moment in between, we are taking in oxygen and exhaling carbon dioxide. All the green plants around us take in the carbon dioxide and give out oxygen. We cannot survive without them and yet we often forget how interconnected we are, as we engage in deforestation at a faster scale than ever.

4. All sentient beings want to achieve a state of happiness.

Children often become deeply immersed in what they are doing when they play (acting out make-believe, building Legos, arranging doll houses). We describe them as "playing happily" and their happiness is part of their state of being, not something they are actively seeking. Something actually needs to happen to take them out of this flow—they get hungry or hurt themselves. Somehow as adults we lose the ability to flow happily, and instead, we define happiness as a *pursuit*. Something now has to happen in order to feel happy: a promotion, a compliment, a new purchase. When does this change occur, and how can we return to our base state of happiness?

We all claim we do things and make choices because "it makes us happy." But too many of us pursue happiness at too high of a cost, falsely believing that happiness is about "doing" in order to achieve more or have more. By rediscovering our natural state of being, we can harness our valuable childhood state of play, our happiness flow, and realize that what we have been seeking all this time is present right inside of us.

5. Suffering arises from attachment, aversion, and ignorance to things, people, and events.

Buddhist teachings describe the three primary causes of suffering as attachment, aversion, and ignorance to things, people, and events. We get attached to people, objects, life conditions—if it feels good, we want more of it! When life takes away our attachments, we can feel anxious or angry at the situation or individual behind our loss. Just like we crave attachment to things that bring us joy, we have aversion against those individuals or situations we believe will hurt or threaten us. We are willing to go to great lengths to protect ourselves, even hurting others in the process. By being ignorant of the true nature of existence as constantly changing and deep interconnection, we construct a false reality that causes anxiety and fear. We fight change versus embracing change as being a natural unfolding.

In our ignorance of the true nature of our self as anything more than the countries, religions, skin color, castes, economic wealth, or political affiliations we identify with, we create anxiety and loneliness. We perceive anything that is not "like us" as a threat. If instead, we could reflect on what unites us—we all fundamentally want to be happy and avoid suffering—we could see past our differences and create closer connections with all.

Meditation Exercise:
I Am Not My Body, I Am Not Even My Mind

The practice of meditation is extremely powerful in increasing your self-awareness. As Dr. Jon Kabat-Zinn defines it, meditation is "paying attention in a particular way: on purpose, in the present moment, and non-judgmentally." If you've never meditated before, remember that there is no right or wrong way to do it. There are plenty of helpful apps out there (my favorites are Headspace, Calm, and Simply Being), and I also recommend in-person meditation classes like those offered by Art of Living, or The Isha Foundation, as well as Dr. Jon Kabat-Zinn's virtual Masterclass course.

Duration: five to thirty minutes (I recommend starting with a five-minute practice and slowly increasing in five-minute increments to the full thirty minutes).

1. Sit in a comfortable position, either a Lotus with your legs crossed or on a chair with your back straight. Keep your shoulders relaxed, your chin facing slightly upward, and close your eyes. Keep your jaw relaxed with your lips slightly open.
2. Take three deep breaths, feeling the air fill your lungs and your stomach, and then slowly exhale with an open mouth letting all the air out and feeling your stomach contract.

3. Continue breathing normally for the next ten breaths, focusing on your inhale and exhale. With each inhale, notice your lungs and stomach expanding and rising. With each exhale, allow yourself to relax completely as your body contracts with the exhalation of air.

4. As you continue breathing, repeat the mantra silently. With each inhale, "I am not my body" and with each exhale, "I am not even my mind."

5. Start to bring awareness to "who is saying the words and who is hearing them" and notice if anything shifts within you and a space opens between you, your body, and mind.

6. If you find that the mind becomes distracted with some other thoughts, do not cling to them but also do not push them away. Just bring the focus back to your breath and your mantra and resume your practice.

7. At the end of the meditation, when your timer goes off, slowly open your eyes, and take in the surroundings around you. Notice what you are feeling in your body, the emotions that are present, and the quality of your thoughts.

8. Set an intention to maintain this awareness throughout the day, before getting up and going about your daily chores.

Internal Self-Awareness:
How Do You Experience the World?

Through my studies to become an ontological coach, I discovered that we are all unique observers and see the world with our unique set of eyes. By cultivating self-awareness, we can start to view the world with fresh eyes. If you feel stuck, you can step back and polish your lens, addressing breakdowns or issues which stand in the way of getting the results you want. You'll start by bringing awareness to the three underlying elements of language, mood, and body that collectively shape our perceptions of the world.

Language

The words we use to describe the world are informed by the core beliefs we hold about ourselves, others, and the stories we tell about them. By bringing conscious awareness to these beliefs, the formative life experiences that shaped them, and how these beliefs color the lens through which we see the world, we can start to break their hold on us.

One important distinction that is particularly helpful in disaggregating our stories is to separate **assertion** from **assessments**. Assertions are facts that anyone can verify independently using universally recognized standards. ("The meeting lasted two hours and fifteen minutes.") Contrast that with assessments, which are your versions of the truth, based on a standard that is specific to you and not necessarily shared by others. ("The meeting went on forever!") Holding your assessments as "truths," especially about a person, an event, or a behavior, can drive so much suffering, anger, resentment, anxiety, and loss of connection.

One of my coaching clients, Rob, was very frustrated with his direct report, John, who showed up repeatedly late for their 8:00 a.m. Friday team meeting without a real excuse. Rob could feel his anger rising even before the meeting started as he anticipated John would not show up on time. John's repeated tardiness felt like a sign of disrespect, and Rob started to develop a deep resentment toward him. I encouraged Rob to share his frustrations and his beliefs with John but to remain curious about his side of the story and to listen without judgment.

When the two men spoke, a completely different reality emerged. John was a single parent to his six-year-old son, and on Fridays he had to drop him off at daycare much earlier to make this particular meeting. Unfortunately, traffic at that hour always made him late, no matter how he rushed. John knew how important the meeting was, and he deeply admired Rob. He was afraid to come off as high maintenance if he asked for a time change and remained stuck between his duties as a loyal father and a team member. Armed with this insight, Rob simply shifted the meeting by thirty minutes.

By retelling the stories about the life experiences that have shaped you, you can uncover meaningful patterns that bring awareness to these stories. You can then drop the ones that are not accurate or not serving you anymore and adopt new stories that might serve you better. As novelist John Barth reminds us, "the story of your life is not your life. It is just your story."

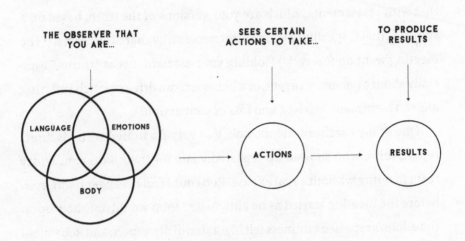

Ontological model on "Who am I?"

Figure 1.1: Source: Newfield Network

Moods/Emotions

Like the stories that we hold about what is happening, our moods and emotions predispose us toward certain actions. Emotions usually are a result of some event that breaks the flow of life that we expect. When things turn out better than we expect, we feel pleasant emotions like joy and excitement. On the other hand, when things turn out worse than we expect, we experience unpleasant emotions like those of anger, fear, disgust, and sadness, among others. Practice 7 will cover tangible actions you can take to overcome some of the unpleasant emotions and moods that can overpower us and limit our possibilities for the future. To get familiar with the range of emotions we can experience, I have found the following website based on the work of Dr. Paul Ekman and the Dalai Lama (http://atlasofemotions.org/) very helpful.

We often use the terms moods and emotions interchangeably, but they are two very different things and need a different set of interventions to move through them. Emotions are usually the result of some event that breaks our flow of life. (You receive good news = happiness. Your car is rear-ended = anger.) Over time emotions can become moods. Moods don't need an event; they can come on just by themselves. But the effect is still the same: they preclude us from taking certain actions or might push us toward other actions. However, emotions often last for short periods of time, even moments to hours or days, whereas moods can linger on for months, years, and even lifetimes. When the news about COVID-19 first broke, you may have felt fear (emotion). Two years later, despite the progress of vaccines and masking protocols, you may still be living in a fearful state (mood).

Unlike emotions that usually are triggered by an external event, you might find yourself in a mood without being able to pinpoint anything specific that triggered that mood. In this way, just like you can have moods, *moods can have you.* For about three months, I woke up every morning in the grip of high anxiety with my body crunched up in a ball, feeling as though I might throw up. I couldn't point to a reason for this; everything seemed to be going great at work and home. The more I tried to figure out the problem, the more anxious I felt. However, once I discovered this mysterious property of moods, I stopped worrying "Why am I feeling this way?" and started to explore "How do I shift my mood?"

The field of ontological coaching identifies four primary moods that you can experience based on whether you accept or oppose the past and future: Resentment, Acceptance, Resignation, and Ambition. To experience the power of moods in shaping yourself as the observer, think about a time you found yourself unable or unwilling to accept a situation. Was your ability to come up with creative solutions limited? When friends, colleagues, or experts stepped in to offer suggestions, were you quick to dismiss them? Looking back, it's very likely that you were in a mood of Resignation. Similarly, if you found it difficult to coordinate with someone (a coworker or your boss) or assumed they were causing you harm, you may have been in a mood of Resentment.

	Past events	Future possibilities
Oppose	Resentment	Resignation
Accept	Acceptance	Ambition

Table: Based on work done by Newfield Network

Body

The last and final unique observer element is our physical body. Mainstream science and healthcare practices tend to treat the mind and body as two separate entities with the mind controlling the body, but increasingly, research is pointing toward a potential bidirectional relationship between the two. Did you know that 95 percent of the chemical messenger serotonin, that is believed to act as a mood stabilizer and commonly linked to feeling good, is produced in our gut? It is well accepted in the therapy world that our bodies keep score of all our life experiences, both positive and negative. When we suppress an unpleasant emotion, say anger or resentment, it can result in a physical tension or stress, and over time, the embodiment of the mood could be the root cause of a chronic ailment.

Your body not only allows you to "see" your emotions and moods by connecting you with bodily sensations, but more importantly, you can engage your body to shift your mental and emotional state. This is why they tell marathoners to smile at certain points because it relaxes them and lowers the pain and fatigue they might be experiencing. The next time you feel nervous or anxious, try this: breathe in for a count of four, hold for the count of four, and breathe out on the count of four. Do this three to four times. See how a simple somatic practice shifts your experience in that moment. Similarly, next time you are feeling sad or down, put on some upbeat music and dance, or sing along in the car—go on, nobody's judging! How do you feel afterward?

Journaling Exercise:
Becoming More Aware of Who You Are

Keeping a daily journal has been a key habit of successful people throughout the ages. Writing down your thoughts and feelings is a powerful tool to process things that are bothering you and can help you identify patterns you can't seem to break away from. Mastering self-awareness requires you to be able to look deeply into the unique observer you are and how you make sense of the world. Taking just a few minutes of your day to be introspective and record your progress can go a long way toward answering that question, "Who am I?"

Here are some prompts to get you started:

1. What are my unique gifts? How am I using my gifts to make a difference in the world around me?

2. What are my spiritual beliefs about myself and the world around me? Who are my spiritual teachers? How can I increase my connection and union with the world around me?

3. What are the major life events in my life that have shaped me into who I am today? How have they shaped me into the unique observer of the world that I am? How have I benefited? What is it costing me?

4. What mood do I usually wake up in? What is the effect of that mood on my thoughts and my energy levels?

5. When do I feel the most happy or joyful? What can I do to increase the joy in my life?

6. How do others see me? What are the things they don't know about me?

7. With which situations, behaviors, and people do I find myself getting triggered—upset, anxious, angry, fearful? What happens to me as a result? What does that feel like in my body?

8. How often do I find myself trapped in a fixed mindset or one of scarcity, victimhood? What is the effect of these mindsets on the actions I can take?

9. What are my biggest fears? How have they served me in my life? How have they held me back?

You can examine your thoughts (language), your mood states, and your bodily physical sensations to create stronger, internal awareness into any obstacles or sources of suffering in your life. You ground your assessments, improve your emotional fidelity, and are able to "name" and "tame" your emotions. You can also develop strategies to tackle moods that hinder your ability to achieve your objectives. These days, when I feel anxious, I listen to music, go for a run, or call a friend.

External Self-Awareness: How Does the World Experience You?

Equally important to understanding how you make sense of the world is to understand how the world experiences you. Dr. Tasha Eurich, a preeminent organizational psychologist, differentiates between two types of self-awareness.[12] The first is *internal self-awareness* representing how clearly you see your own values, thoughts, feelings, needs, passions, fears, strengths, and weaknesses. The second category, *external self-awareness*, represents your understanding of how others view you on the same dimensions. Based on her research, there was no relationship between these two views. In fact, only 10–15 percent of people she studied fit the definition of being truly self-aware.

The higher up you are in an organization, the greater the chances that you suffer a disconnect between the two views—your internal view and that of those who work with you or for you. Dr. Eurich found a negative correlation between both experience and power on self-awareness. A higher level of experience can make leaders overconfident in their level of self-knowledge to the detriment of themselves and their organizations. Similarly, the more power they hold, the higher the probability for them to overestimate their capabilities.

A coaching client, Bill, had always felt that he was loved by everyone who worked for him. He cared deeply for people and was willing to make time for anyone. He reached out to me because he had recently received 360-degree feedback from his office that told a very different story. The report said he was inflexible, transactional, overly demanding, unappreciative, and not a good listener. His coworkers appreciated the high bar he set for everyone but felt that his approach pushed them too hard and didn't allow them to solve problems on their own.

Bill was upset. He felt misunderstood and unappreciated. He worked long hours and made himself available late at night or early in the morning when needed. I encouraged him to do a listening tour with his teams and engage nondefensively and with a deep sense of curiosity. He soon realized that several of his beliefs about his role as leader and his contributions were completely wrong.

As a leader, Bill didn't feel that he could share his sixteen-plus hour daily schedule, which included meetings from 7:00 a.m. to 9:00 p.m. He believed that his teams would appreciate his engagement at any time of day, but it also required his teams to accommodate his overloaded schedule. He was role modeling a 24/7 work lifestyle that inspired no one. Bill took action right away. He worked with his team to create transparency about how much was on his plate and offloaded some to get back to a more normal schedule. He also frontloaded and blocked off team problem-solving time first as well as time for wellbeing and renewal collectively as a team.

Bill also wrongly assumed that solving problems efficiently and at a high level was helpful to his team. He would cut to the chase and give his own input without listening to his associates. As a result, he came across as transactional and not collaborative. To address this, he started creating time in his calendar explicitly to check in with his teammates so they could connect as humans and friends. These conversations, whether personal or professional, added to his team's experience and offered another way for him to lead in a more authentic way.

In her article published in the *Harvard Business Review*, "What Self-Awareness Really Is (And How to Cultivate It)," Dr. Eurich offers two most-held explanations by researchers which resonate with me. First, as one rises in the hierarchy of an organization, there are fewer people above them who can give them constructive feedback. Second, junior colleagues are fearful of repercussions from their boss by offering critical feedback. So most people keep their thoughts and feelings to themselves. When things get really bad, they just quit and find another job. Other research backs this up. In a survey conducted by Development Dimensions International, Inc. (DDI), 57 percent of employees cited that they had quit a job because of their boss.[13] A study by the American Psychological Association found that 75 percent of Americans say their "boss is the most stressful part of their workday." I can only attribute these extremely depressing statistics to a lack of self-awareness on the part of more senior leaders on how they are perceived and the effect they are having on others.

Increasing your self-awareness with 360-degree feedback can prove highly effective in collecting input from bosses, peers, and those more junior to you. My personal favorite tool is the Leadership Circle Profile,[14] which was created by Bob Anderson more than thirty-five years ago and has been used by over 175,000 leaders globally. The Leadership Circle Profile integrates many of the best theoretical frameworks from the leadership, adult development, psychological, and spiritual bodies of knowledge.

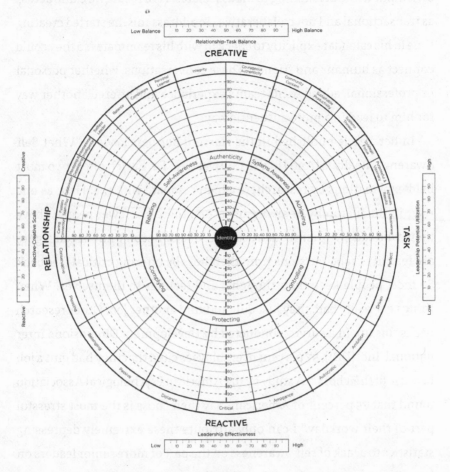

Figure 1.2

HARDWIRED FOR HAPPINESS

The top half of the circle highlights Creative Competencies that contribute to a leader's effectiveness and include their level of self-awareness; how they achieve results; bringing out the best in others; and leading with vision among others. The lower half of the circle highlights self-limiting Reactive tendencies and behaviors including risk averseness and caution over creating results; tendency to self-protect versus engage openly; and tendency to control versus collaborate. These tendencies are proven to limit effectiveness, authentic expression, and empowerment. The left half of the circle provides insights on how you relate to others on a daily basis. The right half of the circle maps the ability and style through which you engage with work to drive tasks and results. Visit https://leadershipcircle .com/ for more information on working with a certified coach who can help you deploy the Leadership Circle Profile in your organization, interpret results, and work with you to support you in shifting your observer to one that is a more effective leader.

Initiating feedback conversations directly with your colleagues can work just as effectively. You can ask for feedback from those who you know have your best interests in mind and are willing to give you honest feedback. You might need to lay the groundwork by connecting with them, being vulnerable, and sharing the intention behind your request for input. This can be done both directly by making a request to your colleagues and asking them to send you their feedback, or through using a coach who can maintain anonymity but do a series of interviews to extract learnings for you.

Community Exercise:
Become Better Observers

Find a friend or colleague who is willing to support your journey and may also be interested in becoming a better observer. You will take turns sharing your stories and listening. Decide who goes first and have that person choose a situation they are struggling with. Tune into your thoughts, moods, and body sensations as you answer the questions below. Describe who is involved, what you are trying to accomplish, and what is getting in the way. Your partner will act as your coach, helping you methodically separate your stories and the underlying beliefs driving them, naming your emotions and moods, and suggesting a shift that might support you in overcoming the challenge. Use the following coaching script:

1. What are you assuming about yourself? About the world? About this situation?

2. What evidence do you have to prove/disprove/ground this assessment? How is this assessment serving you?

3. How can you validate this assessment based on conversations with others? What two other stories could you hold that might explain what is happening?

4. What is the mood present with you? Where does this mood reside in your body?

5. What are the body sensations present for you? Help the other person conduct a body scan to check in with their body. Do you feel a sense of tightness? Where do you experience this—in your jaw, chest, stomach?

6. What is the story running through your body? If your feelings could speak, what would they say to you?
7. What are you solving for? What's most important for you at this moment?
8. What is the smallest action that you can take that might allow you to move in the direction that will serve you?

Building Your Self-Awareness Practice

At its core, the practice of self-awareness is all about breaking the transparency through which you see life in order to create a separation between the reality and your perception or belief around it. Mastering self-awareness will allow you to focus clearly on what matters to you and live a more purposeful life. You can consciously shape your experiences, alleviate suffering and fear, and tune into a natural state of happiness and love. Use the three self-awareness practices in this chapter—journaling, meditation, and partner dialogue—to help guide you on your inner journey.

KEY TAKEAWAYS

- Self-awareness is the ability to step back and observe yourself and the world around you objectively.
- Self-awareness is proven to reduce stress and to improve well-being,[15] resilience,[16] and our ability to meet goals.[17]
- Self-awareness occurs on three levels:
  - The true nature of Self

- ▸ How your Self perceives the world and the actions that you take
- ▸ How the world perceives you through the actions you take.
- By creating space between your consciousness and the thoughts, emotions, and bodily sensations that you might be experiencing, you can gain higher agency to do something about that experience.

Define Your Purpose

"The purpose of life is a life of purpose"

—Robert Byrne

One-third or more of our lives are spent working. In our quest to have more, do more, and be more, we pour so much of our energy into the daily grind that there is no time or space for introspection toward the deeper meaning in our lives. Most people show up to work not because they are truly motivated, but because their job offers a necessary means to an end—money to afford things they want, take care of their families, and save for retirement. According to a 2020 Gallup poll on employee engagement, only 30 percent of people are actively engaged at work. Fifty-four percent of people put in the time at work but without energy or passion. Another 13 percent were actively disengaged with an unhappy work experience that spilled over into their home life. This is a sad state of affairs. For too many people, the activity that occupies a significant part of their waking hours—their job—holds little joy or meaning. Instead it is something they must bear with. Living a life without meaning has serious consequences on our wellbeing both physical and psychological. Scientific studies find that individuals without a purpose in life are more likely to suffer from depression, boredom, loneliness, and anxiety.[18]

As I find myself navigating the world emerging from the COVID-19 pandemic, I've observed that more and more people are feeling stressed, burned-out, disillusioned, and undervalued at work. In fact, they're so unhappy, they are quitting in droves. This mass exodus has been termed "The Great Resignation," and close to forty million people have quit their jobs in 2021 alone.[19]

What if we could find the jobs that truly engaged us and allowed us to live with a bigger purpose? How would it feel to work in coherence with our values and be inspired by what really matters to us, not just our paychecks? If these questions have pulled on your heart strings, you are in the right place. In this chapter I will outline the steps that you can take to discover your passions and unique strengths to design a life filled with meaning. You will be able to reinvent yourself where you currently work or completely reimagine your career to fill it with joy, success, and meaning.

The Science-Based Benefits of Living a Life of Purpose

We are all united as human beings in our search for meaning in our lives. In the 1940s, Abraham Maslow, a renowned American psychologist, proposed a hierarchy of human needs to identify behavioral motivation. At the bottom is physiological (food, water, shelter), followed by safety, then by belonging and love. The fourth basic need is self-actualization, which drives us to reach for our true potential and achieve our "ideal self." Reaching self-actualization allows us to find our purpose, and at the end of our days, it gives us the satisfaction that we truly *lived*, that our lives made a difference. Around the same time, Viktor Frankl, renowned psychotherapist and founder of the school of Logotherapy, found in his research that around 80 percent of people believed that human beings needed a reason for living, and 60 percent believed they had something or someone in their lives worth dying for.[20] Since then, extensive scientific research conducted over the years has time and again validated that purpose is fundamental to physical and mental health, happiness, and success in professional lives. Let's explore each of these benefits in detail.

First, purposeful living has been linked to physical wellbeing, including lower risk of cardiovascular diseases, better sleep, healthier behaviors, and an overall longer, better life. A 2009 study conducted in Japan found that those who had a strong connection to their sense of purpose tended to live longer than those who didn't.[21] Another study in 2014 conducted by researchers Hill and Turiano tracked adults over fourteen years and validated that purpose in life promotes longevity across the adult years.[22] Similar research conducted by neuropsychologist Dr. Patricia Boyle at Rush Medical College found that people with a low sense of life purpose were 2.4 times more likely[23] to get Alzheimer's disease than those with a strong purpose.[24] In other studies, people with purpose have been found to manage pain more positively[25] and were less likely to develop impairments in daily living and mobility disabilities.

Second, having a sense of purpose contributes to a strong psychological wellbeing. People who rate their lives as more meaningful have higher life satisfaction and a sense of self-worth. They also are happier and live with more energy and passion. Studies have validated the strong negative effects of a lack of purpose, including higher incidence of depression, boredom, loneliness, and anxiety.[26] Those with a sense of purpose are also more resilient and better able to handle the ups and downs of life. Finding meaning in things can enable people to find the strength to carry on through the most extreme, horrible circumstances, such as what Viktor Frankl experienced in the Auschwitz concentration camp. Friedrich Nietzsche, the renowned German philosopher, wisely said, "He who has a why to live for can bear almost any how." The impact of purpose on resilience has been independently validated by Dr. Ed Diener, also fondly known as "Dr. Happiness," on the science of wellbeing, and also by Anthony Burrow, Associate Professor of Life Course Studies in the Department of Psychology at Cornell University.

Finally, having a sense of purpose can lead to higher professional success with positive correlations on both the starting household income and net worth but also a higher likelihood of increases over the nine years between assessments.[27] Having a life purpose provides clarity on what is important versus unimportant among the millions of tasks calling our attention and hence a critical first step to live our most conscious life. First-century Roman philosopher Seneca said it beautifully, "When a man does not know what harbor he is making for, no wind is the right wind."

The Power of *Ikigai*: Living a Purpose-Driven Life

Ikigai is a Japanese concept that stands for "a reason for being" or "that which makes life worth living." In other words, it's having a purpose in life. The word consists of "Iki" (to live) and "gai" (reason).[28] The term *Ikigai* dates to the Heian period (794 to 1185) according to research done by clinical psychologist Akihiro Hasegawa and is formed by compounding two Japanese words: iki (生き) meaning "life; alive" and kai (甲斐) meaning "(an) effect." *Ikigai* catapulted into mainstream popularity in 2009 after the Dan Buettner's TED talk on the Blue Zones—areas of the world with the longest-living residents—like Okinawa, Japan, where he found a strong link between having a purpose in life and longevity.

At its core, *Ikigai* means to design your life around the intersection of four main things: what you love, what you are good at, what the world needs, and what you can be paid for. *What you love* is all about those things that make you come alive and bring joy to your heart. *What you are good at* is all about the unique skills that you have individually, and the talents you have cultivated over the years. *What the world needs* is the superset of problems or opportunities individuals, communities, or countries are craving for solutions around. *What you can get paid for* are the skills you possess that are in demand and address a core need that individuals, companies, and countries are willing to pay in exchange for your goods and services.

IKIGAI

A JAPANESE CONCEPT MEANING
"A REASON FOR BEING"

Figure 2.1: *Ikigai based on diagram by Marc Winn*

Most people choose their professions based on convenience, availability, and income potential. They either don't fully know what they are passionate about or need a job that secures a comfortable life. Sometimes people *do* know what they love to do, but they push their passions aside for other reasons: their family doesn't approve; they feel pressure to earn a bigger salary; or they are worried they won't succeed. Unfortunately, people get stuck on a one-way track of promotions and pay increases to support an ever-expanding lifestyle (bigger homes, more things) and responsibilities (taking care of kids, aging parents). At some point, it just feels too late to make a change. In my experience, about 20 percent of people have found careers that bring them joy, leverage their strengths, fulfill the world's needs, and get paid well for it. The rest of us can redesign our life to leverage our strengths, make work become play, and transcend this difficult work-life balance.

Finding Your Ikigai: A Hero's Journey

As I reflected on my own process toward finding my *Ikigai* and finding the courage to transform my work and life, I realized my journey followed the archetypal story pattern first identified by Joseph Campbell in 1949. *The Hero's Journey* goes like this: A hero ventures forth from the world of common day into a region of supernatural wonder. Fabulous forces are encountered there, and a decisive victory is won. The hero comes back from this mysterious adventure with the power to bestow boons on his fellow man. This arc plays out in most mono-mythological texts over the ages including *The Odyssey*, Siddhartha's journey toward becoming Buddha, and the legend of King Arthur, as well as in popular movies like *Rocky*, *Star Wars*, and even *Lilo and Stitch*.

The
HERO'S JOURNEY

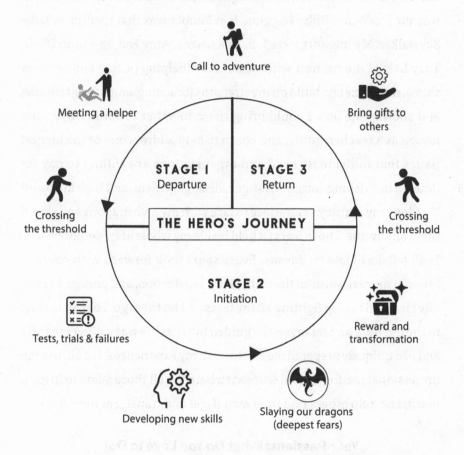

Call to adventure

Meeting a helper

Bring gifts to others

STAGE 1
Departure

STAGE 3
Return

Crossing
the threshold

THE HERO'S JOURNEY

Crossing
the threshold

STAGE 2
Initiation

Tests, trials & failures

Reward and
transformation

Developing new skills

Slaying our dragons
(deepest fears)

Figure 2.2: The Hero's Journey

I found many similarities between my own experience and the three key stages of the Hero's Journey: Departure (call to adventure), Initiation (being tested, picking up new skills), and Return (transformed with gifts for the world).

In the Hero's Journey, mentors and helpers play a critical role in helping the Hero cross the threshold and begin the adventure. Gandalf played that role for Frodo and Bilbo Baggins; Ben Kenobi was that mentor to Luke Skywalker. My mentors were Johanne Lavoie, Amy Fox, and Julio Olalla. They helped me connect with what I love (helping people and relationships), recognize and build on my strengths (coaching, empathy, gratitude), and showed me how I could bring these together toward reinventing myself as a teacher, guide, and coach to help address one of the biggest issues that individuals need and organizations are willing to pay for (human flourishing, burnout, fatigue, disengagement, and high attrition).

Along my journey, I came face to face with my own dragons and slayed them one by one. Those fears I'd held inside my whole life: *I am not enough; I will fail; I will lose my friends.* Every step I took forward with courage brought more rewards in the form of joy, satisfaction, and energy. Eventually I learned to stop fighting all my fears and let them go. I began to trust in the universe and let myself be guided by what life was calling me to do and had uniquely prepared me for through my experiences. I could use the professional platform I had worked so hard for all those years to inspire, teach, and help others find their own *Ikigai* and transform their lives.

Your Passions: What Do You Love to Do?

Discovering your passion is easier said than done. If you have no idea what your passion is, or you feel passionate about many things and cannot decide what feels strongest, don't despair. Passion is actually something that can be built over time and practiced. Let's take a look at what you love to do from a macro level (high points from your past) and a micro level (recent, daily experiences) and identify the activities and environments that make you come alive and engage you so deeply that you lose track of time. To find your passions, you first have to start with reconnecting with what you love.

First, think back over the past ten years and identify three to five of your most memorable experiences and proudest achievements. Some of these might have pushed you to the limit and left you physically and mentally exhausted but also made you extremely proud because of the impact you made. Write down each of these experiences and then underneath, write your response to the following questions:

- What were you doing at that moment?
- What were you thinking about?
- What were you feeling during those moments? What about this high-point moment stands out for you?
- What does the experience say about you?

Read back over your notes and search for patterns across all of your answers. Can you identify what you valued most about yourself and/or the work you did? What seemed most important: your own success or that of the people around you? What conditions helped you thrive? How could you spend more of your time on these peak experiences?

Now let's examine things on a micro level. Get out your journal and record an activity log for two weeks. Every day, write down the moments you felt completely engaged in something, as well as times when you felt drained by a task or activity. I like to capture the granular details before I go to bed when I am relaxed and can remember things clearly. When the two weeks are up, read back through your journal, keeping the following questions in mind:

- What were the nature of activities you were involved in (solving a tough unsolved problem, winning a new account, convincing others, researching topics)?
- What was the role you were playing (individual contributor, team leader, stakeholder, consultant, or expert providing input)?
- What was the setting (in an office, at a lunch, outside) and over-all environment (level of chaos/distractions, quiet solitude, temperature, lighting)?
- What was the nature of your interactions with others involved (contentious or harmonious?) as well as time constraints (did they feel spacious or rushed?).

Journaling Exercise:
The Ingredients of Your Purpose

Discovering your purpose is a journey of self-exploration that can last a lifetime, and the beginning of the journey really began when you first arrived here on Earth. Taking a deeper look at yourself as a child and young adult can spark core memories and realizations that serve as key ingredients in the recipe of your *Ikigai*. Oftentimes we forget what we were like before we became all-consumed with the corporate ladder. As you ponder the following prompts and journal your responses, it may help to dig up old photos of yourself so you can really reminisce and remember when you just experienced the world without thinking too hard about it.

1. When you were a very young child, what did you love to do? What brought you the most joy? When did you feel the least self-conscious?

2. What were your hobbies as a child, teenager, and young adult? What activities did you lose yourself in where time just flew by?

3. In school, what subjects did you not only enjoy but exceled in? Do you remember any feedback from teachers that really made you feel proud and happy?

4. What was your dream and vision for life when you were in high school? What did you think you would accomplish in college? What job did you envision yourself doing?

5. What aspects of yourself as a young adult do you miss the most?

6. What challenges about yourself as a young adult are you most proud that you have overcome?

Your Strengths: What Are Your Unique Gifts?

There is extensive research done by the Gallup organization and others that shows that when you focus on developing your strengths, you can grow faster than when trying to improve your weaknesses. Using your strengths every day can be a highly effective gateway to living a life of purpose.

Your family, friends, and colleagues can be good sources of insights on your strengths and how you can use more of them. Often they see you more clearly than you see yourself. Approach them and explain that you are seeking input, and offer the following three questions as a guide:

1. What are my unique gifts?

2. When I am at my best, what do you see me doing and which strengths am I leveraging?

3. What would be your advice to allow me to bring my best self forward all the time?

Alternatively, you can also use a third-party survey to identify your strengths. My personal favorite that I have used extensively with my clients is Gallup's CliftonStrength Finder. The CliftonStrength Finder identifies what you are naturally best at based on your natural patterns of thinking, feeling, and behaving. The assessment identifies your unique combination of thirty-four different strength themes which sort into four domains (strategic thinking, relationship building, influencing, and executing). The themes are a culmination of decades of research led by Don Clifton to study and categorize the talents of the world's most successful people. Each theme identifies both what one does best, actions that can be taken to maximize potential, and key blind spots to watch out for. If you're interested, you can find out more at the Gallup website (https://www.gallup.com/cliftonstrengths/en/home.aspx).

Your Calling:
What Does the World Need from You?

You can start to discover your calling by exploring unmet needs that can originate from the world of business enterprises or be in the domain of nonprofits meeting a social, economic, or ecological need. Start to identify those that are coherent with your core values and what matters to you. Ask yourself the following questions and write your responses in your journal:

- If time, money, or capabilities were not an issue, what problem would you dedicate your life to solving? What business venture would you start?
- Is there an idea or a possibility that keeps tugging at your heart or something you can't stop thinking about?

- Is there a topic or issue which is a source of extreme pain, anger, or frustration for you?
- What or who inspires you? What's worth doing even if you fail?

Personally, as I did this exercise, I felt myself called to address a rising epidemic of loneliness, anxiety, stress, and burnout. I was saddened to see so many individual leaders reeling under fatigue and living with resentment against peers and resignation at the growing bureaucracy and slow pace of change. Not only were they making their own lives miserable living in anxiety and fear, the environments they were creating accidentally at home and work reflected their energies and were also caustic.

Your Livelihood:
What Can You Get Paid For?

If you are gainfully employed, you may feel like this piece of your *Ikigai* has already been solved. Your work is creating value and meeting a need in the world for which your company is willing to pay. That's important, but a paycheck alone won't fulfill you the way your true purpose will.

Having already identified what you love, your strengths, and calling, you can try to reshape your current job to infuse more of what you love and what you are good at into your daily work. You can minimize things that drain your energy, find opportunities to better utilize your time, and engage with your colleagues to see how your work is making a difference in the world around you.

Minimize Energy Drain

Ideally your passions journaling exercise has already identified a set of activities that fill your day and give you energy and others that sap energy from you. Go back to your journal entry and add some notes about what aspects of the activity are draining and how you might be able to re-engineer them. Can technology help automate something that is very manual and cumbersome? Can you eliminate, excuse yourself from, or assign others to attend meetings which are not value added? Can you change the environment to be more energetic or inspiring (moving meetings outside, adjusting lighting, or temperature)?

Find Opportunities to Increase Time on Activities That You Are Passionate About

Initiate conversations with your boss, peers, and other colleagues who are already working on activities or are in departments that you find exciting. Explore small ways in which you can start to get involved and get exposure to work that is energizing for you. It might start with volunteering for a project in addition to your day-to-day job, shadowing someone to learn, or participating in a brainstorming session. Invest in building relationships and actively enlist their support to help you upskill yourself and make the switch into doing what you love full time.

Reframe Your Job By Anchoring to the Bigger Impact and Purpose Story

There is a commonly told story of three bricklayers working at a construction site. When asked what they were doing, the first one replied, "I am working hard to feed my family." The second one replied, "I am building a wall." The third one said, "I am building a beautiful cathedral for God." They all had the same job, yet each had a fundamentally different meaning behind it. Initiate a conversation with your team and collectively expand meaning-making by seeing how your day-to-day actions are connected to the bigger organizational purpose. Examine the benefits the company is delivering to your customers, employees, suppliers, communities, and shareholders.

One of my clients, Tom, was a director in a global IT services firm, and he had a deep passion for coaching younger team members. He liked working in teams where he could teach the young programmers the tools and tricks of the trade to help them become great. As happens to many people, he was promoted from team leader to project manager, and finally to a program management role. His days looked nothing like the days from his early time at the company. Now instead of a team dynamic, he faced back-to-back calls with clients, resolving issues and negotiating change requests. Tom was miserable.

Tom wanted a change and considered joining a much smaller company or becoming an independent coach so he could get back to doing what he loved. But those routes would mean a big pay cut and he would have to start over again, establishing credibility and learning completely new programming languages.

I encouraged Tom to think about how he could infuse more of what he loved into his daily routine by offloading activities that were energy drains. Tom identified two tasks that occupied almost half his time: tracking and following up on issues and writing summary memos for key stakeholders each week. He decided to delegate both tasks to deserving junior colleagues who welcomed the growth opportunity.

With 40 percent of his time now available, Tom began actively coaching younger project managers and junior team members. They loved his advice and mentorship, and soon word started to spread. Eighteen months later, Tom was asked to take on a completely new role as a senior director of learning and development. In this new role, Tom could really scale his impact and the people he could help by operationalizing what he was doing out of his passion and teaching others how to mentor and coach. He set up the infrastructure where anyone who needed help could ask for it and get connected with others across the company who were willing to help or had the experience or expertise. Once completely miserable, Tom is now the happiest he has been in his career and so grateful that he didn't quit his job, but reinvented it to fill it with more of what he felt passionate about.

Community Exercise:
Engage in Purpose Dialogues at Work

According to research conducted by McKinsey, approximately 70 percent of people say they define their purpose through work.[29] However, there is a big disconnect when it comes to *living* their purpose at work. Compared to 85 percent of executives and upper management who feel that they are living their purpose at work, only 15 percent of frontline managers and frontline employees agree. Almost 50 percent actually disagree with that sentiment.

We all have a unique opportunity to connect organizational purpose to our own individual purpose and bring more meaning to our lives. Start with your core team that you work with every day and share the tools and content from this chapter.

Prework for discussion:

1. Use Gallup CliftonStrengths Finder assessment tool to identify your individual strengths and develop ideas on how you can better utilize those talents and develop them into strengths.
2. Keep a journal for two weeks to identify activities that energize you and get you into flow, and those that you find

draining. Identify actions you can take to improve your overall experience by increasing focus on activities that you love; choose options for reducing all energy-draining activities.

3. Third, review your personal sources of meaning (company, customer, team, society, self) and link to how being part of this company helps you achieve your meaning.

Discussion: Now that you have completed the prework, engage with your team over a series of discussions (could be once a month over lunch) to collectively reflect and support each other in living into our purpose at work.

1. How is our work making a difference in improving the community, the environment, and humankind?
2. How is our work making a difference in the lives of our customers so it makes it easier, better, safer, and healthier?
3. How can we support each other by leaning into each other's unique talents and developing them into real strengths?
4. How can we reconfigure what I work on to make it more energizing? More connected? More trusting? More authentic and open?
5. What opportunities do I want to create and shape for myself that will give me energy to sustain myself over the next six months? How can this team collectively support me in achieving my aspirations?
6. What steps can we take to support each other on our purpose journey over the next six months and longer?

7. When we look back on the next six months, how will the team have led with purpose and inspired others to do the same?

Use Your *Ikigai* to Make a Bigger Change

It would be ideal if you could infuse more passion and meaning into your current job, but sometimes there are real constraints that prevent you from living your purpose without a fundamental reimagination. Maybe your company doesn't provide enough opportunities to leverage your strengths. You might be highly gifted in relationship building and find yourself stuck in IT coding in a backroom, with little avenue to move laterally into sales. Maybe 80 percent or more of your workday is filled with back-to-back meetings, intracompany politics, and activities that you find draining. You might not have the ability to shape that environment. It might be that your company's culture is not coherent with your values or what matters to you. Let's take a look at how to identify what else is out there for you and how to go after it.

Create a Mind Map

Having identified what you love to do, your strengths, and issues you find yourself called toward, it is time to generate a range of ideas and options that could potentially take you toward your *Ikigai*. I really like how Bill Burnett and Dave Evans[30] use "Mind Mapping"—a terrific design-thinking tool that generates a range of ideas—in the course on life design they teach at Stanford University. In a nutshell, here is how mind mapping works (more details in the journaling section at the back):

- Start with one of the activities that leverages your strengths and which you enjoy doing. Now write down five to six things related to it in a ring around the central idea.
- For each of the things you wrote down in the second ring, generate an additional five to six ideas for each to create a third ring.
- Draw three to four lines from each word and free associate new words related to the prompts.
- Repeat the steps above until you have created three to four rings around your core idea.
- As a final step, take this random association of words and highlight a few that might be interesting to you or jump out at you. Ideally, pick them from the outermost layer, as these are farthest from our conscious thinking. You can now start to mash these up to generate a few concepts.

I started my own mind map around the core activity of "helping others." Within ten minutes, I had over twenty different ideas. The most obvious was "pivoting to do more coaching and leadership development work with the firm." But as I looked over my map, two additional concepts began to emerge. First: could I create a company that supports others in pursuing their own journeys toward discovering greater meaning and purpose? Second: could I leverage my network of connections and twenty-plus years of diverse business management experience to launch an Impact fund/Accelerator that focused on supporting companies focused on doing good in the world?

The final step in the process to redesign your work life and infuse it with meaning is to **test commercial viability** of the different options you are excited about through a mix of primary and secondary research. The primary research can take multiple forms, including having conversations

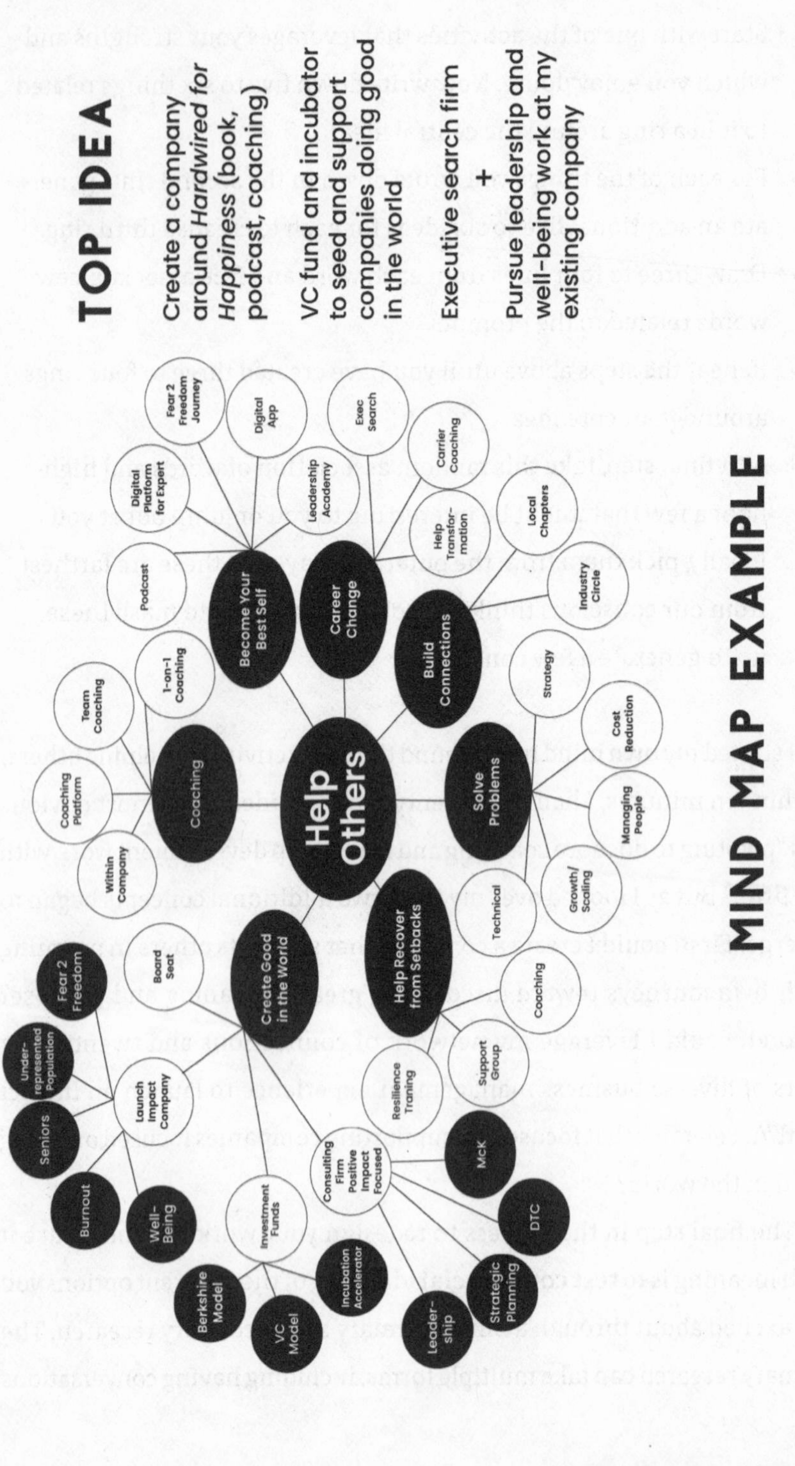

TOP IDEA

Create a company around *Hardwired for Happiness* (book, podcast, coaching)

VC fund and incubator to seed and support companies doing good in the world

Executive search firm

+

Pursue leadership and well-being work at my existing company

MIND MAP EXAMPLE

Figure 2.3: My mind-mapping output

Help Others (central node)

- Become Your Best Self
  - Fear 2 Freedom Journey
  - Digital App
  - Digital Platform for Expert
  - Podcast
  - 1-on-1 Coaching
  - Team Coaching

- Career Change
  - Exec Search
  - Leadership Academy
  - Carrier Coaching
  - Help Transformation

- Build Connections
  - Local Chapters
  - Industry Circle
  - Strategy

- Coaching
  - Coaching Platform
  - Within Company

- Solve Problems
  - Cost Reduction
  - Managing People
  - Growth/Scaling
  - Technical
  - Coaching

- Help Recover from Setbacks
  - Support Group
  - Resilience Training

- Create Good in the World
  - Board Seat
  - Fear 2 Freedom
  - Launch Impact Company
    - Under-represented Population
    - Seniors
    - Burnout
    - Well-Being
  - Investment Funds
    - Berkshire Model
    - VC Model
    - Incubation Accelerator
  - Consulting Firm Positive Impact Focused
    - McK
    - DTC
    - Leadership
    - Strategic Planning

with others already pursuing something like your idea; designing a small experiment to test the viability of the idea; and allowing yourself to feel what it would be like to live this new life. Secondary research involves talking to experts and reviewing market research that might exist in the area you are interested in exploring.

Talk to Others Who Are Pursuing the Field That Interests You

Start by identifying a set of individuals who are pursuing careers in areas that are of interest to you and who would be willing to share their insights with you. You could ask your immediate friends, family members, or colleagues for any recommendations they might have or possible connections to individuals you might identify. LinkedIn can also be a terrific resource to research and connect with others. It is important to gather input from eight to ten people to ensure you get a diverse set of perspectives. As you engage with these individuals, ask them what it is like to work in that field, what a typical workday looks like, the amount of travel, the level of flexibility they enjoy, what they like about their jobs, and what they don't enjoy. They can also share advice on the skills you will need to acquire, top companies that operate in that field, and how you might go about breaking into them.

Design Small Experiments

I would also encourage you to test your idea and play the roles you are considering, even if for a short amount of time. One of the benefits of this approach is the ability to truly immerse yourself and experience firsthand what working on this idea would entail. There are several ways to create these experiences, such as shadowing someone else who is already in this role, volunteering or taking on an unpaid exploratory project, running a workshop, taking a part-time job, or freelancing on weekends or after hours and creating a minimal viable product to test with prospective customers.

Conduct Market Research or Talk to Experts in the Space You Are Interested In

There are several market research and expert network firms like GLG, AlphaSights, and others that can make deep experts available to you who can be valuable sources of insight. You can also buy market research reports on the different industries/verticals you are interested in that profile these segments in terms of revenue, profitability, growth, level of investment (venture capital, private equity), and top companies operating in the space.

In my case, one of the concepts I was interested in exploring was to pivot toward pursuing leadership consulting within my firm. I wanted to test the commercial viability of this offering, as it was almost nonexistent at my firm at that time. Before jumping in, I wanted to make sure there was sufficient market demand for this offering. I identified about fifty individuals across six different organizations to get their perspectives both within and outside my company. Second, I also knew that most search firms like Egon Zehnder and Heidrick & Struggles also have vibrant leadership consulting practices; so I found leaders in those practices to connect with. Third, I decided to connect with others who had gone the entrepreneurship route as well as those who were working for boutique leadership development firms. Finally, there are lots of technology-based startups that are using artificial intelligence and other virtual models to improve leadership and team effectiveness. Using a mix of my personal network and LinkedIn, I was able to find individuals within each of these companies who gave me a very rich perspective on the space of leadership development.

The information I gathered not only helped me identify whitespaces to target with the leadership development offering we were creating, but also gave me insight on what life would look like, were I to launch my own entrepreneurial venture in the domain of the Impact Accelerator or a stand-alone advisory and coaching firm. Even more importantly, it extended my network within the leadership development, wellbeing, and happiness space, identifying several collaborators and thought partners who I could lean on, if I were to launch my own venture someday.

Meditation Exercise:
Your Eightieth Birthday Party

This visualization practice is a powerful technique to sense what you value most in your life and tap into the wisdom of your older self. Imagine that you are arriving at your own eightieth birthday party where your friends, family, coworkers, customers, and others from your community have gathered to celebrate with you. You can allow yourself to imagine anyone you would most want to be there irrespective of age (your parents or grandparents), or those you might not have met yet (your grandchildren).

Duration: fifteen to thirty minutes

1. Sit in a comfortable position that allows you to be relaxed but also alert. This is a good meditation to just practice sitting in a chair with your back straight. Keep your shoulders relaxed, your chin facing slightly upward, and close your eyes. Keep your jaw relaxed with your lips slightly open. You can rest your arms on your legs with palms facing downward.

2. Take three deep breaths, feeling the air fill your lungs and your stomach, and then slowly exhale with an open mouth, letting all the air out and feeling your stomach contract. Let yourself relax completely.

3. Resume breathing at your normal pace keeping attention on each inhale and exhale, feeling your belly rise with each inhale and fall with each exhale.

4. Now imagine that you are floating down a river in a boat running through a beautiful forest. The sun is shining, and the forest is alive with noises of birds and little animals moving through it.

5. Feel the sun on your face and let the sounds of the river and surroundings lull you into the rhythm of nature— slow, peaceful, ever changing. Let yourself just relax into the moment.

6. Imagine now as you float down the river, you hear some sounds of a beautiful harp from a distance. You row your boat to the bank so you can explore where this sound is coming from.

7. As you get off the boat, you see a little path that leads through the woods toward a house. The sound seems to be coming from there and you decide to follow it.

8. As you arrive at the gates, you realize music is coming from a party inside and people have gathered to celebrate your eightieth birthday party.

9. As you enter the house, you see so many familiar faces who are all excited to see you. Your family is here—your kids,

parents, grandparents, siblings. Your friends are here—from school, college, and adult life. Your coworkers, customers, and suppliers you worked with over the years are all here. You also notice others from the communities that you are a part of—the local barista, kids benefiting from the donations you have made.

10. As you make your way through the room, acknowledging each of them, they pull you aside and whisper in your ears what you have meant to them. They share with you what you have stood for as a person and the impact you have had. Let the words of each individual or group sink in and land.

11. The last person you meet is your older self. If you were to be bold in this moment, what would your eightieth, wiser self say to you?

12. Gently bring your attention back to the present moment. Take a moment to get centered here and then slowly open your eyes.

13. Use the next five minutes to journal and capture what you heard people say, what the words meant to you, and how it affected you. Also jot down any actions you want to take going forward to live into what matters to you in the end.

Building Your Purpose Practice

For most of us, discovering our purpose is not something that suddenly turns on like a lightbulb overhead. It is a perpetual quest that brings up a lot of existential questions that need to be wrestled with. It requires us to be brave and courageous to pursue them, while still navigating our current professions in a fiscally responsible way. You may already have thoughts on your purpose and what you truly have always wanted to pursue but have never brought the opportunity to do it to fruition. Now is the time to seize the moment, take the reins in your hands, and explore your passion.

I would strongly encourage you start by first seeing if you can transform your current job. Think about pivots that you can make over the next three to five years that continuously help you realign your current job with your *Ikigai*. Have the bold conversations with your manager or leadership team on what you are passionate about and how they can support you in living into your purpose.

In case you do decide for one reason or another that you can't align your *Ikigai* with your current job, make sure you are realistic about the plan you are laying out for pursuing your new venture and have the right foundation in place: financially, new skills you will need, strong relationships, and the support from your family and friends. Seek the advice of experts and mentors on the path you are outlining. Doing the right diligence before action will ensure you never regret turning over that stone you always thought about.

If you were to sit with your grandchild on your knee one day and they would ask you what you do, you want to tell them with excitement and passion what you do, that you have followed your heart, and have made full use of the time you have spent in this world. By taking deliberate actions now, you can create a career which keeps you engaged, growing, and serving others till your last breath. The best part of it all is you get to enjoy the journey every step of the way versus waiting for the next career milestone or promotion. Your joy and happiness do not depend on the actions of others. It solely stems from living into your *Ikigai* from moment to moment.

KEY TAKEAWAYS

- Purposeful living has been linked to:
  - ► Physical wellbeing, including lower risk of cardiovascular disease, better sleep, healthier behaviors, and an overall longer, better life.
  - ► Higher life satisfaction and a sense of self-worth, energy, and passion.
  - ► Higher professional success.
- To develop your *Ikigai*, or reason for being, design your life around the intersection of four main things: what you love, what you are good at, what the world needs, and what you can be paid for.
- Always start by reimagining your work at your current job by increasing focus on activities that can bring you joy and energy, reducing time on activities that are energy draining, and stepping back to connect the overall organizational purpose to your individual purpose.
- If living your purpose isn't possible where you are, reimagine your career or life using thoughtful mind mapping, market research, leveraging relationships, and testing the viability of your options.

Embrace Mindful Living

"Our appointment with life is in the present moment.
The place of our appointment is right here, in this place."

—Thich Nhat Hahn

Consider this Zen parable: one day, while a farmer was working in the field, his horse ran away. That evening his neighbors came to console him and said, "So sorry for your loss." The farmer seemed unperturbed. He just said, "Maybe." The next morning, the farmer was surprised to see that the horse had returned and had brought with him seven other wild horses. Again his neighbors gathered to congratulate the farmer on his good fortune. The farmer didn't seem overjoyed, but he replied, "Maybe."

Later that week, as the farmer's son tried to tame one of the wild horses, it bucked and threw him off its back. The son was badly injured and suffered a broken leg. The neighbors offered their sympathies and said, "That's too bad—now you will have to till the field alone." The farmer just said, "Maybe."

That weekend, soldiers came to the village looking to enlist young adults into the army to fight the neighboring king who had declared war.

Many of the friends of the farmer's son were enlisted, but his son was spared as he was injured. All the neighbors cried, "Isn't that wonderful?" And the farmer said, "Maybe."

The moral of the story as taught by Gautama Buddha is to not dwell in the past or dream of the future, but instead concentrate the mind on the present moment. Life consists of both good and bad moments. We can never predict what the outcome will be. We can avoid a lot of suffering by taking things moment by moment versus jumping to conclusions and maintaining our equanimity regardless of what life serves us.

How often do you find yourself thinking of something other than what you are doing? If you're like most people, you spend almost half your waking hours distracted, according to research done by psychologists Matthew A. Killingsworth and Daniel T. Gilbert of Harvard University.[31] "A human mind is a wandering mind, and a wandering mind is an unhappy mind," Killingsworth and Gilbert wrote in the report. Whether you're lost in the past or worried about how the future will unfold, chances are you're missing out on life in the present moment. The problem isn't that we have a rich memory or a vast imagination, but that we have lost the ability to direct our brains consciously to what we want. Imagine if our hands or legs moved on their own volition, without our control, 50 percent of the time? Would we not be rushing to the doctor to regain mastery over our limbs? Then why do we accept our wandering minds?

The good news is that you can develop the superpower of mindfulness to transform your life and fuel your journey forward. Dr. Jon Kabat-Zinn, considered the father of the modern mindful movement, coined a definition of mindfulness that is easy to understand and quite universally accepted: *the awareness that arises from paying attention, on purpose, in the present moment and nonjudgmentally.*" When we meditate, we are practicing mindfulness more formally by carving out time and using one of numerous approaches of paying attention. Today, mindfulness/ meditation are well-known practices across the globe and are used to improve mental health, stress, and burnout. However, despite the high level of awareness of mindfulness and meditation and the many benefits, only 14 percent of American adults practice meditation.[32]

Over the course of this chapter, I will share several best practices and actions that you can take to increase your ability to focus and bring the power of mindfulness to transform your experience from moment to moment, day to day, hour to hour. I have curated these from the works of leading masters from the east and the west. Having experimented with every one of these practices, I can attest to their effectiveness in improving your ability to focus and turn the mundane moments into magic.

The Science-Backed Benefits of Mindfulness

Mindfulness has been proven to lead to better performance, higher innovation, and the ability to better manage stress and anxiety in our day-to-day lives. It is no surprise then that leaders across almost every domain from business (Bill Gates, Arianna Huffington) to sports (Lebron James, Steph Curry) to celebrities (Will Smith, Jennifer Lopez) have integrated mindfulness practices into their daily lives. Recognizing the power of mindfulness, Google created a program called Search Inside Yourself that has been running since 2007 and has trained 100,000 people around the world.

One of the pioneering studies on the benefits of mindfulness was conducted in the early 2000s by Dr. Jon Kabat-Zinn, the founder of the UMass Memorial Health Center for Mindfulness, in collaboration with Dr. Richard Davidson from the University of Wisconsin–Madison.[33] They found that participants who went through an eight-week mindfulness-based stress-reduction program experienced less anxiety and more positive moods compared to the control group. These self-reported improvements originated from physiological changes to their brains. Specifically, the researchers found that participants had a significantly higher activity in the left side of the prefrontal cortex—the part associated with complex emotional, cognitive, and behavioral functions—as compared to the right-hand side.

Countless scientific studies since then have identified the long list of psychological and physiological benefits of mindfulness. The top psychological benefits include an increased ability to concentrate, self-confidence, social skills, and an overall sense of optimism and happiness. On the physiological side, mindfulness has been proven to increase our immunity, better manage pain and other physical ailments like psoriasis, irritable bowel syndrome, fibromyalgia, and even chronic heart failure. Using advanced neuroimaging techniques like fMRI, EEG and others, researchers have been able to study how practicing mindfulness produces fundamental changes in our brain structure that are behind many of these benefits. A research paper published in 2014 by a team of scientists pooled data from more than twenty studies and identified several distinct areas of the brain that were affected.[34] (See the following table.)

Brain Structure	Function	Changes Observed with Regular Meditation
Prefrontal cortex	Thinking brain—Rational decision-making, accomplishing goals	Increases in thickness and gray matter[35]
Insula Cortex	Responsible for awareness of body sensations from hunger, breathing, heartbeat	Connections in the right insula strengthen increasing awareness

Anterior Cingulate Cortex (ACC)	Self-regulation and ability to ignore distractions and pay attention; also play a critical role in learning from the past to support better decision-making[36]	Higher activation while meditating suggests greater ability to handle distractions[37]
Brain Stem	Mood regulation	Gray matter increases linked to higher self-acceptance
Amygdala	Process stress and responsible for fight-flight-freeze response	Shrinks in size; reduction in connectivity to the ACC resulting in greater emotional control[38]
Hippocampus	Critical role in learning, memory, and emotional processing	Gray matter concentration in left hippocampus increasing, suggesting meditators better at mood regulation[39]
Thalamus	Processes sensory information, including pain	Higher activity in the thalamus region combined with decreased activity in regions associated with processing pain,[40] suggesting ability to endure pain without psychological/emotional suffering

Table: How mindfulness/meditation practices affect brain structure

Aetna, the major US health insurer, is renowned for embracing the mindfulness movement and reaping its benefits in productivity and stress reduction. According to a study published at the Wharton School, Aetna estimated an annual productivity increase of $3,000 per employee and a 28 percent reported reduction in stress levels after implementing mindfulness practices at work.[41] Andy Lee, the former Chief Mindfulness officer at Aetna, reportedly began every meeting with a minute of mindfulness practice: sitting quietly and paying attention to the breath. Aetna also promotes this practice across the company—taking a mindful minute to calm and refresh the mind, multiple times during the day.[42]

With the strong evidence backing the effectiveness of mindfulness in rewiring the brain to live healthier and happier lives, I highly recommend making a habit of exercising your brain daily with mindfulness exercises just as you would give your physical body a workout. Mindfulness arguably does more for the brain than brushing does for your teeth—and most of us brush our teeth *twice* daily!

How to Sit: Meditation as a Path to Mindfulness

The easiest way to practice mindfulness is to bring awareness to the present moment, no matter what you are doing. You can do this by simply focusing on your breath as it is always with you—you can only breathe in this moment, not in the past and for sure not in the future. You take about 20,000 breaths in a day, most of them mindlessly. But if you take even a single breath mindfully, it provides a beautiful path connecting your wandering mind to your stationary body.

A formal sitting meditation practice can play a big role in helping you gain greater control over your wandering mind and experience increased calmness, clarity, and joyfulness. Almost all spiritual texts recognize that happiness is our default state of mind. If you want real life evidence, just look at a baby or a young child. You will notice that for them, they are always in the present moment, happy, smiling, and intensely involved in whatever they are doing. Something must happen to make them *unhappy* (e.g., they get hungry, fall down, feel discomfort). However, if you shift attention to yourself or other adults, we need something to make us *happy*. Somewhere along the way to adulthood, as we lose our ability to focus and just be in the moment, we find ourselves constantly worrying about the future or replaying the past. We lose sight that there was a time we were happy just "being." Meditation can allow you to rediscover that base state of happiness that you can reach, not by doing more, but by letting yourself be and fall into the present moment.

You can practice sitting meditation in a variety of places, including sitting down on the floor, on a chair, lying down on a mat, and even while walking. What is important is that you take a posture that embodies wakefulness and allows you to both remain alert and relaxed for a long period of time. One such posture—developed over thousands of years and my go-to posture for meditation—is called the seven-point meditation posture:

1. **Legs: sit in a comfortable position.** The most important thing when meditating is to find a position which is comfortable to you. Formal practice suggests using a cross-legged position also called the Lotus position, where you sit with your legs crossed, each foot placed with the sole facing upward on the opposite thigh. I find this to be difficult. So I use an alternative position where I sit with both feet crossed resting on the floor and under the opposite thighs. You can also use a cushion that raises your buttocks higher to release the tension on the knees, or even sit on a chair with your legs on the ground.

2. **Back: keep the back straight.** Keeping your back naturally straight enhances alertness during meditation practice and enables energy to move more freely through your body's subtle energy channels.

3. **Shoulders: relaxed and spread slightly back.** Try opening your chest slightly and relaxing your shoulders so that they are spread slightly back, almost as if you are pinching a pencil with your shoulder blades. You can practice raising your shoulders up

to your ears and then roll them back so that your shoulder blades move downward. This motion helps to guide the upper body into position and fosters an alert, attentive mind, rather than one that is distracted or dull.

4. **Arms: folded with hands resting in your lap or on your knees.**
Place your hands loosely on your lap, with your right hand resting in the palm of your left hand with thumbs slightly touching. Alternatively, you can place your palms on each folded leg in one of several *mudras* (hand positions). My personal favorite is the *Gyan mudra*, which is performed by touching your index fingertip to the tip of your thumb, while holding your other three fingers straight.

5. **Eyes: closed or slightly closed in a relaxed, neutral gaze.**
When starting meditation, many people find it easier to concentrate with their eyes fully closed to tune out any distractions. However, if you find that this produces drowsiness for you, you can also leave your eyes slightly open to admit a little light, and direct your gaze downward.

6. **Mouth: closed or slightly open mouth with relaxed jaw.**
Your mouth can either be closed or just slightly open so air can escape, as if you were saying softly, "Ah." Let your jaw relax (actively clench and unclench your jaw to see how much it may be stressed). Try a small smile at the beginning of your meditation to instantly relax and bring joy to your practice. Let your tongue touch your upper palate to reduce the flow of saliva.

7. **Face: looking slightly down with chin tucked in or slightly up.** Maintain a peaceful expression on your face, looking slightly down. Keep your chin slightly tucked in. Alternately,

you can also experiment with tilting your neck so your face is slightly upward, till you feel your attention shifting to a point between your eyes (this is also known in some texts as the third eye).

The Seven-Point
SITTING MEDITATION
POSTURE

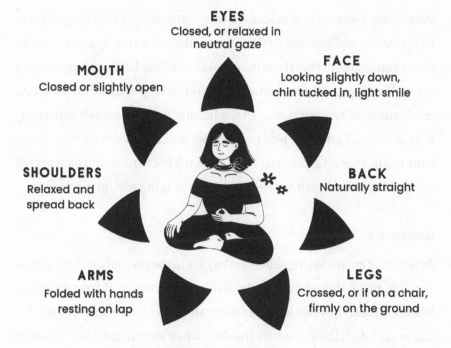

EYES
Closed, or relaxed in neutral gaze

FACE
Looking slightly down, chin tucked in, light smile

MOUTH
Closed or slightly open

SHOULDERS
Relaxed and spread back

BACK
Naturally straight

ARMS
Folded with hands resting on lap

LEGS
Crossed, or if on a chair, firmly on the ground

Figure 3.1: Seven-point meditation posture

The Attitudes of Mindfulness

Equally important as the posture is our attitudes and mindsets that we bring into the meditation practice. In his book, *Full Catastrophe Living* (1990), Jon Kabat-Zinn outlined seven specific attitudes that form a foundation for mindfulness. These attitudes are non-judging, patience, a beginner's mind, trust, non-striving, acceptance, and letting go.[43] The three mindsets people most commonly struggle with (my clients and I included) are non-judging, acceptance, and adopting a beginner's mind, so I'll elaborate on those here.

Non-Judging

We are judgment-making machines, constantly categorizing everything as those we like and approve, or those we dislike and do not approve. I would invite you to accept that there is no good or bad meditation. Stop judging yourself, as it goes fundamentally against the very spirit of mindfulness meditation. When I first started meditating, I found myself constantly judging myself on my ability to maintain focus on my breathing. Every time I found my attention wavering from my breath, I would beat myself up. I had to learn to just notice when I was judging and let it go.

Acceptance

Acceptance means seeing things as they are in the present moment versus how you think they should be. In meditation practice, if you can accept rising and falling of thoughts as a natural aspect of the human mind, you can accept with the same ease the days when your mind is calm, just as much as accepting the days when your *monkey mind* is constantly jumping from one thought to another. Paradoxically, when I stopped trying to force my mind to clear my thoughts, I found myself being able to access a deeper, calmer state of mind. It is no different than picturing the calm waters that lie deep beneath the ocean surface, no matter how choppy and stormy the waves on top.

Adopting a Beginner's Mind

Buddhist monk Shunryu Suzuki wisely said, "In the beginner's mind there are many possibilities, but in the expert's, there are few." To practice a beginner's mind means being open to the experience in each moment as if meeting it for the first time, versus anticipating something to happen and getting frustrated when it does not. Adopting a beginner's mind allowed me to stop comparing my meditation sessions from one to the next and expecting each to be "better" than the last one.

It is not uncommon during our meditation practices, at the outset, to get easily distracted by our monkey minds. A recent study conducted in 2020 by psychologists at Queen's University in Kingston, Canada,[44] suggested that an average person has 6,000 thoughts per day or more than six thoughts per minute, excluding sleeping time. Personally, when I started my meditation practice four years ago, I could not focus for even six breaths before losing my concentration. Once my attention had wandered, I got lost in self-judgment and critical self-talk. What helped me a lot was accepting that I could not *force* my mind to go blank.

Finding our attention is like a muscle that we train every time we become aware that our mind has wandered and bring it back to our breath. It is the act of bringing back that strengthens the muscle and experiencing the moment while dropping the judgment and reacting. Even today, there are days when I find myself in a calm state and others when my mind is like the choppy sea. But all I need to do is drop down deeper past the surface (like diving twenty to thirty feet below the ocean's surface) and find the calmness that is always there.

Meditation Exercise:
Four Dimensions of Stability, Dignity, Connection, and Wisdom

Too often we encounter situations that make us feel unstable, not enough, alone, or lost without a clear direction forward. It's important to ground yourself and find your center despite what's happening around you. This sitting meditation can help you find your center by directing attention to the four dimensions of stability, dignity, connection, and wisdom that all exist within you.

Duration: ten minutes

1. Sit in a comfortable position that allows you to be relaxed but also alert. This is a good meditation to practice sitting in a chair with your back straight. Keep your shoulders relaxed, your chin facing slightly upward, and close your eyes. Keep your jaw relaxed with your lips slightly open. You can rest your arms on your legs with palms facing downward.

2. Take three deep breaths, feeling the air fill your lungs and your stomach, and then slowly exhale with an open mouth, letting all the air out and feeling your stomach contract. Let yourself relax completely.

3. Resume breathing at your normal pace keeping attention on each inhale and exhale, feeling your belly rise with each inhale and fall with each exhale. You don't need to manipulate it. Let the inhale take as long as it needs to— it might take three, four, five seconds. You don't have to

interfere with your breathing. If your inhale is short, allow it to be short. If your exhale is long, let it be long. Keep breathing at your normal pace for the rest of the meditation.

4. While maintaining attention on your breath, shift your attention to the bottom of your feet. As you send your breath and your attention to the soles of your feet, feel the ground supporting you. You can imagine little roots growing from the bottom of your feet into the ground connecting you to Mother Earth, nourishing you and providing **Stability**. If you ever lose your footing, know that the stability is right here for you always. Take five sets of inhales and exhales, relaxing into this dimension.

5. Shift attention now to the top of your head. You can imagine a string attached to your head, gently pulling you upward. Stretch into the full dimension of your length— this is the dimension of **Dignity**. This is a dimension that says, "You are enough, just as you are. You don't have to do anything to be worthy. You are worthy just as you are." Next time you feel insecure or feel unworthy, remember you always have access to this dimension of dignity. Take five sets of inhales and exhales, relaxing into this dimension.

6. Shift attention now to your width and feel the edges of your shoulders. This is the dimension of **Connection**. As you breathe into this dimension, think about your family,

your friends, your colleagues, and others in your life who will always be there for you, cheering you on, supporting you. So, even at this moment if you feel alone, know that there are so many in your life to whom you can reach out and connect. They will be here for you just as you are here for them. Take five sets of inhales and exhales, relaxing into this dimension.

7. Shift attention now toward your back. We spend so much of our time leaning forward that we forget to feel our back. This is the dimension of **Wisdom** and contains all the lessons life has taught you through your trials and your successes. You possess the wisdom within you to handle anything the world throws at you. When you feel uncertain about the path forward, lean into this dimension and see what is waiting to emerge. Take five sets of inhales and exhales, relaxing into this dimension.

8. Finally, bring attention back to your heart center and take three to five breaths, breathing in and breathing out, letting your heart feel connected to the four dimensions: Stability, Dignity, Connection, and Wisdom.

9. Slowly open your eyes and take in the environment around you. Notice what you are feeling in your body, the emotions that are present, and the quality of your thoughts.

10. Set an intention to be with this awareness through the day before getting up and going about your daily routine.

Practicing Mindfulness Off the Mat

We live in a world filled with shiny objects that are continuously pulling our attention from one thing to another. Over the last twenty years since smartphones arrived on the scene, most of us have become dopamine addicts: constantly checking our social media, email, or text messages in search of the next dopamine hit. We have lost our ability to focus and bring awareness for an extended period of time to a particular task. Consider this statistic: Americans on average check their phones 344 times in a day, which translates to once every four wakeful minutes.[45] While meditating on the mat each day is necessary, it is critical to stay in a mindfulness practice *off* the mat as well, in order to continue making progress toward a happier, more fulfilling life.

Another big reason for practicing mindfulness off the mat is that it addresses one of the most common excuses I hear from professionals when asked to practice meditation: "I'm too busy." Trust me, you are never too busy to stay mindful. By simply doing what you do on any given day, but bringing conscious awareness to it, you can convert any activity into a mindful activity and really enjoy the moment. Rumi said it best: "Look past your thoughts, so you may drink the pure nectar of This Moment."

Journaling Exercise:
Mindful Coloring

One of the simplest and most fun ways to practice mindfulness is by investing in a coloring journal. Coloring is yet another opportunity to train your mind to be mindful, focus your awareness on the pre-drawn illustration, and suspend your inner dialogues. Coloring of mandala designs (geometric configurations of symbols, usually in a circle or rectangle) has been proven to lower your heart rate and blood pressure[46] while reducing some symptoms of stress and anxiety.[47]

Here are some suggestions on how to practice mindful coloring:

1. Find a time and a place where you will not be interrupted and set aside ten to fifteen minutes to practice.
2. Sit comfortably at a table and gather your coloring materials.
3. As you color in the mandala, simultaneously bring attention to your breath and notice the quality of your inhale and exhale. You will notice that without trying, your breath will become deeper.
4. Try and sync your coloring strokes with your breath and enjoy the spaciousness and calming quality that emerges.
5. Be aware of any thoughts that might arise as you are coloring. Let them go, imagining them gently drifting away with each exhale, while you focus on the act of coloring.

Figure 3.2: Hiding Pangolin by Shaveta B from Mondaymandala.com

Everyday Mindfulness

Over the last five years, I have experimented with bringing mindfulness to many of my day-to-day activities to turn my life into a living *dojo*. If you feel you don't have time for formal meditation, I would like to invite you to bring mindful energy to one or more of these ideas that require no additional time from you.

Mindful Brushing, Bathing, Shaving, or Getting Dressed

Your morning or evening grooming routine is the perfect practice ground for mindfulness. Each of these activities take two to four minutes and offer a wonderful opportunity to practice mindfulness. For example, as you start brushing your teeth, take a deep breath and bring your awareness to how the toothbrush bristles feel touching your teeth. You can also experience the freshness or tingling caused by your toothpaste. Focus on the in and out motion of your hand as you gently glide the toothbrush across your teeth. Bring a sense of curiosity to fully experience any sensations that might arise.

Eating or Drinking Mindfully

Every time you eat or drink is a wonderful opportunity to practice mindfulness and be fully present. Who is not guilty of eating a meal while busy reading, talking, watching a film, scrolling social media, or working through lunch? Mindful eating is about reaching a state of full attention to your experiences, cravings, and physical cues when you eat. Fundamentally, mindful eating involves eating slowly and without distraction, engaging your senses by noticing colors, smells, sounds, textures, and flavors, and being fully present. Eating mindfully can turn eating into a far richer experience, satisfying more than the need for nutrition.

Next time, before you start eating, take three to five deep breaths and bring your full attention to the food or drink in front of you. You can start by drinking a glass of water and tuning into the level of hunger you are feeling. Bring attention to the plate in front of you, taking in the different colors, textures of the food on your plate, and express your gratefulness for the food you are about to eat and where it may have come from. In the yogic traditions, one would even touch their food mindfully and pay thanks to each of the items which were alive and are in a sense offering their life energies to us. Take your first three bites mindfully, experience the taste, flavors, textures, and how much enjoyment you are receiving from a certain food. Make a mindful choice about what to eat based on what you really enjoy.

Mindful Walking

Whether you are walking in the office from one meeting room to another, walking from your office or home to your car, or just walking around your neighborhood, you can bring awareness to it and transform it into a mindful moment. To practice mindful walking, start by setting your intent to walk mindfully before you even get up from the seat. As you stand up, allow yourself to fully become aware of your body and the sensation of standing. Now take a deep breath in and take one step forward, putting all your attention on the sole of your foot. Exhale as your foot touches the ground, and continue to connect your breath with your step, starting out slowly.

While walking, practice conscious breathing by counting steps. Do not try to control your breathing but keep track of the number of steps you take with each inhale, and the number of steps with each exhale. As you walk, pay attention to the details in your surroundings—the nature around you, including the trees and plants, sounds including those of birds singing, architecture of the buildings, etc. In the words of Thich Nhat Hanh, "Walk as if you are kissing the Earth with your feet."[48]

Mindful Meetings

We live in an overscheduled world where if you are like any of my clients or colleagues, your calendar every day is filled with back-to-back meetings. You might even find yourself multiple times in a day scheduled to attend two meetings starting at the same time. In a rush to get from one meeting to another, you might find yourself struggling to catch a breath and be fully present in any of them. There are three things that you can start to bring more mindfulness in your day at work. First, start scheduling meetings to be only forty-five minutes (instead of sixty minutes) and twenty-five minutes (instead of thirty minutes), keeping a buffer of five to fifteen minutes between meetings. Second, use the break to capture any remnant thoughts from the meeting that just finished in your notepad. You can also use this time to calm your nervous system—in case it was an intense meeting with lots of emotions—by the mindful breathing techniques I described earlier. Finally, you can integrate a mindful check-in before key, high-stakes meetings, where you want everyone to be at their best and bring their whole creative selves.

Community Exercise:
Practice Mindful Listening

Often when we are conversing with others, our tendency is to already start to formulate a response to what we are hearing, even while the other person is still talking. Even if we do not interrupt the other person, we might still tune out. How often do you really stop what you are doing and give the gift of your full attention to the other person? You can do this exercise in groups of six to ten individuals from your professional or personal community.

- Start by doing a centering exercise. Have everyone plant their feet and collectively take three deep breaths together while fully arriving in the moment.
- Ask one of the members of your group a question from the list below and give them three minutes to respond verbally.
- The role for you and the rest of the group after asking the question is just to listen deeply. Give your undivided attention to the person speaking. Silence all notifications for phones, emails, etc. You can acknowledge by nodding, through your facial expressions, or simply saying a few words like, "I understand," or "I hear you." If the speaker finishes before three minutes, it is fine to let silence fill the space.
  - ▸ **Listen with your ears:** Listen to the words and what is being said. Listen also to the song beneath the words. Notice what is *not* being said?

- **Listen with your eyes:** Take the whole person in. Look for non-verbal cues like body language, pacing of words, and flow of energy in their way of being.
- **Listen with your heart:** Listen to the emotions/moods present. Look for what is waiting to emerge.

- After the person finishes, thank them for sharing and ask them to choose the next person whom they want to invite to share.

You can use any of the questions below for the exercise:

1. How are you feeling?
2. What does a life well lived mean to you?
3. What makes you smile when you get up in the morning?
4. What fills you with joy?
5. What are you most excited about in your life right now?
6. What is the most important thing I should know about you?
7. What is one of the most cherished memories of yours growing up?
8. What is a life experience that has played a big role in shaping who you are today?
9. What are you most proud of in your life?
10. Who are the heroes in your life?

My client Carla was the CIO of a large bank and led a team of twelve senior executives. Every week, Carla held a sixty-minute team meeting to check on progress being made across the different priority technology initiatives that each of the leaders were responsible for and to collectively take actions, including reprioritizing resources, adjusting timelines, and resolving cross-functional issues. Carla was frustrated as the team often seemed distracted and inattentive. The quality of dialogue and decision-making was suffering. Carla invited me to attend a meeting and help her refocus the team.

Right away, I could see a couple of issues that were plaguing the team. Most people were only half paying attention: their laptops were open, and they typed emails frantically on their mobile devices. It was a classic pattern I had seen with overscheduled leaders trying to multitask their way to success. I could also see that the attention spans were the lowest in the first and last ten minutes of the meetings. In the first ten minutes, people seemed to be processing whatever had transpired in the meeting they had just come from. Similarly, I could see that people were already checked out in the last ten minutes, thinking about the next meeting.

Together, Carla and I came up with three simple things she could implement to introduce mindfulness into these meetings. First, she condensed the meeting to forty-five minutes and got the commitment from her team to keep the first ten minutes and last five minutes of the time she had freed up as buffer. They were not to schedule anything during these times. Second, they agreed to turn electronic devices OFF during the meeting. This was easier said than done, as some leaders were responsible for critical infrastructure or applications. However, Carla's assistant was listed as an emergency contact and could reach them right away if needed. Third, Carla instituted a mindful check-in at the beginning of the meeting for the group to "fully arrive." To do this, I encouraged them to integrate a STOP practice which I had discovered as part of a mindfulness workshop at my work.[49] **S**topping; **T**aking five to ten mindful breaths, while feeling their feet; **O**bserving the sensations in their body, emotions present and just using the power of breath to calm themselves; and **P**roceeding with more awareness and checking in with each other using a question. They chose from a list of questions like: How do I feel at this moment? Is there anything that is stopping me from fully being here? What's our intention for today?

The results were immediate; the team was able to accomplish more in forty-five minutes than they had ever done in an hour. More importantly, the quality of dialogue was much higher, and the environment was not as tense. By taking a few minutes to breathe and be attentive in the moment, the group reached a collective state of calm and could engage productively.

Building Your Mindfulness Practice

Mastering your ability to flex your mindfulness superpower on and off the mat is a critical step on your journey. Living mindfully will help you look deeply within yourself to discover who you are, face your deepest fears, and get more of what you want out of life. As you read further, you'll see that many of the other practices including gratitude, letting go of negative feelings, fueling up through love, compassion, and kindness, and investing in wellbeing require us to shine the light of mindfulness. My clients and I have benefited significantly in our capabilities for self-awareness and regulation, in being able to connect with others through empathy and listening deeply, and in being able to perform at a high level through the power of concentration. My only regret is that I did not discover mindfulness earlier in my life, despite growing up in India, where many of the mindfulness practices originated more than 2,000 years ago.

My invitation to you is to make mindfulness a core part of your everyday life and create twenty-five to thirty minutes in your schedule to "take the seat," no matter how busy you are. Start with a ten-minute daily practice and give it a try for thirty days. I am convinced you will benefit tremendously and not look back.

KEY TAKEAWAYS

- Mindfulness has been proven to lead to better performance, higher innovation, and the ability to better manage stress and anxiety in our day-to-day lives.
- The easiest way to practice mindfulness is to bring awareness to the present moment, no matter what you are doing, using seated meditation or just focusing on your breathing.
- Practicing mindfulness off the mat is just as critical and can be done during everyday activities, such as brushing your teeth, eating, walking, and conducting meetings.

Practice Gratitude

"He is a wise man who does not grieve for the things which
he has not but rejoices for those which he has."

—Epictetus

H ow often have you found yourself thinking *"I'll be happy when..."*? And how often, very quickly after getting or doing that thing, it no longer holds as much value, and you start thinking about the next thing? When we feel good, our brains are triggered to want more of that feeling, and we tend to forget about what we already have in favor of chasing an ever-moving target. But if we rely solely on the external things themselves to bring us happiness, we're doomed to run in circles, unaware that happiness is an inner game. Gratitude is a powerful antidote to the current culture of *more*—doing more, wanting more, buying more. Practicing gratitude changes our focus from what we don't have, to all that we are already blessed with.

Consider the following story: one day, a philosophy professor walked into his classroom and announced that he was going to give the students a surprise test. He handed each student an examination paper with the text facing downward. Once everyone had their papers, he asked them to turn them over. Every paper was the same: blank, with an inch-wide black dot in the center. He gave the students five minutes to write down their thoughts about what they saw and turn their answer sheets in.

Once he had collected the papers, he started reading out loud how the students described the black dot—some literally described the shape of the dot (it was actually an oval, not a circle), its location on the page, its size, and other physical attributes. Others approached it more figuratively in terms of what it represented for them—a difficulty in life, a failure, or a weakness, something they were afraid of.

Once he was done reading, he imparted a valuable lesson. Even though their descriptions were different, every student focused on the small, black dot. Not one student had written about the large, white space on the page. We often take the same approach in life, fixating on specific problems or issues with our health, our jobs, or relationships. We miss all the positives surrounding us—our friends, our families, our jobs, our communities, miracles we see every day. Gratitude helps us recognize the white space around the dots.

Dr. Robert Emmons of the University of California, Davis is one of the leading experts in the world on gratitude and has spent over a decade researching it. In his paper published in the *Greater Good* magazine, he defines gratitude as having two components.[50] The first is an affirmation of goodness in life—we acknowledge that while life is not perfect, we routinely benefit from the good things in the world, the gifts, and other benefits we receive. When you see a half-empty cup, you can appreciate not just the half of the cup that is full, but also bring attention to the hundreds, if not thousands of other cups representing our life that are actually overflowing. Helen Keller expressed this perfectly when she said, "I cried because I had no shoes until I met a man who had no feet."

The second part of gratitude is recognizing that the source of this goodness is outside of ourselves. We acknowledge the role that others, including a higher power if you are spiritual, play in the many gifts we receive. When enjoying a tasty takeout meal, we can enjoy the food itself and also bring attention to all the people who were involved in procuring the ingredients, cooking the meal, and delivering it to us. We can always acknowledge our advantaged starting points and even the most basic needs as compared to those living in war-torn countries or facing threats of violence, famine, or other devastation.

When you cultivate your capacity and ability to be grateful, you will find that your mindset shifts from one of scarcity to one of abundance. You will feel a stronger sense of being enough and having enough, and you will find the courage to jump off the hamster wheel of running harder and harder to get more and more. You will find yourself content with what you have and really start to enjoy the gifts that have been bestowed on you. You will also experience a shift in how you experience the world and start to see an interbeing nature of our existence with others and the universe. Lao Tzu, an ancient Chinese philosopher, said, "When you realize there is nothing lacking, the whole world belongs to you."

In an age of consumerism, we are constantly bombarded with messages of things we need to buy or things we need to do to feel happy, satisfied, and enough. Manipulated by machines, we are consuming at levels we never have done in the history of our civilization, and these are unsustainable in the long term. We have come a long way from the nomadic lifestyle of 20,000 years ago, when small groups of twenty to thirty people had to move constantly to search for food almost every day. With the advent of farming, we settled down and started accumulating things. An awareness of abundance and a regular gratitude practice help you break free from the shackles of possessions, pare back the excessive drive to over-consume, and win back control over your life.

Science-Based Benefits of Practicing Gratitude

Gratitude is a common thread that runs through many religions and philosophies across the east and west. Eastern wisdom traditions like Buddhism and Yoga Sutras extol virtues of gratitude and contentment. "Santosha" is the second of the Niyamas of Patanjali's Eight Limbs of Yoga and roughly translates as contentment. Buddha often preached, "let us rise up and be thankful, for if we did not learn a lot today, at least we learned a little, and if we did not learn a little, at least we did not get sick, and if we got sick, at least we did not die; so, let us all be thankful." Similar wisdom can be found in the words of Marcus Aurelius, in Meditations, 9.6: "all you need are these: certainty of judgment in the present moment; action for the common good in the present moment; and an attitude of gratitude in the present moment for anything that comes your way."

Scientific research led by Dr. Martin Seligman, Dr. Robert Emmons, and others they have collaborated with over the years have outlined several tangible benefits from a regular gratitude practice. In his article titled "Why Gratitude is Good," Dr. Emmons highlights several benefits from practicing gratitude:[51]

Physical health. Practicing gratitude leads to stronger immune systems. Grateful people are also less bothered by aches and pains, lower blood pressure, better sleep, less fatigue, lower levels of cellular inflammation.

Psychological/Mental health.[52] Grateful people have higher levels of positive emotions like joy, pleasure, and happiness. They also experience lower levels of negative emotions like envy, resentment, frustration, and anger. Practicing gratitude is proven to reduce stress, depression, and anxiety, and increases the ability to overcome trauma and experience post-traumatic growth.

Social/Emotional health.[53] Grateful people have a higher ability to regulate emotions, show higher empathy and reduced aggression, enjoy greater social cohesion and friendships. They are also more forgiving, more helpful, generous, and compassionate.

Professor Robert Emmons, together with his colleagues Michael McCullough and Jo-Ann Tsang, found that grateful people don't ignore the negative aspects of life or struggles; they just choose to appreciate what is positive as well. Brother David Steindl-Rast, a Catholic Benedictine monk, very wisely said, "it is not happiness that makes us grateful, it is gratitude that makes us happy."

Gratitude is not just limited to humans; it's also found consistently in animals. Charles Darwin suggested in 1872 that all humans, and even other animals, show emotion through remarkably similar behaviors,[54] even the more complex ones, such as jealousy, gratitude, and suspicion. Given animals cannot use words to express when they are feeling grateful, researchers study reciprocity as a good proxy for gratitude. After decades of observing ape behavior at Gombe National Park in Tanzania (as well as other wild chimpanzee populations), researchers have concluded that chimpanzees also can feel and display gratitude.[55]

Advances in neuroscience are providing the clues behind this powerful effect that gratitude has across our physical, psychological, and emotional wellbeing. In a 2015 study conducted by Dr. Glenn Fox and his team,[56] participants' brains were scanned while they were feeling grateful to see where gratitude shows up. They found a high level of activity in the parts of our brain which are known to play a big role in processing emotions, interpersonal bonding, rewarding social interactions, moral judgment, and empathy. Giving and receiving gratitude releases the "good" hormones dopamine and serotonin in our brain, which make us feel good. The Mindful Awareness Research Center of UCLA found that gratitude actually changes the neural structures in the brain, making us feel more joyful and content.

Gratitude is clearly an important quality and one that can dramatically change our lives for the better. But is it as easy as simply feeling thankful for what we have? What if you've always felt like a "glass is half empty" type of person? How can we actively recognize that we live in a world of abundance?

Cultivating an Everyday Gratitude Practice

Every day when you wake up in the morning, how often do you take a moment to celebrate that you are still alive? Nearly 150,000 people around the globe do not wake up each day. As you get out of bed and your feet touch the ground, look around at your home and express gratitude for being there. Did you know that an estimated 150 million people world-wide are homeless,[57] and another 1.6 billion people around the world live in "inadequate shelter" based on estimates by Habitat for Humanity. Now shift your attention to your physical body—is everything working normally? According to the World Bank, nearly 1 billion people, or 15 percent of the world's population, experience some form of disability. As you have breakfast, think about the millions around the world who are hungry and will not have something to eat. According to research published by the Food and Agriculture Organization (FAO), globally, about 8.9 percent of the world's population—690 million people—go to bed on an empty stomach each night.

These simple, yet profound moments of gratitude can be practiced in the first five minutes of your day. Think about how your experience of the world would change, if you could bring attention to all the things that today you might take for granted. I was particularly moved after reading an essay that Helen Keller wrote in 1933 for the *Atlantic Monthly* titled "Three Days to See." Keller, who became blind and deaf because of an illness when she was nineteen months old, learned fingerspelling, Braille, and Tadoma, or feeling vibrations and movements on the face associated with speech. In the essay, she tells the story of a friend who visited with her and had just been back from a walk in the forest. When Helen asked her what she saw, her friend replied (as would many of us), "Nothing in particular." Keller responded:[58]

> How was it possible, I asked myself, to walk for an hour through the woods and see nothing worthy of note? I who cannot see find hundreds of things to interest me through mere touch.... At times my heart cries out with longing to see all these things. If I can get so much pleasure from mere touch, how much more beauty must be revealed by sight. Yet, those who have eyes apparently see little.

Keller then describes how she would live and what she would do if she were given three days to see and hear again. Her writing is inspiring, and I was astounded to start to experience the wonders of sight, sound, touch, taste, and smell that I am blessed with and the wonders of the world I get a chance to experience daily.

We take so much for granted that we need a little bit of support to start noticing things. As I started on my gratitude journey, I challenged myself to think of three things every day that I could feel grateful for. But after a few days I couldn't think beyond the basics: my family, my job, my parents, my health, where I lived, my friends. Luckily, I discovered an app called Gratitude 365 that gave me daily prompts that focused on different aspects of my life in a microscopic way. So, for example, instead of just health, it encouraged me to really think about my sight, my eyes, and my ability to see. The next day, it asked me to think about a personal appliance that I used and how it improved my life. I thought of a dishwasher. I remembered growing up in India without a dishwasher and washing all the items by hand. Pretty soon I realized the list of amazing things I was blessed with was endless.

It is easy to be grateful when things are going well, but you can find things to be grateful for even in your suffering. Khalil Gibran wrote in *The Prophet*, "your sorrow is your joy unmasked. And the selfsame well from which your laughter rises was often filled with tears. And how else can it be? The deeper that sorrow carves into your being, the more joy you can contain." Remember, that to get to the highest purity gold which has the most value, gold goes through multiple cycles of heating, melting, and solidification to allow for all impurities to be removed. Think back to some of the hardest times in your life when you felt that things could not get worse. Now think about the growth that period enabled in you in terms of new skills you learned, a realization of what really matters in your life, or you developed empathy and compassion for others going through similar suffering.

People often ask me if I could recommend only one practice that has the biggest short-term impact in increasing happiness, and I always say "gratitude." Integrating gratitude has had a profound change in how I experience life. By acknowledging all the things that I used to take for granted, I feel more joyful, peaceful, and truly cared for by the universe. Even when things don't go well, the lows no longer seem as low. Even in adversity, I can see the goodness and how much worse it could have been. One night it all became very clear to me.

It was 11:00 p.m. on a Thursday night, and I was driving home from Denver after a team dinner. There was not a lot of traffic, and I was making good time. A thought of gratitude flashed through my head for the fact that there was no debris on the road. In India, driving could be dangerous. You always had to watch for cows, dogs, people, potholes, and a long list of other things. I never worried about that in Colorado.

Literally five minutes later, I found myself staring at what looked like a one- to two-feet-tall concrete block in the middle of the highway. At 65 mph, there was little I could do but slam on the brakes and swerve to the next lane to avoid it. Unfortunately, my car went over part of it with a huge thud and scraping noise. I was pretty shaken up, but I kept on driving. It was dark, the car seemed OK, and I was only twenty minutes from home. Despite the "check engine" light flashing, I arrived safely.

When I inspected my car, I was shocked to see that the entire fender from the passenger side of the car was gone. The hood was stuck shut, and coolant and oil pooled underneath the car. Five years prior, I would have been in a foul mood: my car was ruined! *Why did this happen to me? I would have thought. Who was the idiot who dropped a giant piece of debris on the highway?* It might have been days or even weeks before I recovered.

Instead, thanks to my investment in my gratitude practice, I actually felt completely at peace. My thoughts immediately went to a calm, positive place: an angel was on my shoulder. How lucky am I to have made it home unscathed! In twenty-five years of driving, this has only happened to me once. I was better able to handle repairing my car and moving on without the incident hanging over me like a cloud.

The following are a set of curated practical exercises that have made a big difference in my life and which I hope will enable you to experience the magic of everyday gratitude. Choose one or try them all and see what works for you.

Gratitude Journal

See the Journaling Exercise on the following page to get started. Nothing you list is too mundane (e.g., grateful for our garbage collection company that took the weekly trash away). The goal of the exercise is to bring attention to all the simple things that you might be taking for granted and enjoy the positive feel of connection, joy, and happiness that come from that.

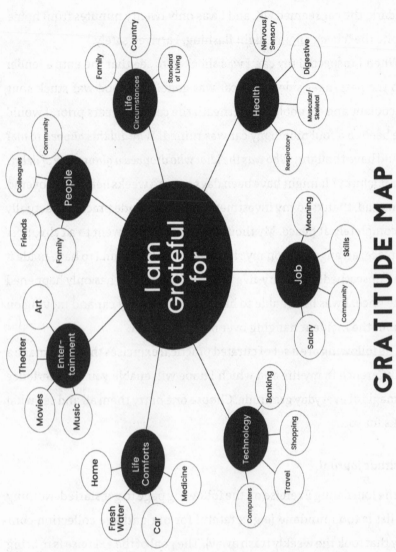

GRATITUDE MAP

Figure 4.1: What am I grateful for?

Journaling Exercise:
What Am I Grateful For?

Keeping a gratitude journal can be a wonderful way to bring awareness to all the blessings in your life that you otherwise might be taking for granted. Martin Seligman and his team at the Positive Psychology Center pioneered the "what went well" or "three blessings" exercise and confirmed the significant positive effects on life satisfaction and depression levels from this practice. You can use it as a daily ritual to bring awareness to all the blessings in your life that you otherwise might be taking for granted. Try to write down three things each day using the chart and prompts below to help inspire you. Make it as specific as you can. Then add a line or two about how that thing makes your life better.

1. **People:** Who are the individuals in your life who play a key role in who you are today? Family, friends, colleagues, those you interact with daily (e.g., bus driver, barista, others). Others in your community.

2. **Health:** What are all the different body parts, organs that are functioning today that we take for granted? Our five senses (eyes, ears, touch, taste, smell), our arms, legs, different body organs (e.g., kidneys, heart, lungs, liver), physical abilities, memory, etc.

3. **Job:** What are the different aspects about our jobs that we can be grateful for? Financial resources, growth opportunities, social community, ability to make a difference in others' lives, others.

4. **Technology and services:** What are the different technological gadgets or services we use that make life convenient, fast, and efficient? Devices: laptops, phone, television, refrigerator; services: Uber/Lyft, food delivery, online ordering, online banking.

5. **Life comforts:** What are all the life comforts we enjoy that we take for granted that many others wish they had? House, warm bed to sleep in, hot water, clean drinking water, access to healthcare, car, television.

6. **Creative Media:** What are all the creative things that bring us joy? Music, movies, books, paintings, dance, theater, others.

7. **Life:** What are all the life events that have shaped you? Remember the good times, the acts of kindness we benefited from; the hard/tough times and the lessons they taught you.

Gratitude Jar

This is a similar exercise to journaling for those of you who may be more visually inclined. Find a large jar or a box and decorate it as elaborately or as simply as you like. Every day, take a pause every so often to bring your attention to anything that brings you joy or helps you in your daily life. For each of these, write what happened and its effect on you on a little slip of paper or sticky note and put it into the gratitude jar. Choose a timeframe (Sunday evening, or the last day of the month) to open your jar and see the abundance of blessings pour out right in front of you.

"Give It Up" Exercise

This is a practice I picked up from the Greater Good Science Center at UC Berkeley. Each week, choose something that you enjoy on a regular basis: a morning cappuccino, text updates with a friend, a favorite pen. On day one, allow yourself to indulge as you normally would. Then, for the next six days, do not allow yourself to indulge in that item or activity at all. On day seven, allow yourself to indulge again and pay attention to how you feel physically (savoring the taste of the coffee) and emotionally (happiness at hearing from your friend). Try giving up a different thing the following week. With continuous practice, you will start to savor the many pleasures you become desensitized to and re-create the moment when you first discovered them. As I'll discuss later in this chapter, simplifying your life can help deepen your gratitude practice.

Gratitude Meditation

The human body is the most extraordinary machine in the world. Nothing we have created has come close to the complexity that resides in our own bodies. Did you know that our bodies are comprised of more than 200 bones, more than 600 muscles, and seventy-eight different organs (including five that are vital for survival—heart, brain, kidneys, liver, and lungs) organized around ten major organ systems (e.g., reproductive system, cardiovascular, etc.)? If any of these parts stops working due to an injury or a disease, our body shifts immediately to try to heal what's ailing us. Yet we go through most days unaware of the wonders that reside within us. If you haven't done so yet, I would strongly encourage you to see the Body Worlds' exhibition (https://bodyworlds.com) to discover the wonders that live within our own skin. Gratitude meditation exercise number four, below, is a powerful technique to intentionally focus and bring awareness to the different body parts and systems that make life possible.

Meditation Exercise:
Gratitude Body Scan

Gratitude meditation is a powerful technique to intentionally focus and visualize those things we are deeply grateful for. I have combined a gratitude practice with a traditional body scan meditation to slowly bring awareness to the different parts of our body that we often take for granted. For each body part, you can use the following mantra Thich Nhat Hahn frequently uses in his teachings: "Breathing in, I am aware of my X; breathing out, I smile to my X."

Sometimes when we connect with the body, we can become critical. If you find yourself noticing any judgment or negative thoughts arising during this exercise, just let them be. Try not to suppress any feelings or thoughts that emerge. Allow any dark thoughts, doubts, or negative self-talk to be cleared away with each exhale.

Duration: forty-five minutes

1. Get into a comfortable position which allows you to be relaxed but also alert. I recommend a seated, cross-legged position (Lotus position) on the floor. If it is not comfortable, you can also just practice sitting in a chair with your feet flat on the floor. Keep your back straight, your shoulders relaxed, your chin facing slightly upward, and your eyes closed. Keep your jaw relaxed with your lips slightly open. You can rest your arms on your legs with palms facing downward.

2. Take three deep breaths, feeling the air fill your lungs and your stomach, and then slowly exhale with an open mouth,

letting all the air out and feeling your stomach contract. Let yourself relax completely as you breathe.

3. Resume breathing at your normal pace, paying attention to each inhale and exhale, feeling your belly rise with each inhale and fall with each exhale. Take a few moments to be aware of your whole body from head to toe. Keep breathing at your normal pace for the rest of the meditation.

4. Bring your attention now slowly to the top of your head. Repeat the mantra internally: "Breathing in, I am aware of my head; breathing out, I smile at my head." Take three to five breaths maintaining your attention to the top of your head.

5. Slowly shift attention to your forehead and to your face. Take three to five breaths maintaining your attention to your forehead. Take three to five breaths maintaining your attention to your face. Repeat internally: "Breathing in, I am aware of my face; breathing out, I smile at my face."

6. Now bring attention to your eyes. Become aware of how important they are to you—everything they allow you to see and accomplish, how they gift you the wonders of nature, beauty, the people you love. Take three to five breaths maintaining your attention to your eyes. Repeat internally: "Breathing in, I am aware of my eyes; breathing out, I smile at my eyes."

7. Shift attention to your ears and appreciate the ability to listen to music, birds chirping, wind softly blowing, and your children's voices. Notice how your ears have increased your

ability to interact with those around you. Take three to five breaths maintaining your attention to your eyes. Repeat internally: "Breathing in, I am aware of my ears; breathing out, I smile at my ears."

8. Connect next with your nose and mouth. Take a nice deep breath in through the nose and breathe out through the mouth. Express appreciation for the natural ability of the nose to not just help you breathe and filter out impurities, but also to reveal the amazing world of smell. Offer thanks for your lips, your strong teeth, the tongue that allows you to enjoy taste. Take three to five breaths maintaining your attention on your nose, mouth, teeth, tongue. Repeat internally: "Breathing in, I am aware of my nose and mouth; breathing out, I smile at my nose and mouth."

9. Shift your attention to the chest now. Notice the gentle rise and fall of your chest and abdomen as you breathe. Feel the air filling your lungs, providing oxygen and taking away carbon dioxide. Notice your heart that beats 24/7, circulating oxygen and nutrients through your entire body. Take three to five breaths giving appreciation to your lungs, heart, and all the organs that your chest holds. With each inhale and exhale, repeat internally: "Breathing in, I am aware of... breathing out, I smile at my..."

10. Continue the meditation with relaxed breathing and bringing attention to each body part. Your abdomen, which forms the core of the body. Your liver, stomach, small and big intestines, all of which have important functions. Your spine, your

shoulders, your arms, hands, legs, all the way down to your fingertips and toes. Connect with the different bones and muscle structures that give us the ability to hold and manipulate objects and send appreciation to each of them. "Breathing in, I am aware of... breathing out, I smile at my..."

11. Slowly open your eyes when you're ready. With your next inhale, allow yourself to see your whole body in its majesty. It protects you, nourishes you, and allows you to experience everything that life has to offer. Take a few moments to treasure this feeling. Feel your whole body pulsating, glowing, feeling the warmth of your gratitude.

12. Return to your day with a renewed appreciation for your amazing and unique body.

Integrating Gratitude at Work

Many companies today are battling with 20–30 percent attrition in their workforces. Based on research conducted at McKinsey, two of the biggest drivers of why employees are leaving at this rate have to do with feeling undervalued by their company and undervalued by their boss. There is a very powerful yet relatively simple solution to this problem: integrating gratitude boosts motivation and engagement. Taking a moment from the busyness of our days to sincerely thank a colleague for their contributions can go a long way.

Adam had recently joined a $2 billion company as the chief transformation officer. It had been a hard five years for the company, and management had to undertake a series of layoffs. From day one, Adam could sense a high level of exhaustion, fatigue, and disillusionment. He knew he would have to engage each and every one of the employees to recommit to the company and dig in harder to collectively push the company back into profitability. He reached out to me for help as one of the major issues was that most employees didn't feel valued. Attrition was starting to pick up, and it was getting harder to recruit talent. We brainstormed ideas, and I encouraged Adam to institute two key gratitude practices.

First, team leaders asked for weekly nominations for those who had gone above and beyond to make a difference (i.e., filling in for a sick colleague, taking on additional work to move an initiative forward). Then Adam published their names in an all-company email, and one of the executive team members would personally call each person to thank them for their contribution. Within three weeks, the positive buzz and halo effect started to spread. Many of the employees were happily surprised to speak directly with senior executives, and higher management began to build a personal bond with these individuals and empathize with their situations.

Second, Adam launched a "Thank-a-Ton" program. Every employee got thirty thank-you post cards that they could personally give to a colleague who helped them out. The cards outlined a simple structure they could follow to give thanks by recognizing the specific act and the effect it had on them. Employees were encouraged to personally handwrite and deliver the card. If that was not possible, they could send it via interoffice mail. Soon, thousands of cards were exchanged within the company. More importantly, it wasn't just the recipients who benefited—the senders felt good too and found themselves paying it forward more often.

Within three months, Adam had managed to turn around engagement scores from an all-time low to an all-time high.

Community Exercise: Gratitude Visit at Work

A gratitude visit is a wonderful way to show appreciation to someone you are deeply grateful for, who believed in you and might have supported you at a pivotal moment in your life. This exercise is based on the series of interventions designed by Dr. Seligman as part of his positive psychology work and is proven to be highly effective in improving overall wellbeing.[59]

1. Choose someone at work who has been helpful and kind to you, yet you have not had an opportunity to express your gratitude. This person can be someone in your company (your admin, someone who reports to you within your department, a peer from another department) or someone from outside your company (e.g., a supplier, a customer, someone in a government agency).

2. Take a moment to think about the things that this person has done that make you extremely grateful. Write a letter of gratitude (approximately 300 words) to this person, making it concrete about what the person specifically did and how this person's behavior and actions have affected your life. Let them know what you are doing now and how often you remember what they did.

3. After you have written the letter, plan a visit with the recipient (ideally in person or virtually through Zoom). Let them know you would like to see them and that you have something special to share. Be vague about the purpose of the visit to keep the surprise element and up the fun factor.

4. When you meet, give the person a hug and thank them for the part they have played in your life. Tell them you would like to read a letter expressing your gratitude and request that they don't interrupt until you are done reading.

5. Take your time reading the letter. While you read, pay attention to their reaction as well as your own. After you have read the letter, discuss the contents, their reaction, and your feelings for each other. Remember to give the letter to the person when you leave.

Deepening Gratitude through Simplicity

Over the centuries, we have accumulated more and more. According to Regina Lark, one of the leading organizing specialists based in Los Angeles, the average American household has 300,000 or more items.[60] Today, we consume twice as many material goods as we did fifty years ago.[61] Despite the size of homes tripling over the last forty years, one in ten Americans rent off-site storage facilities to house their many possessions. In fact, if the rest of the world consumed at the level of Americans, we would need 5.3 times the number of planets to survive. Mahatma Gandhi, who brought the British empire to its knees by leading the nation through *satyagraha* (insistence on truth) and simple living, said it beautifully: "there is enough in this world for everyone's need but not for anyone's greed."

To be content with what you already have and not look outward is a universal message across all scriptures and wisdom traditions from Christianity, Buddhism, and the Yoga Sutras, among others. In Christianity, one of the ten commandments specifically reminds us to not worry about keeping up with the Joneses: "You shall not covet your neighbor's house; you shall not covet your neighbor's wife, or his male servant, or his female servant, or his ox, or his donkey, or anything that is your neighbor's." Similarly, in yogic traditions, *Aparigraha,* or non-hoarding, is one of *Yamas* (restraints), and *santosha,* or contentment, is one of the *Niyamas* (observances) on the eight-limbed yogic path that helps us live into our authentic self and support a journey toward our bigger purpose. Epicurus, the famous Greek philosopher, was onto something when he said, "do not spoil what you have by desiring what you have not; remember that what you now have was once among the things you only hoped for."

Scientific research backs up what we already know from spiritual treatise. One, money matters, but it doesn't necessarily make people happier.[62] Based on research done by Kahneman and Deaton in 2010, salary ceases to matter above $75,000 in the United States.[63] Two, interpersonal relationships are a much more significant predictor of life satisfaction,[64] and those who adopt a minimalist way of life can dedicate more time toward fostering these incredibly important relationships. Three, the happiness of buying a new object, like a car or a laptop, fades quickly over time due to two drivers: decreased pleasure and increased aspirations as our brain adapts and reacclimates to our new level of prosperity.[65]

Embracing practices of simplicity and contentment in the domains of what you own and how you spend your time can free you up to deepen your gratitude practice, as well as pursue your higher purpose and calling. To make sustainable changes, you must first change your mindset and internal definition of success from having *things* to having *time.* You can also reframe your journey toward simplicity by asking the question Greg McKeown does in his book *Essentialism:* "what do I want to go big on" versus "what do I have to give up?"

I recommend learning more about the benefits of a minimalist or essentialist lifestyle. Some of my favorites are *Minimalism: A Documentary about the Important Things* (Netflix), *Tidying Up with Marie Kondo* (Netflix), Greg McKeown's podcast, *What's Essential*, and the Minimalists' blog, https://www.theminimalists.com/start/. As you explore these sources for yourself and hear the inspirational stories of others who have adopted this lifestyle, start to minimize, or eliminate all things that are not in service of your purpose and "bigger why."

Finally, you can take back control over what you consume. Marketers have become good at creating advertising campaigns that cleverly capture our attention and get us to purchase items we probably don't need. Digital marketing experts estimate that most Americans are exposed to around 4,000 to 10,000 ads each day.[66] Here are some ideas:

Minimize social media. Powerful algorithms are constantly working to feed us ads perfectly tailored to our likes and desires, and to encourage us to buy things with a simple click. Try to take a break from social media when you can to reduce this relentless pressure to get and do more things.

Try a shopping sabbath. Periodically abstain from purchasing things in certain categories or for a specific amount of time. For example, you could commit to online-shopping-free weekends or a clothes shopping moratorium for nine months. You can also make a commitment and build in a mandatory waiting period of a day or week, between your desire to buy something and the moment you click to purchase. Do you still want it then, or can you pass?

Shop your own house. Sometimes you just need a fresh perspective to see that what you already own is enough. Try rearranging your furniture, dig through your closet for something you haven't worn lately, or try a new recipe with a tool you haven't used in a while. Chances are the "newness" feeling may be satisfied without having to spend a dime.

Building Your Gratitude Practice

Cicero called gratitude the parent of all virtues. As you learn to appreciate all the things that are going well in your life, you will find yourself experiencing more positive emotions. Developing an "attitude of gratitude" is one of the simplest ways to improve your satisfaction with life and feel happier. Over the last four years, I have maintained a daily gratitude journaling practice (I like to record mine at the end of the day) and can attest that it works. I feel better, *especially* when things don't go according to plan. My invitation to you is to make gratitude a core part of your everyday life.

KEY TAKEAWAYS

- Gratitude is one of the most powerful practices for achieving happiness.
- Those who regularly practice gratitude are happier, experience more positive emotions, and are more optimistic.
- Gratitude rewires our brain from a negativity/scarcity bias to one of abundance. This in turn allows us to simplify our lives and gain freedom through financial flexibility to pursue our dreams.
- The key to practicing gratitude long term is to develop our capacity to notice the little things around us that we often take for granted. In addition, changing how we express our thanks periodically can keep our practice fresh.

Master Your Moods
and Emotions

"God, grant me the serenity to accept the things
I cannot change, courage to change the things I can,
and wisdom to know the difference."

—Reinhold Niebuhr

How much of your average day is spent in a heavy mood (anxiety, fear, anger, and resentment) versus a buoyant one (calm, joy, and optimism)? I am always moved by the lightness with which most other animals—birds, fish, deer, rabbits, squirrels, and others—go about their daily business. In contrast, as I reflect on other human beings, so many of us seem to trudge through life feeling down. Despite being at the top of the evolutionary food chain, we seem to have the most trouble getting through our days with emotional ease. For most of us living in the Western world, a majority of our suffering is psychological, not physical, and is often created by ourselves. We worry incessantly about what will happen next at work, at home, in the world, or we hold on to a past hurt.

A Zen story comes to mind that beautifully captures the weight of holding on to the past. Two monks were returning to their monastery. It had rained heavily that day and there was a gushing stream of water running across the road, six inches deep and flowing very fast. As they came to a crossing, they saw a frail, old woman standing there, unable to cross the road without getting soaked. The elder of the two monks went up to her, lifted her up, and carried her in his arms to the other side of the road. The monks then continued to the monastery.

That evening the younger monk said to the older monk, "Sir, as monks, we cannot touch a woman."

The elder monk responded, "Yes, brother." The younger monk replied, "But then sir, why did you carry that woman across the road?"

The elder monk smiled at him and said, "I left her on the other side of the road, but you are still carrying her."

The Latin derivative of the word emotion is "emotere," literally translated as "energies in motion." It is no surprise then that emotions are experienced as energy moving through the body. Emotions are often triggered based on something happening in the external world that is different than what our minds were expecting. If what happens is better than what we expected, we usually experience a positive emotion like satisfaction, pride, pleasure, or joy. On the other hand, if what happens is not in line with our expectations and reduces our possibilities for the future, we often experience negative emotions like anxiety, sadness, anger, and resentment, among others.

As we discussed in the chapter on Awareness, we often use the terms moods and emotions interchangeably, but they are very different. Unlike emotions, which are usually the result of some event that breaks our flow of life, moods don't need an event to manifest themselves. In fact, if we experience an emotion over and over, it can become a mood and preclude us from certain possibilities, or it might push us toward other actions.

To develop mastery over our moods and emotions, it is important to understand where emotions come from. Lisa Feldman Barrett, a leading neuroscientist and professor of psychology at Northeastern University in Boston is rewriting what we have historically known about emotions. She recently published her groundbreaking research in the book *How Emotions Are Made*. According to Dr. Barrett, humans are not prewired with certain emotions, but instead, these emotions are constructed by our brains to make sense of the stimulus we receive and other ingredients. These ingredients include our overall context (situation and people involved), sensations in our body, our history (memories, past experiences, culture, overall environment in which we grew up), and the language we have learned to describe our feelings. Dr. Barrett explains that our brains are effective prediction-making machines, and we use this mechanism heavily to conserve energy it consumes while parsing through the enormous amount of data it is receiving from our five senses. It is through these predictions that the brain constructs the world we experience.

What I love about the new research is that we can go much further than just learning to ride our emotions better. Given that our brains use our past to construct our current emotions, by revisiting our past beliefs and assessments to test their validity and by creating new experiences in the present moment, we can retrain our brains to manifest different moods and emotional states in the first place. So, in effect, rather than focusing on controlling the external world, which we know is impermanent and out of our control, we can develop mastery over shaping our internal world and meaning-making apparatus. We can also develop a finer understanding of the different moods and emotion states and what differentiates one from the other in order to better regulate them.

Over the course of this chapter, I will share practical tips and suggestions that can help you gain mastery over six of the most common moods and emotions that often create a lot of suffering for people: Anger, Resentment, Fear, Anxiety, Guilt, and Shame. I will also share how you can cultivate positive emotions of ambition and optimism. It is my hope that as you embed these practices into your lives, you will be able to break free, lighten your load, and move with more energy on your *Hardwired for Happiness* journey.

The Science-Based Benefits of Mastering
Moods and Emotions

Significant research points to the long-term ill effects of chronic Fear, Anxiety, Anger, and Resentment on our overall quality of life and physical and mental health. On the physical health side, Fear and Anxiety weaken our immune systems; cause gastrointestinal issues like stomach aches, ulcers, and irritable bowel syndrome; reduce fertility and change menstrual cycles; and cause cardiovascular damage. In the grips of anxiety, our breathing becomes shallow, and we can experience panic attacks resulting in heart palpitations, chest pain, and lightheadedness. On the mental health side, anxiety can produce frequent feelings of impending doom, reducing our ability to concentrate, and making us more irritable. Fear and anxiety can reduce our ability to form long-term memories, negatively affect several parts of the brain like the hippocampus, and make us more reactive and less able to regulate our emotions. We also become more prone to high stress, fatigue, burnout, and depression.[67]

We can let go of these emotions by being less attached to our expected or desired outcomes and surrendering to what's emerging. This approach, long practiced in Buddhism and Eastern philosophy, has been proven to reduce symptoms of depression, anxiety, and stress[68] and increase empathy, kindness, wisdom, and self-actualization.[69] Surrendering at its core is the willingness to meet life just as it is in the moment, and stop fighting or resisting what is present. Surrender provides a counterbalancing force to the tendency of our human mind to try to control everything, which is nearly impossible in our fast-changing world.

Like fear and anxiety, chronic Anger puts a person into a fight-or-flight mode, generating the stress hormone cortisol, which results in numerous changes in heart rate, blood pressure, and immune response. Those changes then increase the risk of depression, heart disease, and diabetes, among other conditions. Research conducted by Yoichi Chida, MD, PhD, found that anger and hostility are linked to a higher risk of heart disease, and poorer outcomes for people with existing heart disease (*Journal of the American College of Cardiology*, 2009).[70] Similar research conducted by Chris Aiken, MD, at the Wake Forest University School of Medicine found that the chances of having a heart attack double in the two hours after an angry outburst. Anger suppression doesn't help either. In a study conducted by Ayano Yamaguchi and colleagues, suppressing anger produced more negative, not positive, emotions, more inauthentic feelings, and increased stress. Like Anger, Resentment has been proven to weaken the immune system and increase stress, anxiety, risk of heart disease, hypertension, stroke, cancer, weight gain, mood swings, depression, and burnout. In addition to health impacts, Resentment also corrodes relationships, destroying intimacy and trust and making one more and more lonely.

Letting go of our Anger and Resentment and practicing forgiveness calms stress levels, leading to improved health. Loren Toussaint, Everett Worthington, and David R. Williams dedicated an entire book[71] to the state-of-the-art research on forgiveness and mental and physical health and wellbeing. On the physical side, forgiveness helps improve heart health, lowers anxiety and stress levels, lowers blood pressure, and strengthens our immune system. On the psychological side, forgiveness improves mental health—including lower anxiety, stress levels, and symptoms of depression—relationships, and self-esteem.

Mastering Anger and Resentment

The harmful effects of Anger and Resentment are well-known, appearing in every wisdom tradition over the ages. Seneca captured it well when he said, "Anger is like an acid that can do more harm to the vessel in which it is stored than to anything it is poured on." Like other emotions, Anger and Resentment are experienced in our bodies and in our minds. As we become Angry, our bodies tense up. Inside our brains, neurotransmitter chemicals called catecholamines and adrenaline are released, resulting in the burst of energy we usually associate with the "exploding outward feeling" of anger. Our heart rate accelerates, our blood pressure rises, and the rate of breathing increases. Our faces or necks might become flush as blood rushes to our limbs, preparing us for protective action. Our attention narrows toward the person who is the source of our anger or resentment, and we lose broader perspective. The famous neuropsychiatrist Daniel Siegel said, "Anger makes us flip our lids," which helps us imagine our prefrontal cortex actually losing its ability to regulate our emotions and make wise decisions.

Anger and Resentment are close cousins, and both originate from a belief that someone or something is unfair and has harmed us or others we care about. The difference is that anger is most often expressed, versus resentment, or the "silent emotion," which is more easily repressed because of a felt sense of hierarchical difference which makes it unsafe to truly share what we are feeling. While the adrenaline-caused arousal that accompanies anger can last hours or days, Resentment can last weeks, months, or even years, eventually becoming a mood. Every time we think back to something that happened, we reinforce those pathways in our brain of feeling angry and wanting revenge.

Anger and Resentment often ride together in an emotional storm. Instead of accepting and moving on from a negative experience, we get caught in a loop of resentment, anger, hopelessness, and emptiness. These feelings can become toxic in two key ways: one, people succumb to them and blow off the fury and steam, exchanging harsh words in an email or taking other actions they might later regret when cooler heads prevail. Second, they might suppress them by internalizing the hurt and suffering, and numbing themselves through the use of substances (alcohol, drugs, food), or through social media, or excessive television. Neither of these approaches are productive ways to handle anger and resentment. When we act out of Anger, we are operating with ten to fifteen less IQ points and reduced decision-making and cognitive capacity.[72] We also know from research that when we suppress our emotions, it only makes them stronger, in addition to the significant physical harm we are causing to ourselves with high amounts of cortisol surging through our bodies. When we numb to reduce our mental discomfort, we instead hurt our health long term through the ill effects of substance abuse, overeating, and other maladaptive coping behaviors.

However, not all Anger is bad at its core. It alerts us to a boundary that we deeply care about and has been breached. Positive Anger that is motivated by compassion and a sense to right the wrong against an individual, group, or system can be a powerful force for change. If we can harness the energy in anger to move us to action swiftly and mobilize others in our quest, we can persevere for long periods against all odds. We need to look no further than the inspirational examples of Martin Luther King Jr., Mahatma Gandhi, and Nelson Mandela, who overcame insurmountable odds by channeling their Anger and redirecting it toward injustices.

When we feel Angry or Resentful, we can very quickly move into blaming someone or something and holding them responsible for causing us to feel this way. However, when we point a finger to another person, the other three fingers point back at us. What is our own role in the situation? When we replay the same incident over and over again, it extends the suffering. Buddha, in one of his teachings, compared this resentment and repetition to being wounded by two arrows. The first arrow represents the actual incident that caused us the hurt. The second arrow is our own self-imposed suffering that we create by reliving that experience. This is especially true in work settings where after an incident has happened, we load another arrow in our bow every time we see the other person and wound ourselves again.

We have to learn to resist the temptation of placing blame on ourselves or others. By deepening our awareness of the other person, ourselves, and the world around us, we can explore different perspectives that might allow us to let go and move toward a solution to address our suffering. To think more clearly, we have to get over what Daniel Goleman calls the "Amygdala hijack." First, become aware of the bodily sensations that are present when you feel anger or resentment building: you may have tightness in your chest, a racing heart, shortness of breath. Second, create a pause, center yourself, and take four to six deep breaths. Let your breath allow your emotional energy to calm down and create space to bring your cognitive brain back online. Finally, once you are out of the heat of the moment, use your cognitive capabilities to explore the source of the anger and resentment you are experiencing.

I want to share an approach leveraging learnings from Julio Olalla and the Newfield Network that is proven to be highly effective in working through triggering situations, discovering the source of your suffering, and taking action to address it.

MANAGING ANGER IN THE MOMENT

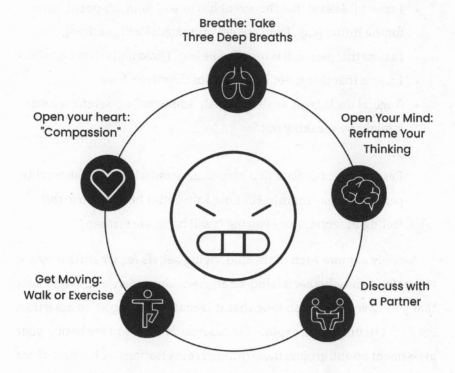

Figure 5.1: Managing Anger in the moment

Get Curious

Next time you find yourself in a mood of resentment that is not serving you, write down the story that you are telling yourself. Be particularly careful to state the assertions (facts) and assessments (beliefs) that are part of the story. In the grip of Anger or Resentment, your mind can be agitated and centered around your ego self. You might find yourself holding a story that looks like the following:

- I assert that something has happened or is happening (e.g., my boss is not supporting me in achieving my goals).
- I assess (believe) that this event has or will limit my possibilities for the future (e.g., I will not get promoted; I will get fired).
- I assess that person X is responsible (e.g., I hold my boss responsible).
- I assess that this is not fair, and I am the victim here.
- Anger: I declare my wish to punish "someone" or "set the record straight by speaking out."
  OR
- Resentment: I declare that sometime, somewhere, somehow, this person will pay for this. For now, I am better holding on to this feeling in secret, since voicing it will harm me further.

Actively explore each of the underlying beliefs for whether they are true or false and whether it is indeed an assertion or merely an assessment that you have held for so long that it is masquerading as an assertion. For each circumstance, explore the "standards" that you are basing your assessment on and ground them through conversations with others. Once you have done the work of really investigating your assessments and standards, you can take actions toward resolving the situation. They can involve one of the three actions below.

Make a Request or a Complaint

If your Anger or Resentment stems from someone doing something or not doing something that you would prefer, you can make a request to the other person. Many resentments often stem from expectations that are not shared between two parties. It is important to watch out for our inner dialogue around "I shouldn't have to ask for something" and instead focus on creating harmony and happiness versus preserving a need to be right. On the other hand, if the resentment is stemming from an agreement that was well understood between you and the other person, you can make a complaint to the other person, reminding them of the promise they made. It is extremely important to avoid criticizing and instead adopt a mindset of curiosity to understand what might have gotten in the way or what you can do to support the other in fulfilling the request.

Choose to Forgive and Move On

An act of forgiveness can be a powerful choice to remove the suffering created by holding on to the Resentment. Forgiveness is as much about you as it is about the other person. When you forgive, you do not necessarily stop considering someone responsible for what he or she did. You are choosing to let go of the hurt, close the chapter, and not allow what happened in the past to interfere with whatever possibility may arise in the future. It is important to highlight that I am advocating forgiveness but not necessarily forgetfulness. You cannot choose to forget something that has happened in the past, but you definitely can refuse to hold on to your resentment toward the other person in order to recultivate trust, intimacy, and collaboration.

Choose to Close the Relationship

Sometimes, due to the degree of damage that has been produced, or the systemic recurrence of some type of actions, or the deep distrust that might have developed, you may conclude that neither complaint nor forgiveness will restore the relationship, and it is a cost we are not willing to pay to continue. In this case, you can choose to close the relationship and remove yourself from the situation that is causing you suffering.

Journaling Exercise:
Writing Out Your Anger and Resentment

Journaling is highly effective in dealing with overwhelming emotions and is very effective in managing Anger and Resentment. Journaling allows us to slow down in order to process the unpleasant emotions more effectively, look into the underlying problems, fears, and concerns, and develop strategies to address them. This exercise is inspired by the framework presented by Desmond Tutu and Mpho Tutu in *The Book of Forgiveness*.

1. **Naming it:** Start by naming the hurt that is causing you to feel anger or resentment toward another person or the situation. Be specific about who/what it is directed toward (e.g., I am feeling angry toward Joe) and the specific role they/it played to trigger this emotion in you.

2. **Telling the story (Part 1):** What assessments are you holding about the other person or the situation unfolding that is causing the unpleasant emotion to arise? When was this negative emotion triggered? If a large amount of time has passed since that incident, why are you still dealing with it?

3. **Telling the story (Part 2):** What is this emotion trying to teach you? What lessons can be learned from this experience?

4. **Granting Forgiveness to Let Go (Part 1):** What would become possible if you let go of the underlying belief driving this emotion? How would your life be different a year from now if you let go of what no longer serves you?

5. **Granting Forgiveness to Let Go (Part 2):** When you think about letting this go, what fears come up? How can you celebrate the courage that letting go required?

6. **Renewing or Releasing the Relationship:** How do you want to move forward with your relationship to the offender? Do you want to renew it by sharing what you felt and making a request? Or do you want to close the relationship because too much harm has been done or due to irreconcilable differences?

You can "walk" the finger labyrinth on the next page as an aid for your exploration before or after journaling with the finger of your nondominant hand.

1. Set your intention to stay open for the Forgiveness journey as you enter the labyrinth.

2. As you trace the path, notice if there are any places where you lose your way, get stuck, or meet with resistance. Pay attention to what is emerging in you.

3. Pause once you reach the center, asking for a blessing from the universe to help you forgive. Remember, forgiveness is not forgetfulness.

Follow the path back out offering thanks as you exit.

Resentments can be particularly damaging in family relationships. In my coaching session with one of my clients, Rosie, she expressed that one of her biggest Resentments involved her younger brother. She grew up in Poland and had moved to the United States twenty years ago. Since then, she had supported her parents in Poland by sending some money to help with day-to-day expenses. They never asked for any financial help from her, but she felt that given all the sacrifices they had made, it was her responsibility to make their life a bit easier now that she could afford it. She also felt guilty for having left them behind in Poland, especially as they grew older.

She expected her younger brother to do the same after he moved to England for an engineering job. Her brother did not share her view and never offered to send their parents money or pay for their trips. Rosie felt he was "selfish" by letting all the financial responsibility fall on her, but she never explicitly shared her feelings with her brother or asked him to "do his part" because she was afraid of conflict and feeling disrespected if he said no. Her resentment only grew, and their relationship suffered, even after they both got married and had kids. It caused a lot of suffering for their parents, too, as they could see the rift between their two kids.

I coached Rosie to work through the mood of Resentment toward her brother and asked her to focus on being happy together versus being right. Could she engage with a mindset of curiosity and really try to understand her brother instead of immediately judging him? Rosie began to realize that her original assessment was mistaken; she discovered he had turned down an opportunity to work in the United States and chose a job in England so he could be close to his parents.

She also learned he had offered for them to come stay with him once they were older as the cost to support them through medical insurance was a lot cheaper in the United Kingdom than in the United States. Her brother's key belief was that their parents had a sufficient nest egg and didn't really need financial support. He was fully committed to stepping in if they ever needed the help and never expected Rosie to cover their expenses on her own.

SANTA ROSA LABYRINTH

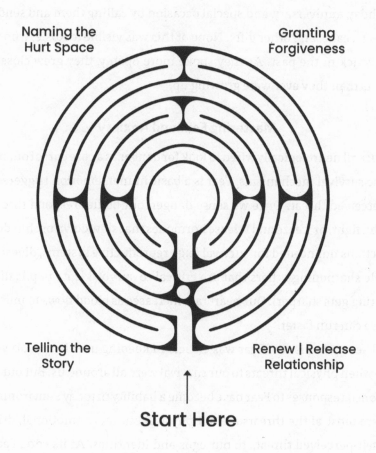

Naming the
Hurt Space

Granting
Forgiveness

Telling the
Story

Renew | Release
Relationship

Start Here

Figure 5.2: Santa Rosa Labyrinth with Heart-Space

Over time as Rosie let go of her own assessments and moved from a mood of Resentment to one of Acceptance, she started to see all the other ways in which her brother provided support for their parents, in many ways even more so than her. His choice to live on the same continent was a big emotional relief for them. He also made efforts to celebrate every birthday, anniversary, and special occasion by calling them and sending flowers, cake, and other gifts. None of this was visible to Rosie, who was still stuck in the past. As they spoke more openly, they grew closer as adults than they ever were growing up.

Mastering Fear and Anxiety

We are all neurologically wired to look for danger as a core part of our most basic survival mechanisms. Fear is a basic human emotion triggered by a perceived threat. Once we sense danger, our bodies respond through flight, fight, or freeze and release hormones that slow down or shut down functions not needed for survival (e.g., reproductive systems, digestion) while sharpening others that are critical to survival (e.g., pupils dilate, hearing gets sharper). Our heart rate increases as blood flows to muscles so we can run faster.

The mechanism of Fear was critical in keeping us safe 20,000 years ago when physical threats to our survival were all around us. But our conditioned responses to Fear have become a liability in today's environment where most of the threats are not physical but more emotional, driven by self-perceived threats to our egos and identities. At its core, Fear is a very healthy emotion, as it provides safety in our lives. The problems arise when Fear gets triggered by something that is quite insignificant or becomes a mood that keeps us from growth and new possibilities.

Fear and Anxiety are often lumped together but they are two very distinct emotions. Fear relates most often to a known, observable danger (e.g., someone pointing a gun at you), whereas anxiety can be seen as an unfocused, objectless, poorly defined, future-oriented fear.[73] Anxiety doesn't require a triggering stimulus and can often become a mood that lingers for long periods, putting a huge toll on our nervous system by keeping you on high alert and ever vigilant. One of the biggest drivers of Anxiety is that most of us don't like uncertainty, and our minds try to control everything to keep us safe. We keep imagining futures that are fraught with risks, or where we will be negatively affected in a bid to solve any and all issues that might arise. But control is an illusion, especially with the pace of change that has increased exponentially around us. No surprise then that anxiety disorders are the most common mental illness in the United States, affecting 19.1 percent of the population every year, or approximately one in five.[74]

Psychologists often describe fear as "**F**antasized **E**xperiences **A**ppearing **R**eal" to illustrate how most fears are stories that we make up. Most of the worst-case scenarios we feel anxious about don't ever come to fruition but make our day-to-day moments miserable regardless. No one is immune from this fearmongering. We all have Fears. Some of the most common fears include: not belonging, not being loved, insignificance (not mattering), fear of not being worthy, fear of not being... enough (smart enough, thin enough, rich enough, strong enough...).

Community Exercise:
Befriending Our Fears

Fear dialogues are a wonderful exercise you can do with a group of friends that you are reading this book with or even your team at the office. We spend most of our time hiding our Fears, as we feel that people would think less of us if they discovered these about us. This wonderful exercise helps you see that fear is a core part of the human experience, and by seeing and honoring the role our fears have played in our success, we can learn to move through them to uncover our fullest potential versus being limited by them.

This exercise is best done in person over a period of sixty minutes but can also be done virtually over Zoom. Feel free to repeat this many times with new friends and colleagues to be able to really discover a part of yourselves that remains hidden from most, and yet guides so much of our outward behaviors.

1. Start the conversation by sharing your perspectives developed through this book or from your experiences on fears and the role they play in your lives.

2. Share a list of eight to ten fears that come up often in different situations. Be vulnerable to create an environment where others can be vulnerable too. For example: for me, the most common fears that show up from time to time are not being loved, not belonging, not being worthy, not feeling smart enough, being wrong, not good enough, not thin enough, fear of not being healthy in my old age, fear of losing respect, fear of insignificance...

3. Invite others to take five minutes to write their list of eight to ten fears as well and then have them choose the "biggest" fear that shows up more often. In the world of ontological coaching, these are also called master assessments and have

the ability to shape our whole being and how we experience the world around us.

4. Have everyone go around the group and share their biggest fear. See if you can discover others like yourself who share your fears. As you listen to others, see if any of their fears resonate with you. Feel free to add to your list if you don't already have it.

5. Next, engage in a dialogue using a set of questions to see more clearly the role these fears play in our lives. Everyone gets two minutes to speak while others listen attentively:

   a. How has this Fear hindered me in the past?

   b. How does this Fear show up in my life every day when I face an obstacle at work or home, and feel stuck?

   c. What do other people observe in my behavior? What am I saying? What am I doing? What energy am I giving when I am in this Fear?

6. At the end of this round of conversations, explore a third set of questions pertaining to the fears:

   a. How has this Fear served you in your life? Can you see how it has helped you be successful at work, at home?

   b. If you could put aside this Fear...what would become possible in your life?

   c. What would that feel like?

7. Have an open, debrief conversation after the second round of dialogues about what you are taking away from this conversation.

Early in my career, I struggled significantly with Anxiety and suffered daily bouts of headaches, heaviness in body, and high irritability. As a newly minted manager I wanted to make sure that everything my team delivered met my high standards of perfection. My drive was fueled more from a fear of not belonging or being loved versus delivering the highest value we could for my clients. Nelson Mandela said it beautifully, "Courage is not the absence of fear, but the triumph over it." Combating excessive Fear and Anxiety in some cases may require seeking medical help through a mix of therapy and medication, especially if your fear is triggered by an underlying medical condition. However, for many of us who struggle with general anxiety, I have curated a set of somatic (body) and cognitive practices that have made a big difference in my life.

1. **Diaphragmatic breathing:** Sit in a comfortable chair with your head, neck, and shoulders relaxed or lie down on the floor or bed. Put one hand under your rib cage and one hand over your heart. Inhale deeply through your nose, noticing your stomach and chest move with each breath. Purse your lips and exhale through your mouth, noticing your stomach fall with each exhale. By focusing on exhaling deeply, you are activating your parasympathetic nervous system, which influences your body's ability to relax and calm down. You can practice diaphragmatic breathing three to four times a day for about ten minutes each to reap the calming benefits.

2. **Movement and exercise:** Integrating movement and regular exercise have a proven effect on reducing anxiety. Next time you are feeling down or stressed, just get moving: go for a walk around the block, hit the gym, go to a yoga class, or take a bike ride. By getting your body moving and sweat flowing, you will activate endorphins that will bring a feeling of calm and a more

positive mood. Studies have shown regular exercise can work as well as medication to control anxiety in some people, according to the Anxiety and Depression Association of America.[75]

3. **Practice letting go:** Negative thoughts can take root in your mind and often make the situation appear much worse than it actually is. It is important to uncover the underlying story that is replaying in your mind when you find yourself in the grips of fear or anxiety. One powerful way to process these moods and emotions is to linguistically reconstruct the emotions of fear and anxiety using an ontological coaching approach. Let me share what a linguistic reconstruction of Anxiety or Fear looks like:

   a. I assert that something has happened or is happening (e.g., my boss is not supporting me in achieving my goals).

   b. Given that, I predict that I might face challenge X that can result in a future loss.

   c. Anxiety: I assess that at this moment, no matter what I do, I can't fully prevent X from happening. I declare that I want to have certainty one way or another.
   OR

   d. Fear: I assess that I might not have enough "Y" (e.g., smarts, good looks) to be able to face the challenge. I declare my desire to run away and not take a risk of exposing myself.

Once you are able to inspect the underlying story behind the core assessments you are making about yourself, the situation, and the future, you can start to take back control by letting go of what is untrue. You can engage in conversations with others (family, friends, colleagues) to share your assessments to test their validity and pressure test the actions you are planning to take. In the majority of cases, when you test the validity of the cause for Anxiety, you will find your worries are overblown and there is really no need to be worried. You can brainstorm all the different actions you can take to prepare yourself to handle what might unfold in the future. Only 20 percent of our fears come true, and when they do, with the right preparation, you will be well placed to handle them. For the remaining 80 percent of the fears, it is much better to surrender to the unfolding of life and avoid the unnecessary suffering that comes from resisting.

LETTING GO OF ANXIETY

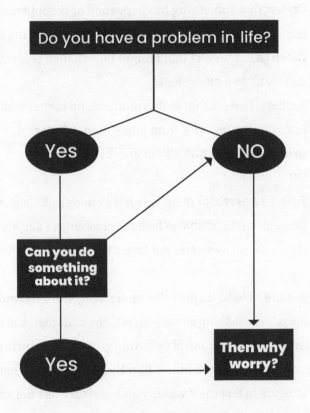

Figure 5.3: Letting go of Anxiety

HARDWIRED FOR HAPPINESS

Rachel was the vice president of banking operations for a bank and approached me for help to prepare her for an important upcoming job interview. Rachel was a highly regarded and trusted executive who had risen through the ranks from a frontline clerk. I had always been impressed by Rachel's communication skills and her ability to influence senior stakeholders successfully on contentious topics. So I was a bit surprised when Rachel shared that she had been turned down after three, in-person job interviews because of a lack of confidence, executive presence, and communications.

I invited her to close her eyes and step back into the moment of her last in-person interview: what were the thoughts running through her head, any bodily sensations, and any moods? Rachel shared the following:

- **Thoughts:** I need to say the "right things" or I am going to fail. He is going to see through me that I am not good enough, like the others. I will ruin my reputation in the industry and will become non-hirable.
- **Mood:** Anxiety at being proven right that I am not good enough; fear of not being able to provide for my family if I lost my current job and won't find a new one (as proven by my failure the last three times).
- **Body:** Pit in the stomach, shortness of breath, feeling unstable/ ungrounded, and on edge.

In our coaching session, we explored the origination of Rachel's Fears, especially her insecurity around not being able to provide for her family. She explained that she'd grown up on food stamps and never wanted that for her own family. I took Rachel through a centering exercise helping her breathe deeply into her belly, feel her feet, and calm her nervous system, as I could tell she was still charged from reliving her experience. From a calmer state, we explored each of her assessments to test their validity. Her rise over the last ten years at her current bank, as well as her top 1 percent ratings consistently were proof that she indeed "was good enough." Her family had saved enough in a rainy-day fund that could carry them forward for three-plus years. We explored what would become possible if, instead of trying to get proof externally by reading visual cues and body language from her interviewer, she could ground herself in her "enoughness" by tuning inward, feeling her feet, and continuing to breathe calmly.

Together we created a daily practice integrating elements of thoughts (practicing a declaration of "I am enough"), body (practicing grounding through breathing deeply and feeling her feet), and mood (wonder and anticipation versus anxiety). Three weeks later, Rachel nailed her final round of interviews and was hired.

Meditation Exercise:
Melting Away Stress and Anxiety

Progressive muscle relaxation[76] is a meditation that relaxes your mind and body by progressively tensing and relaxing different muscle groups. You will tense each muscle for about seven seconds and then relax while visualizing waves of relaxation flowing over you as you release the tension. Pause for ten seconds before each step. If you are suffering from any injury or feel any pain or discomfort in any muscle group, please feel free to omit that step.

Duration: thirty minutes

1. Take a comfortable standing position which allows you to be relaxed but also alert. Keep your back straight, your

shoulders relaxed, your chin facing slightly upward, and close your eyes. Keep your jaw relaxed with your lips slightly open. You can let your arms hang by your sides. Feel the base of your feet grounding you into the Earth.

2. Take three deep breaths, feeling the air fill your lungs and your belly, and then slowly exhale with an open mouth, letting all the air out and feeling your belly contract. Let yourself relax completely.

3. With your next breath, bring attention to any feelings of discomfort, stress, or anxiety that might be present. Hold them in the loving embrace of your mindful attention and repeat in your thoughts:

    a. Breathing in, "I witness my feelings."

    b. Breathing out, "I smile at my feelings."

    c. Take five more inhales and exhales, continuing to witness the feelings that are present. Continue breathing normally as you go through the rest of the steps.

4. Start by bringing the forehead muscles under tension by lifting your eyebrows as high as you can. Hold for seven seconds and then release them, feeling the tension go away.

5. Now squeeze your eyelids tightly shut to put tension on your eye muscles. Hold for seven seconds and release.

6. Now smile as widely as you can, feeling your mouth and cheeks tense up. Hold for seven seconds and release to feel the jaw and all your facial muscles relax.

7. Next, pull your head gently to the left feeling the tension in the right-hand side of your neck. Hold for seven seconds and

release. Next, pull your head gently to the right side, feeling the tension in the left side of your neck. Hold for seven seconds and release.

8. Now lift your shoulders up as if to touch your ears. Hold for seven seconds and release.

9. Next, tense your upper back by pulling your shoulders back as if to make the shoulder blades touch. Hold for seven seconds and release.

10. Now clench your fists tightly, squeezing for seven seconds and then release.

11. Next, tighten your glutes, holding them for seven seconds and release.

12. Now bring tension to your thigh muscles by bringing your knees together and holding them for seven seconds before releasing.

13. Next, stretch your legs out in front of your body and flex your feet, pointing your toes toward your body. Feel the tension in your calves for seven seconds and then release.

14. Finally, point your toes, bringing tension to your feet muscles for seven seconds and then release.

Once you are done, continue breathing normally for the next ten breaths, allowing the feeling of calmness and relaxation to wash over you. Gently open your eyes.

Fortunately, my own story of anxiety had a happy ending as well. I am deeply grateful to my mentors at that time, who helped me manage my anxiety and created an environment of trust and collaboration that allowed myself and others to thrive. I learned to name my fears and openly share my perspectives. I engaged my clients as well as my teammates early in the process, which took away the fear of not meeting expectations, since everyone was involved. It helped in many cases, especially cutting down the extra fear-driven work I was piling on. As I began to face my fears, not only did my anxiety go away, but the deliverables, client, and team experience all improved as well.

Mastering Guilt and Shame

The complicated emotions of Guilt and Shame are deeply rooted in our cultural context. In our cultures, we grow up with certain implicit and explicit customs, conventions, and ways of acting that often serve as a moral compass. These standards are critical for well-functioning societies, given our highly interdependent nature of existence. Guilt and Shame often arise as emotions when we find ourselves violating one of these standards. While they are similar, they are not the same. With Guilt, the standard is usually internal to us and private, whereas with Shame the standard is external and public, resulting in us losing our community standing or identity. Brené Brown, one of the world's leading researchers on shame and vulnerability, very eloquently shares the difference between the two in her book, *Daring Greatly*. She describes guilt as the assessment "I did something bad" versus shame as the assessment "I *am* bad." Both shame and guilt can result in low esteem, low self-confidence, and loss of self-worth.

We can tackle the moods and emotions of Shame and Guilt using a similar approach as with Anger and Resentment.

Get Curious

The next time you find yourself in a mood of Shame or Guilt, write down the story that you are telling yourself. Be particularly careful to state the assertions (facts) and assessments (beliefs) that are part of the story; both about the action you did or did not do, and the standard you are using to judge that action or inaction. It is also important to assess not just your role in the act but also explore other factors that might have been responsible or contributed to it. Carefully assess the standard which is giving rise to the feeling of shame or guilt and who set the standard (you, someone else, community), whether the standard is clear and explicit, and if you want to live by that standard or from something else that you "own." Once you have done the work of really investigating your assessments and standards, you can take actions toward resolving the situation.

Let's say you felt guilty because you were late picking up your child from school after work. Within your guilty feeling, there is a judgment based on what "good parents are expected to do," e.g., not leave their child stranded. But what else was going on to cause your lateness? Perhaps you are minimizing the colleague who needed your help urgently, or the efforts you made to try to have your partner or another parent handle pickup. Was your child in danger or just sitting in front of the school with the teacher's aide? Are you habitually late, or was this a rare exception to your regular routine?

Activate the Power of Self-Compassion and Empathy to Sooth Yourself

You can recognize that just like everyone else, you are not perfect. Bring the soothing force of self-compassion to alleviate your suffering. In the moments when you feel really small and unworthy, it can also help to remind you of key things that you are proud of in your life. By holding this one act in which you failed against the broader backdrop of your strengths and successes, you can remove the sting from the feelings of guilt and shame. I would also encourage you to share your story with someone who has earned your trust and will respond with empathy and understanding.

Ask for Forgiveness from Yourself or Others and Move On

By actively forgiving yourself for the actions or behaviors that caused you to feel guilt or shame, you can start to let them go. You can also formally ask for forgiveness from others and share how you plan to make amends to repair any damage that you might have caused. Once you have made amends, you can declare the past closed and choose to move toward a new future, where you can stop suffering in silence.

Cultivating a Mood of Optimism and Ambition

As important as it is to skillfully navigate the unpleasant emotions like anger, resentment, fear, anxiety, shame, and guilt, you can learn to invite in positive emotions like satisfaction, joy, hope, optimism, and love. These not only make us feel good about ourselves and our lives but also allow us to see the world in an entirely different way, thus opening up a larger set of possibilities.

In my transformation work with client organizations, one of the biggest moods that takes hold in corporate culture and employees is Resignation or Pessimism. In this mood, no one can see any possibility for the future; and as a result, do nothing to change the situation. The most prevalent stories I hear in those organizations or cultures are: "Why bother? What's the point? Nothing will make a difference. We have tried everything before." Any suggestions from others on potential actions that could be taken are quickly rejected. From the point of the view of the employee, resignation shows up as grounded realism.

The field of ontological coaching provides a similar approach as I have described in prior sections to shift away from Resignation to a mood of Ambition and Optimism. Start by examining the underlying thought patterns in terms of beliefs and assessments that are giving rise to your perspective about the situation. You can also investigate your history of past experiences in life that are giving rise to the belief that positive change is not possible. Having nailed the core assessment, you can look for contrary evidence that might prove this belief to be wrong. You can do this by engaging in learning from other individuals, experts, and organizations. For example, if your investment portfolio has not grown in value in the last several years, and as a result you feel you are not good with money, and the stock market is not for you, start by comparing the results to the overall market as well as to others in your friend or social circle. You might find that while your portfolio held value, many others lost value.

You can also start to look for alternative reasons that might explain the results. For example, the market as a whole might not be doing well. Or maybe the time at which you decided to enter the market was at the peak of the market. As a result, while the performance over the last several years has been lackluster, you will do fine as all markets go through cycles.

Even if your beliefs turn out to be true, you can still do one of two things to shift your mood to one of Optimism or Ambition in order to open yourself up to new possibilities. One, you can examine the implications about the future you are making, even if the belief is true. Are you catastrophizing (which many of us often do) and staying fixed because the future you are imagining is the worst-case scenario with a low possibility of happening? Or maybe it is too rosy of a picture. Second, ask yourself how the mood of resignation or pessimism is serving you right now. What good is holding on to that belief serving you?

Building Your Mood-Mastery Practice

Lightening your load by tackling the negative moods and emotions that weigh you down will only help make your *Hardwired for Happiness* journey a smoother one. You have to learn to listen to the wisdom in your moods and emotions, and then let go. Stepping back, you can recognize that often the moods and emotions you find yourself in have less to do with the external world, but more to do with the lens through which you are observing it. Recognize that you will never have full control on the external world and what it throws at you. Instead, start focusing on shaping your internal landscape to change your own experience.

KEY TAKEAWAYS

- We use the terms *moods* and *emotions* interchangeably, but they are very different. Unlike emotions, which are usually the result of some event that breaks our flow of life, moods don't need an event to manifest themselves. In fact, if we experience an emotion over and over, it can become a mood and preclude us from certain possibilities, or it might push us toward other actions.

- The most common moods and emotions that create a lot of suffering for people are Anger, Resentment, Fear, Anxiety, Guilt, and Shame. You can gain mastery over them by learning to be with them versus expressing or suppressing them by grounding yourself in the present. From that place of center, you can get curious, test the validity of the assessments giving rise to the moods, and consciously choose among the actions that will set you free: make a request or complaint; let go and forgive; or close the relationship.

- Cultivating a mood of Optimism and inviting in positive emotions like satisfaction, joy, hope, optimism, and love, not only make us feel good but also allow us to see the world in an entirely different way, opening up a larger set of possibilities.

Fuel Up with Compassion

"Love and compassion are necessities, not luxuries.
Without them, humanity cannot survive."

—Dalai Lama

I n a Zen story, a man wandered down a deserted beach. He saw a boy going back and forth from the beach to the edge of the waves. As the man came closer to the boy, he noticed there were thousands of starfish stranded on the sand, and the boy was throwing them, one at a time, back into the sea.

The man approached the boy and asked, "Why are you throwing starfish into the sea?"

The boy said, "The sun is rising and the tide is going out. If I don't throw them into the sea, they will die."

The man observed the futility of the task, and said, "There are thousands of starfish. There is no way you will make a difference! Why are you wasting your time doing this?"

The boy hurriedly picked up the next starfish and threw it as far as he could into the sea. "It surely made a difference to that one!" he replied.

How has your life benefited from kindness and compassion from others? In what ways are you paying it forward? Compassion and kindness are the doorways through which we can transform the suffering of others and live in interbeing with each other and the broader natural world. Buddha described compassion as the one thing that if we possess it, we must also have all the other virtues. As our capacity for compassion grows, we are better able to tune into the suffering all around us and create a space for others to be able to share and lighten their load. As we cultivate a mindset and habits of compassion and generosity, not only do we help others, but we also get back more than what we give out into the world. As we start living in deeper connection and harmony with the world, love and belonging will follow and transform our lives for the better.

It is equally important to develop the capacity for self-compassion. We are the harshest critics of ourselves and constantly judge our every action, thought, or emotion that we feel. We are judgment-making machines. Any learning or growth journey, especially one that starts within, is bound to have setbacks, and we will experience suffering when we fail. Building a capacity for self-compassion allows us to treat ourselves with kindness and pick ourselves up when we fall, the same way we would for a friend in need. Compassion moves us to act, be kind, and generous in helping alleviate all suffering.

Over the course of this chapter, you'll find practical tips and suggestions that will help you build your capacity for self-compassion and practice compassion and generosity toward others. Science is proving the value and benefits of these practices that have been in the foundation of every spiritual, religious, and wisdom tradition like Buddhism, Yoga, Stoicism, Hinduism, Islam, or Christianity. By making these practices a part of your life, you can tap into a never-ending fuel source to power you on your *Hardwired for Happiness* journey.

The Science-Backed Benefits of Compassion

Compassion comes from the Latin words *pati* and *cum* meaning "to suffer with." Among researchers, it is defined as the feeling that arises when you face another's suffering and feel motivated to relieve that suffering. Over the last fourteen years, one of the research institutes that has become a hub in this field is the Center for Compassion and Altruism Research and Education (CCARE) at Stanford University School of Medicine. Founded by Dr. James Doty, Clinical Professor of Neurosurgery, and influenced by his visit with the Dalai Lama, CCARE supports the explicit goal of promoting, supporting, and conducting rigorous scientific studies of compassion and altruistic behavior. Dr. Thupten Jinpa, a noted contemplative scholar and translator to His Holiness the Dalai Lama for over thirty years, joined the Center as a Visiting Scholar and became the principal contemplative scholar for the effort. I would recommend visiting the center website (http://ccare.stanford.edu/research/) to access not only the extensive research on this topic but also learn more about the formal training on compassion the center offers.

Extensive research conducted over the last twenty years has validated that both animals and humans have a "compassionate instinct." A 2009 study conducted by Felix Warneken (Harvard University) and Michael Tomossello (Max Planck Institute for Evolutionary Anthropology) suggested that young children have a biological predisposition to help others achieve their goals, to share resources with others, and to helpfully inform others of things.[77] Other studies with animals have extensively validated the presence of empathy, the drive to not harm others, and to help others. For example, in a 2011 study published in *Science*, Peggy Mason and her colleagues showed that if a rat is trapped in a narrow plastic tube, the other companion rat will work on the latch until it figures out how to spring the trap.[78]

Research is also revealing that compassion can be improved over time to transform your life and increase your happiness. Dr. Helen Weng and Dr. Richard Davidson from the University of Wisconsin-Madison conducted a study where people participated in a thirty-minute compassion-meditation practice daily for two weeks. They were then shown a film about sharing a pot of money and asked to respond. In the film, they watched as one person who had ten dollars gave an unfair amount of money (only one dollar or two dollars) to someone who had no money. The researchers found that those trained in compassion were more likely to say they would give their own money to help the person who was cheated out of their fair share than another group who didn't receive the training.[79]

Cultivating compassion has tremendous benefits to our physical, mental, and overall wellbeing.[80] Compassionate medical care helps individuals not only recover from illness faster but also live longer lives. A more compassionate lifestyle was also found to be a good buffer against stress. Based on a study led by Michael Poulin at the University at Buffalo, stress was linked to higher chances of dying—except in those who helped others.[81] Compassion shifts our focus from self to others and acts as an antidote toward depression and anxiety that often arise from our fixation on ourselves. When we feel compassion, our bodies release the "bonding hormone" oxytocin, which reduces levels of inflammation in the cardio-vascular system, which in turn lowers the risk of developing cancer and other diseases. The regions of the brain that are linked to empathy, caring, and pleasure also light up, which results in the desire to take action to alleviate the suffering of others by being generous and kind. In a study conducted by David McClelland, a psychologist at Harvard University, saliva collected from students who watched a film of Mother Teresa serving food to the poor showed an increase in Immunoglobulin-A, an antibody that has been known to fight against respiratory infections.[82]

Similar to compassion, generosity and kindness toward others are rooted not just in our individual development, but also in our biology and evolutionary history. We are in fact hardwired for generosity. Several studies have shown that performing acts of kindness activate the same reward pathway as sex and food. Based on research undertaken by Haesung Jung and her colleagues, kindness is also highly contagious, and acts of kindness and generosity have ripple effects through our communities.[83] Researchers synthesized results from eighty-eight experimental studies involving over 25,000 participants and found a moderately strong effect on people witnessing altruism to be altruistic themselves. When we witness kindness, we are inspired to be kind ourselves. When we see someone being kind or generous, it gives us a warm feeling inside. Researchers call this "moral elevation," and it not only feels good but inspires us to want to do good ourselves. I would highly recommend seeing the movie *Pay It Forward*, about a young boy who unleashes a social change that spreads from city to city after simply doing three good deeds for someone and asking them in turn to "pay it forward."

Kind and generous people enjoy higher energy, happiness, life satisfaction, and longevity. Performing acts of kindness is also proven to reduce experiences of pain, stress, anxiety, and depression. A 2013 Harvard Business School global happiness study conducted by Lara Aknin and others across 136 countries found that people who are altruistic were happiest overall.[84] Another recent study undertaken by Lee Rowland and Oliver Curry in 2019 showed that people reported an increase in their happiness after performing or observing acts of kindness even after just seven days. The researchers found that being kind to ourselves or to others, regardless of how well you know the other person, boosts happiness.[85] Another study conducted by Kathryn Buchanan and Anat Bardi at the University of Kent found that people reported increases in life satisfaction after a mere ten days of conducting acts of kindness or novelty each day.[86]

We can clearly start to benefit very quickly from practicing compassion, kindness, and generosity. Why wait another minute?

Cultivating Compassion

Before we discuss how compassion works, let me share a story about just how powerful it can be. There was a prestigious private school in the State of Rajasthan in India which had a reputation for the very best math program under the direction of a renowned professor, Mr. Singh. Each year the school offered a few scholarships to lucky children who could not afford the tuition. One recipient, Ajay, came from a very poor community in Rajasthan. He studied math intensely under Mr. Singh's tutelage and soon became top of his class. The other math students were jealous and not particularly friendly toward Ajay.

One day the faculty was saddened to find out that Ajay had been caught stealing money, and the overall view was that he should be expelled. At first Mr. Singh ignored the case, which angered the other students. They drew up a petition asking for Ajay's dismissal, saying they would refuse to come to school unless he was punished. Mr. Singh summoned the whole school to assemble and told them, "In my heart of hearts, I cannot dismiss Ajay from this school. If he is expelled, he will have nowhere to go, and it will ruin his whole education. Furthermore, he will be an outcast in his village, and it will cause much suffering to him and his family. If any student disagrees with me, they themselves will need to leave the school." Ajay burst into tears with relief, happiness, and huge regret for what he had stolen. Any desire to steal again vanished forever.

Expressing compassion is not always easy, but it's an important lesson to not turn your back on someone who needs help. We must look deeper to see what the consequences of our actions could be. Sometimes people just need a second chance and to be shown the path forward.

Compassion is actually comprised of two key components. The first is empathy, which is the ability to walk in another's shoes, be able to see the world from their eyes, and understand their pain. The second is a desire for action that comes from having that understanding of what the other is thinking, feeling, and wanting to help alleviate that suffering.

COMPASSION

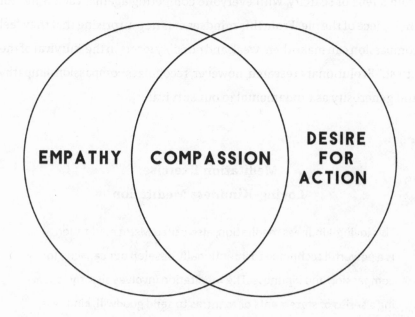

Figure 6.1: Compassion

Genuine compassion is based on the foundation that all human beings want to be happy and free of suffering. So when we see others suffering, compassion automatically arises in us and motivates us to try and relieve the other person's suffering, even if they are not related to us. In every place of human suffering, we do not have to look hard to also find beautiful and moving acts of human compassion from people looking to alleviate that suffering.

It is worth dispelling a couple of myths about compassion. First, compassion is not a relationship between the savior and the one who needs saving. Instead, it is a relationship of equals and becomes real when we connect with the other, not out of pity but out of the realization of our shared humanity with them. Second, compassion does not make one person weaker. A large proportion of the population today sees the world from a lens of scarcity, with everyone competing against each other for their piece of the pie. From this mindset, it is not surprising that they feel compassion can make them weak and possibly losers in the "survival of the fittest." Evolutionary research, however, recognizes compassion, empathy, and generosity as fundamental to our survival.

Meditation Exercise:
Loving-Kindness Meditation

This loving-kindness meditation, also called *Metta* meditation, is a powerful technique to intentionally develop our capacity for compassion and kindness. The meditation involves silently repeating a series of statements or mantras to send goodwill, kindness, and warmth starting from self, to those we love, our acquaintances, and extending out to the whole world. You can use the following mantras for this practice, but feel free to adjust them to make them yours.

"May you be happy.
May you be healthy.

May you be free of suffering.

May you be peaceful."

Duration: fifteen minutes

1. **Sit with purpose:** Sit in a comfortable position which allows you to be relaxed but also alert. This is a good meditation to practice sitting in a relaxed Lotus position with your legs crossed. If it is not comfortable, you can also just practice sitting in a chair. Keep your back straight, your shoulders relaxed, your chin facing slightly upward, and close your eyes. Keep your jaw relaxed with your lips slightly open. You can rest your arms on your legs with palms facing downward.

2. **Preparation breaths:** Take three deep breaths, feeling the air fill your lungs and your stomach, and then slowly exhale with an open mouth, letting all the air out and feeling your stomach contract. Let yourself relax completely.

3. **Breathe normally:** Resume breathing at your normal pace, keeping attention on each inhale and exhale, feeling your belly rise with each inhale and fall with each exhale.

4. **Start with self:** Think of a person who is close to you and who loves you very much. It could be a family member like your parents, siblings, grandparents, spouse, or even a spiritual teacher. Now imagine that they are sitting facing you and sending you wishes for your wellbeing, safety, happiness, and joy. Imagine them speaking the following words to you:

"May you be happy.

May you be healthy.

May you be free of suffering.
May you be peaceful."

Take five sets of inhales and exhales, letting the full weight of each of their wishes sweep over you, and letting their kindness and warmth envelop your whole body and flow through you.

5. **Extend to someone you love:** Now picture a person who you love very much and is near and dear to you. It could be someone from your near family or from your close friend's circle. Silently repeat the mantra for five sets of inhales and exhales and send them your warm wishes, kindness, love, and good vibes.

   "May you be happy.
   May you be healthy.
   May you be free of suffering.
   May you be peaceful."

6. **Extend to neutral people:** Now picture a neutral person who might be an acquaintance. They could be a colleague you work with, a neighbor, the local barista, the bus driver, or anyone else you interact with on a regular basis. Silently repeat the mantra for five sets of inhales and exhales and send them your warm wishes, kindness, love, and good vibes.

   "May you be happy.
   May you be healthy.
   May you be free of suffering.
   May you be peaceful."

7. **Extend to someone with disagreement:** Now picture someone you had a disagreement with recently and left with strained feelings. It might be hard to summon feelings of loving-kindness for this person, and so really give yourself the time you need for these feelings to arise. Remind yourself that despite their differences in opinion, they too, like you, want nothing more than to be happy. Silently repeat the mantra for five sets of inhales and exhales and send them your warm wishes, kindness, love, and good vibes.

   "May you be happy.
   May you be healthy.
   May you be free of suffering.
   May you be peaceful."

8. **Extend to the whole world:** Now picture the whole globe and all the human beings inhabiting this planet with you. You can imagine extending your wishes to all living things, including plants and animals. Silently repeat the mantra for five sets of inhales and exhales and send the world your warm wishes, kindness, love, and good vibes.

   "May you all be happy.
   May you all be healthy.
   May you all be free of suffering.
   May you all be peaceful."

9. **Return back to self:** Complete the loving-kindness meditation by returning to yourself with compassion and repeating the mantra.

"May I be happy.
May I be healthy.
May I be free of suffering.
May I be peaceful."

10. **Take a final deep breath in and breathe out:** Slowly open your eyes and let yourself spend the next several moments feeling the good vibes and warmth from this beautiful practice.

Both the Dalai Lama and Pema Chödrön advise to start from where you are and use your own suffering and aversion to unwanted emotions and things as the means to awaken your compassion. You can start to approach others with what you share in common with them—we all have bodies, minds, emotions; we are all born, and we all die; we all want joy and happiness. You can learn to pause and instead of jumping very quickly into judging the other when facing a breakdown of any sorts, first recognize that just like you, they are probably beating themselves up and feeling bad. You can adopt a mindset of curiosity to really understand the full picture of what might have gotten in their way. You can also start to recognize that the strong feelings you have right now, like all feelings, are illusory and rise and fall like waves in an ocean. But the hurtful words you might say could leave an impression that might be long lasting and affect your relationships.

Be Kinder to Yourself

Cultivating self-compassion is equally as important in our modern world as cultivating compassion for others. According to Dr. Kristin Neff, self-compassion means being gentle, kind, and understanding with yourself; accepting that you are not perfect; and understanding that there is potential for learning and growth in every mistake you make.

Figure 6.2: Three elements of self-compassion based on Kristin Neff's model

She highlights three key elements of self-compassion with suggestions to develop and grow your capacity:

1. **Self-kindness versus self-judgment:** The next time you fail at something or are suffering, practice being warm and understanding toward yourself versus numbing the pain or engaging

in self-criticism. You can always be there for yourself, just like you would make yourself available for a friend who is going through a tough time.

2. **Common humanity versus isolation:** When we suffer or feel unworthy, we tend to also feel shame and self-isolate to protect ourselves. By recognizing that suffering, feelings of inadequacy, and failure are universal and very much a shared human experience, you can bring legitimacy to what you are feeling and face it openly versus shutting yourself down.

3. **Mindfulness versus over-identification:** You can practice taking a balanced, equanimous approach to your emotions versus suppressing them or acting on them. You can wrestle yourself free from the emotional tsunami and see the situation from a broader perspective—is it really that big of a deal? What was your role in creating it? What is the role that others might have played? By just observing your emotions, you can start to mine them for the wisdom they hold in terms of learning, both in your past and actions you can take in the future.

Journaling Exercise:
Practicing Self-Compassion to Tame Your Inner Critic

There are several times during a day when you might beat yourself up over something you have done or regret a course of action. Journaling about those moments to look deeply into the suffering that was part of that experience can be highly transformative.

This exercise can be done over thirty days, and over time it will help you cultivate self-compassion by transforming your relationship with your inner critic.

Toward the end of your day, find a quiet place in your home where you can spend some time in reflection and self-care. Make yourself a soothing drink (a warm cup of herbal tea), put on calm music, and wrap yourself in a blanket or soft sweater. Now bring your attention to one of those events/moments during the day where you felt critical of yourself afterward: an action you took, words you said, a look you gave someone, a missed opportunity to speak up, or even a personal trait (physical, emotional, character).

1. Start by writing down the thoughts that were running through your head at that moment. Try and recall the exact words and phrases you were using when you were being self-critical (e.g., you are so stupid...). Also notice the tone of the voice—was it harsh, angry, loud, hateful? Bring awareness to how familiar you are with these words or phrases from your past. Where did you first hear them? Did a loved one, a teacher, or a friend say those words to you?

2. Now bring attention to what those words made you feel. Which emotions were present for you—sadness, shame, stress, anger, resentment, self-pity, frustration, etc.? Try to bring awareness to your bodily sensations that were present. As you write down your emotions and physical sensations, try to be accepting and nonjudgmental of your experience.

Practice breathing into the place of discomfort in order to be mindfully present with the emotion—neither numbing or making it smaller, nor making it bigger and overly dramatic. (For example, "I was frustrated because he was not listening to me. I lost my temper and hung up the phone. I felt guilty afterward.")

3. Now write down the ways in which your experience is not unique and not isolated to you but deeply connected to the broader humanity. You can bring to mind the universality of suffering—how everyone you know has suffered at one time or another. You can bring to mind the universality of imperfection—how no one is perfect, and everyone makes mistakes that they regret. ("Even monks lose their tempers sometimes; it's only human.") You can also bring attention to the broader context underlying the event and your state of overall wellbeing. ("I was feeling tired because I hadn't slept well last night and was feeling exhausted. If I wasn't so depleted, I would have been more patient.") You can also try to trace the origins of this particular trait to an experience of your past that might have seeded this reaction. ("I never felt listened to, being the youngest of my siblings, and I always had to shout to make myself heard.")

4. Now write three to five sentences to yourself from the perspective of an unconditionally loving friend. You can imagine a close friend holding you in their arms, giving you a warm embrace. You can even gently rub your arm with your other hand to comfort yourself or put your arms around

yourself to hug yourself. Imagine what this friend would say to you when they saw you suffering. What words of comfort and kindness would they offer? (e.g., Relax. It's OK. We all mess up from time to time. It is not the end of the world. I know you are feeling guilty about how you reacted.) Try reframing the perspective of your inner critic in a kind way, extracting the learnings of what you should/could do next time but without the judgment and drama.

5. At the end of the week, go back through your journal entries from the week and read them again, but read them with the intention to really let the words sink in, as if they came from an unconditionally loving friend.

Personally, developing a capacity for self-compassion has been transformative. From an early age, I suffered from "impostor syndrome," worried about not being enough. I constantly judged my efforts, my knowledge, my intelligence, and my work ethic. I did not own my worthiness and felt that my belonging and love from others was always at stake based on what I did. At work, my inner critic was in full force, always pushing me to keep doing more. However, as I developed my capacity for self-compassion, the quality of my life fundamentally changed. I feel lighter and more confident. I learned to hear the voice of my inner critic and glean the wisdom it had to share, but not be controlled by it.

The following are three practical changes that have made a big difference in my life and are integral to how I coach my clients. I invite you to experiment with them so you can also benefit from the uplifting effects they have from cultivating compassion for ourselves and others.

1. **Make peace with your inner critic:** We all are familiar with the inner voice that judges us and puts us down. Our inner critics get their energy from our deepest fears, including but not limited to: fear of belonging (not being loved), insignificance (not mattering), losing control, and vulnerability (not being good enough). Despite possibly trying to protect us from potential rejection, harm, or failure, our fears cause a lot of collateral damage. Next time you hear your inner critic roaring in your ear, you can recognize and honor the positive intent by embracing it and inviting it to take a seat at the table, while also inviting the part of you that is feeling criticized. You can listen to the advice of the critic without all its associated judgment and drama. At the same time, you can tenderly hold that part of yourself that is feeling criticized.

2. **Practice compassionate listening to connect deeply with others:** Listening deeply and giving your gift of attention to others can be a wonderful gateway to compassion. Most of us don't truly listen. We're always interrupting, judging what someone says, or trying to fix the problem they are facing. You can start by being fully present with everyone you encounter. The next time you ask someone, "How are you?" practice deep listening to really check in with the other person. Listen not just to the words they are saying, but also notice the tone (excited, calm, agitated) and their pace (fast, slow). Maintain soft eye contact. Notice if they are gazing directly at you or avoiding eye contact. Pay attention to their body language, their facial expressions, and their mood state. Notice their posture (is it slumped or held straight), their stance (wide, or narrow, turned toward you or away), their hands (composed or fidgety).

As you listen, refrain from giving advice. You can simply say something like, "This must be really tough/hard/painful for you. I'm sorry you're going through this. I am here for you. Let me know how I can be helpful."

3. **Develop morning and evening compassion rituals:** Start every morning by setting an intention to be compassionate to yourself and to others and reflect at the end of the day whether you were successful in fulfilling that intention. Setting an intention is like planning ahead of time, so when an opportunity presents itself, you've already chosen the path you're going to take. You can start by repeating a few phrases to yourself: "I am grateful for the gift of a new day. May I relate to myself and others around me with compassion, kindness, understanding, and less judgment." In the evening, take a few minutes before you go to bed to reflect upon your day. Think about the people you interacted with during the day and the quality of your interactions. Think about your goal that you stated this morning, to act with compassion toward others. How well did you do? What could you do better? Just remember to do this reflection with self-compassion and not be harsh if you were not successful in some cases. By being aware, you are already on your journey.

Robin was the chief marketing officer for a midsized consumer packaged goods company, and Tom was the head of supply chain. They had both recently joined the company after its sale to a private equity company, and right from the beginning, their relationship had gotten off to a rocky start. Their teams were given different objectives in a world of finite resources, and what started as silent fuming had turned into an all-out war with regular arguments and open conflicts in meetings. The CEO of the company asked me to intervene and help coach Tom and Robin to better collaborate.

As I connected with each of them individually and also observed them in meetings, I quickly understood that both were highly talented and wonderful human beings who cared deeply about the success of the company. Their interactions were locked in a pattern of arguments without seeking to understand the other's perspective. They also both held a very vilified image of the other, believing that the other person also held them in low regard.

To help them bridge the divide, I decided to use compassion as a key tool to help them move forward. First, with the help of the CEO, I orchestrated a sixty-minute workshop with the entire leadership team (including Robin and Tom), where I invited each of them to share a compliment ("What makes you great in my eyes is...") with another person and also offer input on what they could do to build trust. After sharing, the two would thank each other and find new partners. Robin and Tom were pleasantly surprised to get positive feedback from each other. Robin appreciated Tom's politeness, his structured thinking, and ability to break down issues simply. Tom appreciated Robin's creativity and out-of-the-box thinking, her flair with words, and her optimistic outlook.

I also invited each of them to play a game to build empathy toward the other's perspective. I asked Robin and Tom to each take a real issue and tell me their side of the story, amplifying the emotion around why they thought they were right: shouting/yelling, stomping their feet, moving around if they needed to. Then I asked them to physically switch places and tell the story from the other's point of view, using the same passion to act it out. They had to be convincing enough until they succeeded.

Both Robin and Tom emerged with new perspectives and a greater understanding of how they both needed to work toward common goals for the company. In meetings, they started asking questions like, "What are you solving for?" and "Tell me more..." before arguing for their own needs. As they learned to listen more deeply and better connect, they discovered truly win-win solutions that were not evident to either before.

Make Practicing Kindness and Generosity a Habit

The world would be a different place without people like Mother Teresa, St. Francis of Assisi, and Reverend Desmond Tutu, who are shining beacons of inspiration and have dedicated their whole lives in service of others. All around us in our communities, we can find people who are making a huge difference in the lives of others, at any scale. Consider Kazi Mannan, who immigrated to the United States in 1996 and runs the Sakina Halal Grill in Washington, DC, and offers free meals to the homeless (and continued to do so during the COVID-19 pandemic). Ashoka Fellow Sarbani Das Roy created an organization called Iswar Sankalpa (God's resolution) to take care of the homeless in India who were suffering from mental illnesses. There is Father Gregory Boyle in Los Angeles, who started Homeboy Industries to help former gang members become productive members of our community.

The Dalai Lama said, "My religion is simple. My religion is kindness." Generosity is seen as a foundational virtue in most spiritual paths and religions. In Christianity, St. Francis of Assisi is known for saying, "For it is in giving that we receive." *Aparigraha*, which means generosity and simplicity, is one of the five *Yamas*, or core social ethics, in yoga. In Buddhism, Hinduism, Sikhism, and Jainism, the practice of "Dāna"—practicing generosity through giving charity and alms to those in need—has been traced back to the Vedic traditions. Most *gurudwaras*, or religious temples for Sikhs, run food halls where anyone who is hungry can get something to eat, even if they are not Sikh.

Generosity and kindness are not just virtues that are reserved for those who have it all. In fact, often those who have very little are the ones most joyfully willing to share a large part of what they have with others. I was so touched by Viktor Frankl's example of such acts of kindness in the worst of human suffering, from his book, *Man's Search for Meaning*:

> We who lived in concentration camps can remember the men who walked through the huts comforting others, giving away their last piece of bread ... They offer sufficient proof that everything can be taken from a man but one thing: to choose one's attitude in any given set of circumstances, to choose one's own way.

Intentionally practicing kindness everyday can go a long way toward turning kindness and generosity into a habit. When you perform small, random acts of kindness, you will experience happiness, which makes you more likely to want to perform them in the future. There are several ways in which you can contribute to others.

Donate Your Money and Resources

One of my dear friends shared a wonderful practice that she has been following with her kids from a very early age. She bought them a piggy bank that has three equal compartments. For all the money they earn, one-third goes into savings, one-third goes into donations to an organization of their choosing, and one-third goes into their account to spend on what they want. Here are some other suggestions:

- Use a digital app like "Roundup" to build giving into our daily routines. Roundup works by rounding up your purchases and directing funds to the nonprofit of your choice.

- Organize or participate in annual United Way drives and other campaigns at work to support a cause you care about.
- Start a fundraiser and use your network to raise funds for people in need. Every day there is a crisis somewhere in the world, where we can make a difference.
- Donate to your local alma mater or get involved with education efforts in your home country, especially if you are from a developing country.
- Actively recycle by donating your older clothes, toys, and things to those in need right in your community.

Donate Your Time and Expertise to Others

This might involve joining a board for a not-for-profit organization, volunteering in local community projects, or mentoring others from your community, alma mater, and sharing your rich experiences.

- Get involved with your alma mater, local university, or industry associations to mentor the younger generation and share your hard-earned wisdom.
- Build relationships and connect with the older people in your neighborhood or through local older people homes to reduce loneliness and help with chores.
- Donate your technical and management expertise to start-ups and other local minority-owned businesses by getting involved with networks like Blackstone Entrepreneurs Network (BEN).
- Actively mentor and sponsor junior colleagues to bridge the gender and racial divides that exist in our world and at our companies today.

Give the Gift of a Smile, Your Attention, and Joy to Others

By showing up with lightness, aliveness, and joy in your interactions, you can transform the experience of those you interact with and brighten up their days.

- Give the gift of your undivided attention and create an environment to allow others to be fully seen and open up. Share your spirit with everyone; you never know the battle each of them is fighting. Set an intention to have people leave every interaction with you in a better mood and emotional state than when they arrived.
- Take a moment to pay a compliment and give a heartfelt thanks to the servers at a coffee shop or restaurant, taxi drivers, house cleaners, grocery workers, nurses, and so many other "invisible" people who make our day-to-day lives comfortable.
- Hold or open the door for someone (it does not matter if they thank you; what matters is the intention to be kind and generous).
- Send a handwritten thank-you note every week to friends, family, and colleagues to brighten up their day.
- Be polite on the road and help others who may be stressed out, or in a rush, by letting others merge, giving a friendly smile, and letting pedestrians cross.

The Greater Good in Action website (https://ggia.berkeley.edu/) is a good resource for more inspiration on not just how to become kinder yourself but also how to inspire kindness in others. Jane Goodall said it best: "What you do makes a difference, and you have to decide what kind of difference you want to make."

Community Exercise:
Engaging in Acts of Kindness in
Our Communities

Community service work can be a great way to make a difference in someone's life and rally others at work, school, and your neighborhood to practice small acts of kindness. Helping others not only increases our happiness, level of energy, and life span, but it also reduces stress, anxiety, and depression.[87] Volunteering can help build deeper connections in your local community, and it's a wonderful way to role model this virtue for your kids.

You can reap these benefits by volunteering in a community effort that you identify with or relate to at least once a month. It could be anything from volunteering at a pet shelter, local soup kitchen, or donating your time toward a nonprofit organization. Even better, you can start a local kindness club in your community and recruit a group of six to nine friends, colleagues, and acquaintances to help you organize monthly random acts of kindness. Once you have the group created, you can take the following steps to get the effort going:

1. Find out what is needed in the community. You can start by asking friends and family members and reading the local newspaper to learn the top issues in the community.
2. Choose a project every month based on what topics interest the group and what you might have an ability to contribute toward in terms of your skills, time you can dedicate, and people you can involve in the effort, among others.

3. Develop a plan on what you are hoping to accomplish and other partners you might want to involve in terms of local nonprofits, government organizations, etc. Identify the resources you will need, including a rough budget, event organizers, and volunteers. Develop and execute a fundraising plan.

4. Publicize the event in your community. You can advertise at your company, children's school, or in your neighborhood. Local radio stations, blogs, and TV stations can also be wonderful ways to get the word out in addition to social media apps, including Facebook or Next Door.

5. Execute the event and reflect with your core group afterward about what went well and things to improve for the next time around.

Building Your Compassion Practice

You come into this world with nothing, and you leave this world with nothing. In the grand scheme of things, no matter where you are, you are always ahead of where you started and have more than what you will end with. We live our lives in great interbeing with others, intertwined and beneficiaries of so many who have given generously to us, from our parents, teachers, friends, and others in our community. We cannot exist without others, and so in many ways, helping others is a way of helping ourselves. Integrating the practices of compassion and kindness toward yourself and others can fill your life with unbounded energy and propel you forward in your *Hardwired for Happiness* journey. By offering others your time, money, and spirit, you can achieve greater happiness and joy.

KEY TAKEAWAYS

- Cultivating compassion, generosity, and kindness provides tremendous benefits to our physical, mental, and overall well-being, and reduces pain, stress, anxiety, and depression.
- Evolutionary research, however, recognizes compassion, empathy, and generosity as fundamental to our survival.
- Compassion is actually comprised of empathy, or the ability to walk in another's shoes, and a desire for action that comes from having that understanding of what the other is thinking and feeling, and wanting to help alleviate that suffering.
- Developing self-compassion is just as important to feel good and keep your cup full in order to pour out for others.

Invest in Your Wellbeing

"Health is the complete state of harmony
of the mind, body and spirit."

—B. K. S. Iyengar

The importance of investing in your health and wellbeing cannot be overstated. Norm Kelly, a Canadian politician, said it best, "You cannot pour from an empty cup." If our ultimate goal is to dedicate our lives to filling the cups of others, we have to make sure we fill ourselves up first. The World Health Organization (WHO) defines health as not merely the absence of disease but "a state of complete physical, mental, and social wellbeing." Wellbeing is a subjective measure with not a single consensus around its definition, but most experts agree that it includes positive functioning at the physical (full of health and energy), mental (feeling content and happy), and spiritual level (satisfaction with life and fulfillment). I have yet to meet a person who couldn't benefit from greater energy and life force.

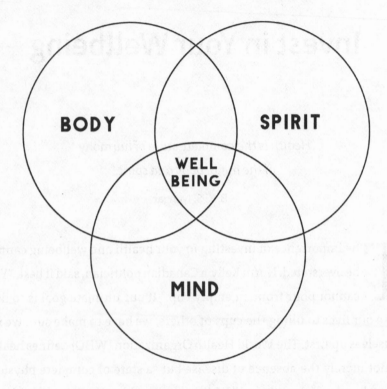

WELLBEING
MIND | BODY | SPIRIT

BODY

SPIRIT

WELL BEING

MIND

Figure 7.1: Wellbeing model—integration of mind, body, and spirit

Theodore Roosevelt, the twenty-sixth President of the United States, offers a wonderful reminder of the importance of investing in our wellbeing to be able to leverage the gifts we are bestowed with for the service of humankind. From early childhood, it was clear that "Teddy" was gifted with a brilliant mind. Unfortunately his brilliant mind was in a body that was weak and plagued with horrible asthma. Even a little physical exertion would bring on an asthmatic attack that would leave the boy bedridden for weeks.

When Teddy was twelve, his father walked into his room and told him, "Theodore, you have the mind but you have not the body, and without the help of the body, the mind cannot go as far as it should. I am giving you the tools, but it is up to you to make your body." Teddy accepted the challenge and said to his father, "I will make my body." From that day on, he worked fervently to build his upper body strength by exercising in the gym his father had built. Over time, he took on boxing, hiking, weightlifting, and mountain climbing. By his early twenties, Teddy had fundamentally transformed his body and overcome his battle with asthma. That physical strength served him well throughout his political career and eventually his presidency. He became an advocate for healthy living and a strenuous life.

The Science-Based Benefits of Wellbeing

Our collective wellbeing faced an onslaught of new proportions in the beginning of 2020 as the world was gripped with the COVID-19 virus. No one was spared across the globe regardless of nationality, race, or prosperity. To protect our bodies from getting infected, we put on masks and started isolating in our homes, and our busy day-to-day lives came to a standstill. As the virus raged through our world, the number of cases and deaths mounted as we lost friends and loved ones. At the time of writing this book, the official count stands at 296 million infections and 5.4 million deaths globally, though the actual numbers are likely much higher than that.

But COVID-19 threatened much more than our physical wellbeing. Mental trauma, stress, and burnout rose dramatically as we faced an uncertain future, loss of connection, and the added responsibility of managing our children's education on-screen at home. The number of people looking for help with anxiety and depression has skyrocketed. According to a report by Mental Health America, in the first nine months of 2020, the number of people screening for anxiety rose by 93 percent, while those screening for depression rose by 62 percent. Even more importantly, eight of the ten screens showed moderate to high symptoms for both anxiety and depression.[88] At work, 40 to 60 percent of employees are reporting burnout and facing high degrees of stress, exhaustion, and fatigue.

Over the course of this chapter, I will share several best practices and actions that are scientifically backed by research and leverage thinking done by experts across a range of fields including traditional medicine, mental health, psychology, yoga, and Ayurveda.[89]

Live Longer, Better

Research done by Dan Buettner on people living in the Blue Zones (geographic areas that are home to some of the oldest people, including Loma Linda, California, USA; Nicoya, Costa Rica; Sardinia, Italy; Ikaria, Greece; and Okinawa, Japan), found that people in these places reach their one hundredth birthdays at ten times greater rate than in the United States as a whole, and many of their lifestyle characteristics that explain their longevity match those in this book.[90] Investing in your physical, mental, and spiritual wellbeing will allow you to unleash your full energies to be able to perform at your best.

Together they will help you live a longer, *better* life—in good health, free from chronic diseases, and disabilities of aging.

It is never too late to start working on integrating practices across mind, body, and spirit that can increase your base level of wellbeing and unleash more energy. I have distilled from my research three actionable practices for each of the three domains (see "Increasing your base level of energy") that are easy enough to integrate into your daily life and have consistently helped myself and my clients increase and maintain their overall level of wellbeing.

Increasing Your Base Level of Energy

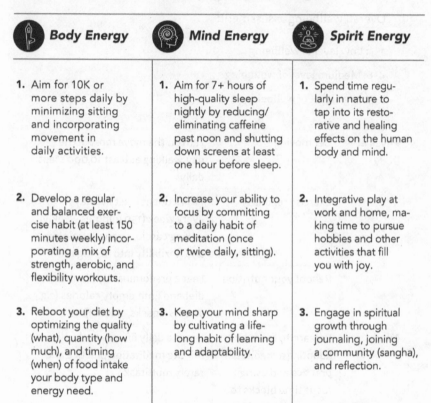

Body Energy	Mind Energy	Spirit Energy
1. Aim for 10K or more steps daily by minimizing sitting and incorporating movement in daily activities.	1. Aim for 7+ hours of high-quality sleep nightly by reducing/eliminating caffeine past noon and shutting down screens at least one hour before sleep.	1. Spend time regularly in nature to tap into its restorative and healing effects on the human body and mind.
2. Develop a regular and balanced exercise habit (at least 150 minutes weekly) incorporating a mix of strength, aerobic, and flexibility workouts.	2. Increase your ability to focus by committing to a daily habit of meditation (once or twice daily, sitting).	2. Integrative play at work and home, making time to pursue hobbies and other activities that fill you with joy.
3. Reboot your diet by optimizing the quality (what), quantity (how much), and timing (when) of food intake your body type and energy need.	3. Keep your mind sharp by cultivating a life-long habit of learning and adaptability.	3. Engage in spiritual growth through journaling, joining a community (sangha), and reflection.

Figure 7.2: Actions to increase energy level

Journaling Exercise:
Take Stock of Your Wellbeing

Start by taking stock of your overall wellbeing by assessing how many of the practices you regularly follow on a weekly basis. Assess your overall level of wellbeing based on the rating score below. Add up the total and divide by nine to get your total score.

Overall wellbeing assessment:

1–3: Low level of wellbeing

4–6: Medium level of wellbeing

7–9: High level of wellbeing

Physical— Body	Get moving	I am on the move most of the day, walking at least 10,000 steps daily
	Exercise regularly	I work out at least five days every week (150 minutes weekly) mixing cardio, strength training, and flexibility into my regime
	Reboot your nutrition	I eat a predominantly plant-based diet and limit empty calories (e.g., sweets, snacks, alcohol)
Mind	Relearn to focus by adopting a meditation practice and using focus time blocks to cut out multitasking	I have a daily fifteen- to thirty-minute meditation practice and rarely multitask
	Sleep to recharge	I sleep between seven to nine hours daily
	Build a learning habit for life	I make time to continuously learn new things and enhance my skills

Spirit	Spend time in nature	I regularly spend twenty minutes daily in nature
	Introduce play into work and home (passions)	I make time daily to do something for myself that energizes and recharges me
	Spiritual growth	I spend twenty to thirty minutes daily if not weekly on a spiritual practice like reading a spiritual book, going to church

Physical Wellbeing: Boosting Your Body's Energy

Your body's energy and physical wellbeing relate directly to your physical body and its underlying systems to work as required. In fact, when our physical energy is depleted, the other two energies are affected too. Think back to the last time you were not feeling well or were in pain—either because you got injured or you came down with the flu or something more serious. Where was your attention and focus? How much mental capacity did you direct toward anything other than addressing the pain or suffering caused by your physical ailment? In order to be at our best physically, we have to focus on making better lifestyle choices and building healthy habits around our physical activity, nutrition, and exercise.

Over the last hundred years, the nature of work has fundamentally shifted from being predominantly physical during and before the industrial age to mostly mental in the information age, resulting in many of us leading highly sedentary lifestyles. A study of some 5,900 adults published in JAMA found that nearly 26 percent sat for more than eight hours a day.[91] We are paying a steep price for our sedentary lifestyles. In a 2012 study[92] conducted by researchers at the University of Leicester in collaboration with Loughborough University, those who sit for long periods were found to have a twofold increase in their risk of diabetes, heart disease, and death, irrespective of the amount of moderate-to-vigorous physical activity that the study participants undertook. So if you find yourself sitting most of the day, you are still compromising your health even if you work out daily for thirty to forty-five minutes. It's no surprise, then, that some are saying, "Sitting is the new smoking."

Get moving: Set a goal for yourself to walk at least 10,000 steps daily. There are many wearable pedometers available that make tracking easy: Fitbit is a popular one, and my personal favorite is the Apple Watch because of the integrated Health app that tracks not just movement, but also calories burned, sleep, heart rate, and other health-related stats. To hit your step goal, invest in a standing or treadmill desk like the ThermoTread GT office treadmill, which allows you to stand or walk while working. You can also look for ways to introduce movement into daily chores at home and work, whether it be parking your car a bit further away from the grocery store/office door or converting sitting meetings to walking meetings with your team. You can also engage in some competitive fun by setting targets with your team at work, family, and friends to motivate each other.

Develop Cardiovascular and Muscular Strength

As part of the natural aging process, we start to lose strength, flexibility, and cardiovascular capacity. According to research published by Harvard Medical School, after age thirty, one can stand to lose as much as 3–5 percent of muscle per decade, with most men cumulatively losing 30 percent of their muscle mass over their lifetime. Many of these declines can be reversed or at least slowed down by embracing movement as a way of life, committing to regular physical practice of strength conditioning, yoga/stretching, and cardio training and improving our nutrition. Equally important to periods of physical exertion is how we integrate recovery into our training programs. Periods of recovery are critical for the body for two reasons: first, it is only during recovery that our bodies rebuild microtears that develop in our muscle fibers into higher strength. Second, by giving time to our body to recover and heal itself, we are reducing injury risk from overtraining.

I would recommend working with a personal trainer to design a program that takes your starting point of fitness and interests into account, and incorporates a mix of strength training, cardio, and flexibility. Join a local gym with a friend so that you can keep each other motivated to show up and push toward improving against the base goals you set for yourself. If it is within your means, I would also recommend investing in select at-home products that are truly wonderful. My personal favorites are Peloton (spinning bike), Tonal (strength training), and Apple Fitness (yoga and other floor exercises).

Reboot Your Diet

In America alone, over 70 percent of adults are overweight, with 30 percent classified as obese. Today more people die or suffer from chronic diseases including diabetes and heart disease than from infections. According to research published by the Centers for Disease Control and Prevention (CDC), six in ten American adults have a chronic disease, with four in ten having two or more diseases, including heart disease, cancer, and chronic lung disease.[93] According to their research, by eliminating the three risk factors of poor diet, inactivity, and smoking, 80 percent of heart disease and stroke, 80 percent of Type 2 diabetes, and 40 percent of cancer could be prevented.

If you need to lose weight, it can be hard to know where to start. There are a multitude of programs out there (Keto, Paleo, intermittent fasting, 5:2

Diet), and they often contradict each other. After consulting eastern and western science nutritionists, doctors, health experts, and scientific publications, I have boiled the best advice down to three key recommendations:

1. Reduce or eliminate meat from your diet. Plant-based diets have been proven to reduce cholesterol and the risk of several types of cancer,[94] lower inflammation in the body, and reduce the risk of developing coronary heart disease, high blood pressure, and diabetes.[95]

2. Watch the number of calories you eat and make sure your intake is not more than what you need based on your lifestyle, how active you are, and your basal metabolic rate. Most adults need 1,800 calories daily or even less depending on the level of your physical activity.

3. Customize a diet that will work for you based on your tastes and how your body metabolizes calories. You can either work with a nutritionist if you have access to one through your doctor's office or healthcare plan, or consider investing in a new device called Lumen, the world's first handheld, portable device designed to measure metabolism. At its core, it is a breathalyzer that analyzes the level of carbon dioxide (CO_2) in your breath. If you are breathing out a high level of CO_2, it means you're burning carbs. A low level then means you're burning fat instead. Lumen uses this data to provide a personalized nutrition and meal plan, to meet your goals.

Mental Wellbeing: Focusing Your Mind's Energy

Mental energy relates to your ability for cognition and focus, and for making conscious choices for yourself and the world around you, including your loved ones, friends, and team members. There is a tight linkage between our mental energy and the emotional states we experience (positive like joy and happiness; negative like stress, anxiety, and depression). To be at our best mentally, we have to explicitly invest in increasing our ability to focus through mindfulness, allowing our brains to recover through healthy sleeping habits, and combat cognitive decline through becoming lifelong learners.

Aim for Seven-Plus Hours of High-Quality Sleep Each Night

We are a sleep-deprived culture, and the trend is only increasing as we get less quality and quantity of sleep. Experts consistently tell us that we need seven to nine hours of sleep daily to be at our best. Yet according to a recent Gallup poll, 40 percent of Americans get less than seven hours of sleep a night.[96] We pay a huge cost both personally and in lost economic output. According to the CDC, sleeping less than seven hours per night is associated with greater likelihoods of obesity, high blood pressure, diabetes, coronary heart disease, stroke, frequent mental distress, and death. When we are not well rested, it takes us longer to finish things, slows our reaction time down, and makes us more prone to errors. Scientists at the University of California, Berkeley have found compelling evidence that there is a link between poor sleep and Alzheimer's disease due to the inability of the body to eliminate toxic compounds produced during the day. According to Matthew Walker, one of the preeminent sleep researchers, our cognitive performance—after ten days of seven hours or less of sleep—drops to the same level as it would be if we went without sleep for a full twenty-four hours.[97]

Over my twenty-five-plus year career in professional services and serving senior executives, I have rarely met anyone who gets more than six hours of sleep each night. It's time to reverse this unhealthy trend. To make sure you are at your cognitive best, I recommend three actions for better sleep:

1. Try to avoid caffeine after 12:00 p.m. Caffeine has a half-life of five to seven hours, meaning that if you drink caffeine at 3:00 p.m., half of it is still surging through your body when you go to bed.

2. Practice digital sunsetting. Turn off screens at least sixty if not ninety minutes before you go to bed, as light plays a key role in regulating our melatonin production, which in turn is key to regulating our sleep-wake cycle (circadian rhythm). At the very least, set your devices to switch to night mode, which reduces the level of blue light that keeps you awake if you use your phone before bed.

3. Create a relaxing routine to unwind before going to bed. This could include reading, journaling, taking a warm bath, or sipping chamomile tea.

Increase Your Ability to Focus for Long Periods

In our world filled with notifications, interruptions, and distractions, it can be hard to focus. Over the last twenty years, with the rise of email and social media, we have all become dopamine addicts—constantly searching for our next hit through checking email, news, or the abundance of red blinking notifications that pop up on our screens. Based on research conducted by reviews.org,[98] on average, Americans check their phones 344 times per day, which is approximately once every four wakeful minutes, assuming we sleep for eight hours (which most of us don't)! The effects of constant switching and multitasking on the brain are very well researched. There is up to a 40 percent reduction in productivity, knocking off up to ten points from our IQ and up to 50 percent higher likelihood of making mistakes,[99] higher degrees of mental stress/fatigue, and lower ability to focus and learn.[100]

By investing in a regular meditation practice and hacking your environment to minimize distractions, you can regain control of your most valuable asset—your mind—and significantly improve your performance by focusing your attention on what matters in that moment.

1. Start your day with an intentional fifteen- to thirty-minute sitting meditation. Any of the meditation techniques I shared in Practice 4 can help you start to master this skill.
2. Adopt healthy digital practices to minimize distractions, including deleting social media apps from your main devices or setting time limits on how long you spend on them. Decide on three to four designated blocks of time in which to check and respond to email versus being always on.
3. Put your phone into airplane mode when working on a focused activity or in meetings. If you must, assign an emergency contact to come find you during this time so you can truly unplug and focus.

Cultivate a Lifelong Habit of Learning and Adaptability

We live in a highly volatile, uncertain, complex, and ambiguous (VUCA) world where the pace of change is accelerating rapidly. Renewing our ability to learn and adapt has never been more important to successfully navigate the ever-increasing tides of change. Charles Darwin wrote in *The Origin of Species* that it is not the strongest or the most intelligent of the species that survives, but the one that is most adaptable to change. Learning comes second nature to us when we are young and growing up.

As we get older, many of us lose curiosity and a desire to learn new things, choosing certainty and routine. However, our brains work the same way as our muscles do: use it or lose it.

With disuse, our learning muscles start to atrophy with lack of use, and we pay the price through decline in our cognitive abilities that starts in our thirties and continues through our end of life. Extensive research has shown that brain aging is actually reversible through intentional learning. Learning to learn is a meta skill that can be developed at any age. As we make learning a lifelong habit, we can help our brains continue to both generate new neurons and create new connections between them improving memory, attention, thinking, language, and reasoning skills. In fact, a learning habit has even been shown to delay symptoms of Alzheimer's.

1. Start by choosing one meaningful skill each from your work and personal life that you want to learn and will help you achieve an important goal.

2. As you engage in learning, make sure to actively cultivate positive learning mindsets of growth ("I can learn anything I put my mind to"), act like a beginner ("it will be hard and take longer since I am new at it"), and flex your curiosity ("every day and attempt is a unique opportunity to learn more about myself").

3. Reflect on your progress, seek feedback from others, and continue experimenting with changing the mode of learning (e.g., reading, listening, seeing, doing) if you get stuck.

Spiritual Wellbeing: Strengthening Your Spiritual Energy

Spiritual energy relates to our ability to step out of the ordinary and everyday world and tap into a boundless source of energy available through connecting with the broader universe, the divine, and our essence of being. Spiritual wellbeing often gets deprioritized in our busy lives, but is easily nurtured through spending time in nature, integrating playful activities that bring us joy, and engaging in spiritual growth through reflection and study.

Spend Time in Nature

Our work and living environments play a critical role in our wellbeing by increasing or reducing our stress, which in turn impacts our bodies. Noisy, cluttered, clinical, and artificially lit environments can cause you to feel anxious, sad, or helpless. This in turn elevates your blood pressure, heart rate, and muscle tension, and it suppresses your immune system. On the other hand, being in nature, or even viewing scenes of nature, reduces anger, fear, and stress and increases pleasant feelings. Exposure to nature contributes significantly to your physical wellbeing, reducing blood pressure, heart rate, and muscle tension, and it lowers the production of stress hormones. New research from an interdisciplinary Cornell University team found that as little as ten minutes in a natural setting can help increase happiness and lower the effects of both physical and mental stress.

In the 1980s, the Japanese Ministry of Agriculture, Forestry, and Fisheries created the term *shinrin-yoku*, which translates to "forest bathing" or "absorbing the forest atmosphere." The practice encouraged people to simply spend time in nature, "bathing" in the energy and clean air of the woods. No matter where you live, you can benefit from this practice as it does not require heading out to a heavily wooded area. You could simply take a trip to a nearby park, your favorite local trail, the beach, or even your backyard. If you don't have access to natural spaces around you, studies have found that just looking at images of nature is enough "natural" stimulus to lower your stress levels. Find a photo of a beautiful natural setting that speaks to you and put it up in your cubicle or your office (or set one as your screen saver). The next time you need a mental break from work, practice *shinrin-yoku*, whether it's relaxing and focusing on the scene in front of you or heading out for a brief walk to experience nature in person.

Meditation Exercise: Walking Meditation

Walking meditation is a formal practice like watching the breath. The practice of mindful walking is a beautiful way to deepen our connection with the Earth and the natural world that surrounds us. We breathe, take a mindful step, and come back to our true home. Walking meditation gives us an opportunity to bring awareness to the sounds, smells, and sights of the natural world around us versus being lost in our thoughts and failing to see its beauty.

Duration: fifteen minutes

1. As you begin, walk at a natural pace. Let your hands hang loosely at your sides. As you take each step, count from one up to ten and then count back from ten to one. With each step, pay attention to the lifting and falling of your foot. Notice movement in your legs and the rest of your body. Notice any shifting of your body from side to side. You might notice your mind wandering. That's OK, let it be, and without frustration just gently guide it back again to the breath and sensation of lifting and falling of your foot. Whenever you are in nature, maintain a larger awareness of the environment around you and stay safe.

2. After two to three minutes, expand your attention to the sounds you hear around you. It might be a bird tweeting, or wind blowing through the leaves, or a squirrel running across the branches of a tree. Just focus on whatever sounds might be present and stay away from judging or categorizing them as pleasant or unpleasant. Notice sounds as nothing more or less than sound.

3. Shift your awareness next to any smells that might be in the air. Every season has a unique smell, as does every flower and tree. Again, simply notice without judging whether you find them pleasant or unpleasant.

4. Next, move your attention to the different hues, colors, and objects that might be present around you. You might notice how the wind has shaped the trunk of the tree. See the various colors of the different leaves, flora, and fauna. Focus on staying present and maintaining a sustained awareness.

5. Continue walking mindfully for another couple of minutes, keeping this open awareness of everything around you, wherever you are. Nothing to do, nothing to fix, nothing to change. Fully aware of the sensations in your body, the sounds, the smells, and the sights.

In the final few minutes, come back to awareness of the physical sensations of walking. Notice your feet again touching the ground and any movements in your body with each step.

Integrate Play into Your Work and Home

Play is what we did when we were children growing up. We could spend hours in fantasyland making up adventures and letting our imaginations run wild. But as we get older, we get preoccupied with our daily routines. Devoid of play, our life loses its magic as it gets crowded with mundane daily chores before we collapse exhausted every night in bed. When we do carve out some leisure time, we are more likely to zone out in front of the TV. When was the last time you remember doing something just for the fun of it?

Stuart Brown, MD, the founder of the National Institute for Play, has studied play for decades. In his research, play has been shown to release endorphins, improve brain functionality, stimulate creativity, help us deal with stress with greater ease, and laugh more often. Integrating play into your life can benefit your relationships, job, and mood.

1. At work, start integrating play by reimagining team celebration events that are typically dinner/drinks into physical play activities or team outings that get people active (going on hikes, volunteering, a ping-pong tournament).

2. At home, engage with your spouse and kids at least a couple of nights a week in a fun activity, whether it's playing games, cooking, or spending time outside together. Spending time with the children in your life, observing them as they play, listening to their conversation, and joining in, will act as constant reminders of your own youth when you could lose yourself in play.

3. Go on mini-adventures. The next time your work takes you out of town, take an afternoon to yourself or take a later flight to explore a museum or go for a run at the local park.

Engage in Spiritual Growth through Journaling, Reflection, Satsang

Another way to tap into your spiritual wellbeing is by cultivating a connection to the divine and the life energies that surge through us and connect us to the universe. Spirituality is the belief in something bigger than what is seen or can be explained—something that we might call God, Goddess, Jesus, Rama, Rahim, Buddha, the Great Spirit, or a myriad of other titles. Regardless of your faith or religion, most ancient and holy scriptures are filled with words of wisdom about living a life on core principles that enhance our life energies, bring communion with nature and our fellow human beings, and shift our focus from self to service.

It is well-known that traditional religious affiliations have declined over the last several decades. But newer data suggests that spirituality itself, or more specifically, a belief in a higher power, is also declining, especially in younger generations. This is cause for concern as research shows that the higher a person's spiritual level, the better his or her quality of life and resilience in facing life's problems. A belief in a higher power can provide relief, strength, and the grit to overcome hardships.

1. Embed a prayer practice at the beginning or end of your day, no matter how busy you are, or if you feel you don't need it. If President Obama, Tony Robbins, and Oprah Winfrey can make time for it, trust me, so can you.

2. Find a spiritual community. It doesn't have to be a church or temple, although many find comfort there. Look for meditation groups, interfaith groups, and spiritual activities that offer a sense of belonging, security, and community. A client of mine sings every Monday evening in a classical choir, which she describes as "her church." Communal singing has been shown

to improve mood, reduce stress, and offer greater connection, all integral to overall wellbeing.[101]

3. Develop a daily spiritual reading habit. Even if you just spend twenty to thirty minutes a day, exposing yourself to a treasure trove of learnings embedded within ancient wisdom traditions like Buddhism, Yoga Sutras, and religious texts can expand your perspective and offer comfort, wisdom, and greater understanding.

Community Exercise:
Forming a Wellbeing Circle

Gather a group of friends, colleagues, or families who you might want to invite on this wellbeing journey together. They can act as both a support mechanism and cheerleader as well as someone who can hold you accountable toward your commitments.

1. Share the wellbeing checklist as well as the set of micropractices for them to read and self-assess their starting point and priorities.

2. Check in with each other using the questions below:
   a. How well have you been feeling over the last three months?
   b. Which wellbeing dimension (mind, body, spirit) is a strength for you?
   c. Which wellbeing dimension (mind, body, spirit) do you struggle with?
   d. What two to three interventions do you plan to incorporate to improve your overall wellbeing?

3. Discuss what has been the biggest roadblock that has or will get in the way of implementing the interventions and what actions you can take to overcome them. It could be any of the following (or others):

    a. Feeling guilty when prioritizing our wellbeing.
    b. Being too busy to practice wellbeing.
    c. Structural factors like financial, housing, personal constraints.
    d. Missing guidance from an expert to help learn something.
    e. Others...

Finally, discuss what help the group can provide to support you and each other on your individual journeys. Be creative and create physical and technology-based support mechanisms. Also, decide how often you want to meet in this group or split off in smaller buddy pairs to check in with each other.

Investments in Wellbeing Have Big Payoffs

When I started my own journey toward happiness, my excesses and under-investment in my wellbeing during my twenties and thirties had caught up with me. I was forty pounds overweight, had developed hypothyroidism, and struggled with high anxiety and stress. Overeating and alcohol had been my go-to vices to unwind and reward myself at the end of a hard day. I rarely slept more than five to six hours a night, even on weekends. My exercise regime was nonexistent. I'd hike a couple easy trails around Boulder maybe a couple days per month, but that was it.

Once I decided to regain my vitality, I invested in a walking treadmill, which has had a huge impact. Now, instead of sitting in my chair, I spend over two to three hours walking while on calls to reach 12,000–15,000 daily steps (versus my baseline of 4,000). I also purchased a Peloton and use it to log my cardio workouts as well as strength training. It took a bit of adjustment, but I now make time to work out six days a week and have never felt better.

I also cleaned up my bad eating habits. First, I adopted a predominantly plant-based diet, reducing eggs, dairy, and animal proteins. By substituting egg with a product called JUST Egg, replacing milk with plant-based milks (almond milk and oat milk), and replacing meat products with others like Beyond Meat, I could still enjoy the taste and texture of many of the same dishes I liked by just replacing the type of protein. I also eliminated most of the empty calories from my diet by replacing processed snacks with fruits and eliminating soda drinks. Yes, I do treat myself to a glass of wine occasionally, and I don't beat myself up for enjoying dessert or a steak on special occasions.

I also began meditating first thing every morning before reaching for my phone. I started with a simple, ten-minute practice, and over the next few months, I had built it up to about forty-five minutes. I incorporated a daily yoga practice to increase flexibility and combat decades of a highly sedentary lifestyle. Finally, I stopped drinking caffeine in the afternoon and put away my iPhone, computer, and iPad by 9:00 p.m. As part of my nightly routine, I spent the last hour of the night reading one of many spiritual texts (you can find a list of my favorite books in the Appendix) and sipping herbal tea to prepare my body for sleep. Before closing my eyes, I wrote down three things I was grateful for in my bedside journal.

Within a month of making these changes, I slept soundly, had more energy throughout the day, and steadily lost about one pound or more each week. Over the next year, I lost most of the excess weight I had gained, and I improved my quality of life. I had more energy throughout the day that allowed me to be more effective at work. I also ended the day with a lot more energy. That meant I could enjoy it with my family, playing with my son, and cooking a meal with my wife in the evening versus collapsing exhausted at the end of the day. The range of activities I could do also expanded, like being able to go on more strenuous hikes and bike rides that opened up more possibilities of exploring the beautiful natural world around me.

While my story is an individual journey, I've also worked with leaders who were able to make positive wellbeing changes across much larger platforms. Chris was the chief procurement officer of a large bank and collectively with his team had worked harder than ever in the eighteen months following the start of the pandemic. As they fought upward price pressures, he and his team had to support a major transition to remote work practically overnight. They had to learn about completely new COVID-19 categories like protective equipment and rapid antigen tests, all while managing the tightest supply chain with vendors.

Most of Chris's teammates were from dual-income working families who also found themselves navigating remote schooling and loss of child-care support systems. Needless to say, eighteen months into the pandemic, 40–60 percent of his employees were exhausted, stressed, and burned out. People were easily annoyed and offended, and the bonds between them were starting to fray. Attritions were up too, with 20–30 percent of the staff at risk of quitting their jobs. Chris knew he needed to take action to quickly stem the tide and infuse new energy back into the entire group. He had to ensure they could deliver against the expectations of their stakeholders while taking care of each other.

Chris introduced the holistic wellbeing framework of mind, body, and spirit to his team, and they all agreed to choose one practice each from mind/body/spirit (see Figure 7.2: Actions to increase energy level) to practice individually. For himself, Chris decided to prioritize better sleep (body), a daily mindfulness practice (mind), and spending more time in nature (spirit). In addition, they also decided to choose practices as a team so they could hone wellbeing as an essential skill. Chris's team launched a 10K steps competition (body), integrated a mindful three-minute check-in before their daily huddles (mind), and engaged in purposeful dialogues across the team to collectively explore the impact they were driving to their stakeholders, customers, suppliers, and community (spirit).

To keep each other accountable, they created a weekly survey to document transparency around these practices, as well as forming peer groups to hold each other accountable and support each other. The results were dramatic. Over the next eight weeks, the team collectively showed improvement in their wellbeing scores by 30 percent, with some individuals showing improvements as high as 70 percent. They also reported a 20 percent improvement in their effectiveness in getting their work done, and a 30 percent increase in group cohesiveness and belonging. Even in the midst of crisis, during a global pandemic, Chris was able to improve and sustain his team's overall wellbeing and in turn, improve the company's success.

Building Your Wellbeing Practice

My invitation to you is to choose at least one practice from each of the domains of mind, body, and spirit to focus on for three months. Once you have mastered them, you can choose to try the next set of practices. Start small and celebrate your successes along the way. Enroll the help of your family and friends to provide encouragement and hold you accountable if you need to stick to your commitments. You can even enlist the help of nutritionists, physical trainers, and health professionals to help you design a custom plan that works for you. Change is hard, but with the right focus and support, I am convinced you will be able to transform yourself and unleash more energy, focus, and joy to fuel your journey forward.

KEY TAKEAWAYS

- People suffering from physical ailments, depression, and anxiety are at an all-time high. Investing in your physical, mental, and spiritual wellbeing will allow you to unleash your full energies to be able to perform at your best.
- Adopting some of the lifestyle characteristics of residents of the "Blue Zones" can increase your chances of living longer and better—free from the chronic diseases and disabilities of aging.
- Spiritual wellbeing is often deprioritized, but deepening your connection with a higher power (whatever you choose) can improve your quality of life and build resilience.

Build a Supportive Community

*"We'll be Friends Forever, won't we, Pooh?' asked Piglet.
'Even longer,' Pooh answered."*

—*Winnie the Pooh* by A. A. Milne

A s children, we thrive on friendships and joy that come from play with our peers. But then we grow up, pursue individual interests and careers, and raise our own families, and there just does not seem to be enough time to keep up with those social connections and friendships that fed our soul previously. In the blink of an eye, decades can pass by without speaking to former roommates, teammates, or those who used to make us laugh out loud, and we realize we have few confidants to share good and bad times with. A study published in May 2021 by the Survey Center on American Life reported that "Americans report having fewer close friendships than they once did, talking to their friends less often, and relying less on their friends for personal support."[102] Nearly 50 percent of all Americans reported having fewer than three close friends, with approximately one in ten reporting zero friends. Compare these statistics to 1990, when 33 percent reported having ten or more close friends, compared to just 13 percent today, and only 3 percent reported having no friends.

If you invest in your relationships early and often to keep them healthy, they will be there to support you and share in your life's joys and sorrows, and vice versa. It is helpful to think of the community that surrounds you as a series of three circles nested within each other (see Figure 8.1: Mapping your relationships): your family, then your friends, and a broader set of acquaintances you are connected to or want to actively cultivate over time. Most of us spend our free time with the smallest circle of our immediate families—spouse, children, and older parents or relatives. The next circle after this is occupied by our friends. According to research conducted by Robin Dunbar, an anthropologist and psychologist then at University College London, about 150 people who you call casual friends might fall in this circle. About fifty of these 150 might be considered close friends, and about fifteen of these might be close enough to turn to for sympathy and share things in confidence. Finally, there are about five individuals who could be considered our best friends (these could also be family members). The last circle is composed of our acquaintances: colleagues, customers, other professionals, networking groups, and others in our community.

There is no one right answer to how many friends and acquaintances anyone should or could have. It depends on your personality (introvert versus extrovert), stage of life (single professional, married with children, empty nester), and the time you have to devote to your relationships. But spending time with those you love and enjoy being with should be an intentional choice, and that time should be cherished. My perspectives have been shaped by tapping the latest and greatest research on the importance of social connections in the fields of happiness studies and positive psychology, as well as tapping the ancient wisdom traditions including Zen Buddhism, Taoism, and Stoicism to name a few. In this chapter, I will share several practical tips and suggestions to deepen your relationships with friends and family while also building a broad network of acquaintances, mentors, and connections who can help you climb your highest mountain, whatever it might be.

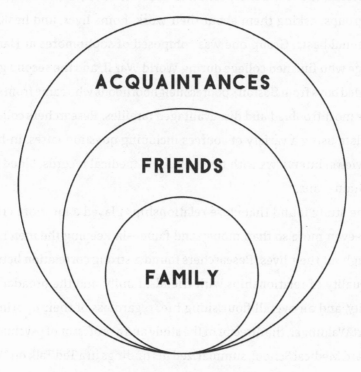

Figure 8.1: Mapping your relationships

The Science-Based Benefits of Community

Humans have always relied on mutual cooperation to survive and thrive, as far back as our hunter-gatherer days. As a result, our need to connect with each other is deeply ingrained in our neurological wiring. Aristotle wisely said, "Man is by nature a social animal." The power of social connections in helping us live longer, healthier, and happier lives has been validated time and again in numerous studies.

The most prominent and longest running studies on happiness have been running at Harvard for over eighty years, following Harvard graduates from the years between 1939–1944, well into their nineties. During this period, the researchers followed the lives of 724 men belonging to two groups, asking them about their work, home lives, and health on an annual basis. Group one was composed of sophomores at Harvard College who finished college during World War II, and the second group included boys from Boston's poorest neighborhoods who came from some of the most troubled and disadvantaged families. Researchers collected rich data using a variety of sources including questionnaires, in-home interviews, interviews with their children, medical records, blood tests, and brain scans.

The study found that close relationships played a far more critical role—even more so than money and fame—in keeping the men happy throughout their lives. Researchers found a strong correlation between the quality of relationships with friends, family, and the broader community, and an overall flourishing life, regardless of their upbringing. Robert Waldinger, the director of the study and a professor of psychiatry at Harvard Medical School, summarized his findings in a Ted Talk on "What Makes a Good Life" that has been viewed forty-two million times.[103] He shared the following advice: "Taking care of your body is important but tending to your relationships is a form of self-care too. The people who fared the best were the people who leaned into relationships, with family, with friends, with community."

Those of us who live in a rich web of relationships are not just happier but also live longer and healthier lives. Julianne Holt-Lunstad, a psychologist at Brigham Young University, concluded after reviewing 140 different studies that those with strong relationships are 50 percent less likely to die early.[104] The loneliness that arises from feeling a lack of connections is as harmful as smoking fifteen-plus cigarettes a day. According to social psychologist Ellen Berscheid, our social nature and our ability to work together and love one another are some of the most important factors in the survival of our species. Cultivating a deep connection to our family and friends can help us tap into one of the most important sources of happiness in our life and provide a buffer to any ups and downs that life throws at us. It helps to know we don't have to navigate the hard times alone—each of the five fingers on our hand don't have a lot of strength, but when they come together in a fist, they can be mighty.

Numerous studies have also validated the important role that the quality of networks plays in our professional success. Those of us with higher quality networks have access to more job and business opportunities, advance faster, and enjoy higher status and authority. Building and nurturing professional relationships also improves the quality of work and increases job satisfaction. Interestingly, the quality of our networks depends on the people we might think are on the fringe of importance.

In 1973, Stanford sociology professor Mark Granovetter, who has been nominated for the Nobel prize, published an empirical paper that introduced the concept of "strong" versus "weak" ties and the critical role weak ties play in the quality of a network.[105] Strong ties are characterized by deep relationships that exist and those with whom we interact with high frequency like our family, close friends, or colleagues. Weak ties are characterized by surface-level relationships or acquaintances, such as industry contacts you may see only at conferences; office colleagues in other departments; or parents you exchange pleasantries with at your kids' school. Granovetter studied whether the strength of ties had an impact on finding a job. He showed that people with "weak ties" not only found jobs that the rest of the network couldn't see, but those jobs also came with higher compensation and satisfaction.

Ronald Burt, an esteemed professor at Chicago Booth who has spent over two decades studying the ways that social networks create competitive advantage, concurs. According to his research, the single most important variable that explains someone's success is whether they are in an open network (lots of weak ties) versus a closed network (lots of strong ties). In a closed network, you are deeply connected to a small set of people who all also know each other, and hence, almost everyone has the same access to information. Contrast this with the diversity of information that those with lots of weak ties enjoy, often bridging or connecting roles that increase their power as they broker and facilitate flow of information across different networks. At its core, the performance differential of individuals with open networks who had lots of weak ties can be attributed to the ability to access a larger and more diverse set of perspectives and viewpoints compared to others. This allows them to be more creative by colliding richer sets of ideas and being better at predicting and picking winners, as well as jumping onto winning ideas first compared to others in their deep networks.

I can attest to the important role open networks have played in creating opportunities. I got my first job out of business school through a friend of a friend, who connected me to a partner at a local consulting firm. It was a business school classmate who invited my group to submit a proposal for a project at his company that would, over a year, become our largest client and responsible for 60 percent of the revenue. Similarly, even in my early days as an associate and engagement manager at McKinsey, I was connected to five different networks (procurement, product development, the industrial sector, the consumer sector, Chicago office), and thus I always had a much larger choice of engagements to choose from when it came to staffing decisions. By investing significant time building relationships across all different parts of my firm, I have been able to successfully leverage the rich knowledge and expertise that already existed.

RELATIVE PERFORMANCE BASED ON OPEN vs CLOSED NETWORKS

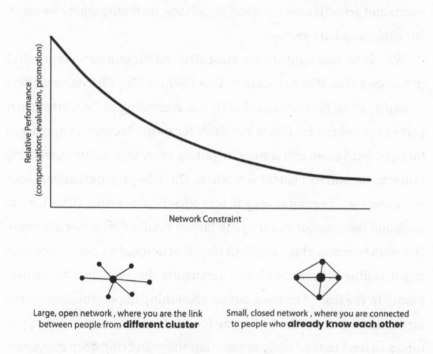

Large, open network , where you are the link between people from **different cluster**

Small, closed network , where you are connected to people who **already know each other**

Figure 8.2: Relative performance based on open versus closed networks (Ron Burt)[106]

Prioritize Your Relationship
with Your Family

Thomas Jefferson said, "The happiest moments of my life have been the few which I have passed at home in the bosom of my family." From my twenty-five-plus years of experience in consulting, coaching hundreds of senior clients, and working with very driven colleagues, most will say that having love-filled relationships with their spouse and children is a top priority for them. Yet most of them actually spend their time working, struggling to spend sufficient time with their families. Even when they are with their families, they report feeling distracted and preoccupied by work issues. The struggle to balance family time with outside commitments and activities is something we all face, no matter where we are in our careers and life journeys.

Why do we lose sight of what most of us call our number-one priority? In his book *How Will You Measure Your Life?* Dr. Clay Christensen offers an explanation that resonated with me. According to Dr. Christensen, part of the reason for this is our drive for overachievement and a way for us to feel valued and worthy by getting external validation, winning promotions, and accolades from others. Our jobs provide that in spades, and unless we are careful, we will find ourselves investing all we have at work and leave nothing in the tank for our families, when we get home. Our work becomes a big part of our identification and we pour everything into it, calling in from vacations, consistently checking emails even over dinner in the fear of missing out on something important. In a search for fulfillment at work or providing for our families, we miss the opportunity to tend to the family foundation that can bring deep happiness and belonging.

Journaling Exercise:
Take Stock of Your Relationships

In the fast pace and grind of our day-to-day lives, it is no surprise that our focus most days is on those who are right in front of us, calling for our attention or shouting the loudest. It is often not our immediate family and friends, but often our boss, our client, or someone reaching out for help. We need to step onto the balcony from time to time to be able to see our life's dance floor and take stock of the health of your relationships and actions we might need to take before it's too late.

In this journaling exercise, I want to invite you to take stock of your relationships across all three domains (family, friends, and acquaintances) by identifying a set of individuals who matter to you. Next, you will assess the health of your relationship based on two criteria: quality of the relationship and your personal satisfaction with the time you get to spend with them. Use a scale of one to five, with one being significantly unsatisfied and five significantly satisfied. For each of these individuals, you will also identify a near-term action you will take in the next twenty, sixty, or ninety days to reconnect or deepen that relationship.

> **Family:** Reflect on your relationships with your family—not just your immediate family (spouse, kids) but also your extended family (your parents, uncles, aunts, cousins, grandparents). Take a journey down memory lane when you were growing up and the special memories you have of joyous times you spent with them. Which ones stand out? Which individuals left a big impression on you?

List the name of each individual family member who holds a special place for you and write down a special memory you shared with them and the impact they had on you.

Friends: Reflect on your relationships with your friends—not just those you spend time with today but also those who played a meaningful role in your formative years growing up in school, college, and early careers. Reflect on those fun times you had and the meaningful moments you shared. Which ones stand out? Which friends have you lost touch with? Which of these friends do you wish you would have spent more time with? List the names of each of your friends who hold a special place for you and write down a special memory you shared with them and the impact they had on you.

Acquaintances: Take stock of your contacts from your broader professional network and local community—alumni from school/university, industry contacts (associations, suppliers, customers, competitors), local organizations like nonprofits, school boards, current and ex-colleagues from places you have worked, among others. Also reflect on your purpose from Practice 2 and aspirations for any career or job changes you aspire to make and individuals/groups who might be able to help you along the way by sharing insights, contacts, and helpful advice.

An inspirational story about a father and his son touched my heart and highlights the importance of prioritizing family time. The father got home late from work, as he often did. Usually his kids were already fast asleep, and he would enjoy dinner with his wife before reading the newspaper.

But tonight, he heard the pitter patter of little feet, and he peered over his paper to see his eight-year-old son looking at him.

Seeing that he had caught his father's attention, the son asked, "Father, how much do you earn per hour?"

The father was a little taken aback, but he replied, "I am paid $150 per hour, my son."

The son then asked, "Can I borrow seventy-five dollars?"

The father, annoyed, said, "For what? Please don't waste money on a silly toy or game. Go back to bed."

Hearing this, the son sheepishly left the room, with tears in his eyes.

The father went back to reading his newspaper, but he felt terrible about speaking harshly to his son. So he made his way to his son's room. He stroked his hair gently and saw the pillow was wet, as the son had been crying.

The father said, "I am sorry I spoke so harshly earlier. I will give you the seventy-five dollars you asked for. But I am curious; why do you want it?"

The son smiled and hugged his father. He ran over to his piggy bank and brought it to the bed and emptied it.

"Daddy," he said, "I didn't have enough money saved up earlier, but now I do. Can I buy an hour of your time so we can have dinner together tomorrow night?"

This time, the father could not stop the tears from flowing down his face. He realized that in his drive to work hard to earn money for his family, he had neglected them, and money would never buy as much happiness as the time he could spend with them.

To live your life in sync with your priorities, it is extremely important to regularly take stock of your priorities and wants from life (see Practice 2), see how happy you are with how things are going, and set hard boundaries to reorient your investments of time and resources toward them.

Like many of my clients, you may also struggle with setting boundaries to prioritize what matters to you, so the following are tips that have worked well for me.

1. **Anchor on the bigger "Why?":** What is the reason you're setting this boundary, and is there any guilt associated with the decision? Are you prioritizing saying yes by saying no to something else?

2. **Start small:** It is important to start small but stay consistent and make it a hard boundary. Saying, "I will commit to one evening a week to spend uninterrupted family time together" is better than saying, "I will prioritize five family days every week" and then beating yourself up for not following through.

3. **Communicate the reason:** Explain the boundaries you want to set with everyone at home and work and engage them into designing a solution that supports the goals of the groups without sacrificing what's important to you. Protect your time against inefficient interactions and interruptions by creating rules for checking emails, turning off notifications, and creating hard stops at the end of the day.

About five years ago, when I took stock of how my life was going, I realized that while I really liked the work I was doing, I was significantly underinvesting in my family. I was on the road three to four days every week working long hours, often with little energy left when I got home to my lovely wife Lizzie and six-year-old son Ashwin. Most of the work of raising Ashwin and running our home fell to Lizzie (who never complained). I also realized that while I always made sure that I was at home for all the big moments like birthdays and school plays, I was missing the little moments of daily celebrations or loving hugs when something didn't go well at school.

The next progression at the firm would have come with more pay, but also more responsibilities and time away from my family. So I made the important decision to change professional tracks and also go part time (70 percent), limiting my travel to two days per week. I set hard boundaries: every day I blocked off time in the evenings when I could be technology-free, have dinner, and play games together (we like cards, and Double Trouble). On weekends, we go hiking, biking, or play basketball games. We take mini-vacations once a month and two to three longer vacations each year to explore new cities and the outdoors. Over the last decade, we have also been able to spend at least five weeks with our parents despite living on different continents. During COVID-19, when travel was not possible, we made up for it as much as we could by connecting daily through WhatsApp or FaceTime. These basic changes have allowed me to reorient my energies toward what truly matters and has brought so much happiness into my life. My family has grown closer, handled adversity better, and created memories that will stay with us forever.

To build a family that provides a never-ending pool of happiness, energy, and support, you will need to be mindful not just about the amount of time you spend but also on the quality of the time you actually spend with them. Here are six suggestions for you to consider when building a stronger, healthier, and more resilient family based on research done by Dr. Dennis Lynn, a senior instructor in human development and family sciences at Oregon State University-Cascades.[107]

1. **Express appreciation and affection toward each other:**
   A warm embrace and daily "I love you" goes a long way. So do

small acts of kindness, like bringing home flowers for your spouse without a special occasion and expressing gratitude for little things they do every day.

2. **Commit to the happiness and welfare of each other:** Spend time and energy in family activities, sharing responsibilities and making decisions together.

3. **Communicate effectively and positively with each other:** Dr. John Gottman, one of the preeminent experts on relationships, recommends following the magic ratio of five-to-one, creating five positive feelings/interactions for every negative one.[108] Try to avoid what he calls the four horsemen of the apocalypse: criticism, contempt, defensiveness, and stonewalling.[109]

4. **Cultivate strong coping and resilience skills to handle crises:** You can role model and teach your children how to bounce back from setbacks. It is never too early to expose them to programs that build resilience like Project Happiness by Randy Taran or growth mindset developed by Carol Dweck. Both are wonderful programs you can do as a family to grow stronger and resilient together.

5. **Develop a spiritual wellbeing practice:** You can develop a strong spiritual practice as a family, whether it's going to a church or temple, saying grace and gratitude before dinner, or taking hikes together to appreciate nature and feel connected to the universe.

6. **Enjoy time with each other:** Set aside time to have fun together, whether it be playing games, traveling together, or other activities that infuse joy into each other's lives.

Meditation Exercise: Family Meditation

Spending time meditating together as a family is a great way to bring more mindfulness to your lives and introduce your kids at an early age to the multitude of benefits of meditation. You can do this practice with children as young as five years old. I would encourage you to start with five minutes and slowly increase it to ten to fifteen minutes, every day before dinner, before watching any television in the evening, or before sleep time for the kids. Below you will find a script you can use for meditation just before bedtime with young kids.

Duration: five minutes

1. Lie down in your bed in a comfortable position on your back with your arms relaxed and by your side. Relax your whole body and let the bed support you.

2. Take three deep breaths, feeling the air fill your lungs and your stomach, and then slowly exhale with an open mouth, letting all the air out and feeling your stomach contract. Let yourself relax completely.

3. On the next inhale, bring attention to your feet and legs. With the next exhale, let go of any tension or tightness and let them relax.

4. On the next inhale, bring attention to your stomach, chest, and shoulders. With the next exhale, let them relax completely.

5. On the next inhale, bring attention now to your arms and fingers. With the next exhale, let them relax completely.

6. On the next inhale, bring attention to your face (your nose, lips, eyes, ears). With the next exhale, let them relax completely.

7. With the next inhale, bring attention to your whole body and let it completely relax with your next exhale.

8. Now imagine you are standing in front of a big tree with deep roots, a strong trunk, wide branches with a vast canopy. This tree is home to your very own treehouse. Picture how you would like your treehouse to look. Over the next several inhales and exhales, visualize all the elements you want to design into your treehouse: size, color, number and types of windows, door, and ladder to reach the treehouse.

9. Next, let's continue breathing in and out and take your time to fill the treehouse with anything that you love. You can place your favorite stuffed animals, pillows, plant, favorite art, and other things that will make you feel good. Take your time placing each item where you want them in the treehouse.

10. Know that when you are inside your treehouse, you can just relax and let go of all your thoughts and worries. Take a deep breath now and allow yourself to completely relax and feel the calm and peace wash over your body.

11. Know that you can just close your eyes any time and visualize your treehouse to feel more peaceful and calmer. Know that your treehouse is available to you any time you would like. You can visit here whenever and as often as you want.

> 12. Slowly open your eyes and maintain that feeling of peace and calm as you get ready to go to sleep.

Unfortunately, one of the big casualties of our culture of hyper-individualism and the rise of nuclear families has been the loss of connection with broader extended families. Our time with grandparents, aunts, uncles, and cousins is often relegated to Thanksgiving, Christmas, occasional weddings, or extended family get-togethers. In our race to improve our lot, we find ourselves drifting from our roots, and often it is too late before we realize that our own parents are at the end of their lives.

Here is a simple exercise to recognize how little time we actually do have with our parents: subtract your parents' age from the average life expectancy in your country. If you are in the US, you can use seventy-eight as the number. Multiply that with the number of days you spend on average annually with them. For me, since I see my parents roughly two weeks per year, it means I have less than four months of time left to spend with them. This immediately made it obvious that I needed to prioritize our visits, even if it meant stepping back from a project or canceling another vacation. Protecting time with our extended families, just as we do with our immediate families, helps us avoid regrets later when they are gone.

Build Strong Ties with Friends

Our friends have a special place in our lives from an early age. In our early childhood years, we got lost for hours together engaging in imaginative play, delighted at finding others who also "saw" our make-believe worlds. These friendships played a critical role in our development and allowed us to practice social, cognitive, communicative, and emotional skills.

In our prepubescent and teenage years, our friends became our closest confidants, supporting us, encouraging us, and standing by us as we navigated the world of crushes and heartbreak. We shared laughs, wiped each other's tears, and made vows to never part ways, to be best friends *forever*.

However, life unfolds a path for us that often diverges from those we thought we'd never be apart from—whether we end up physically in another city or country or moving at vastly different speeds through career and relationship changes. And even though social media promises to let us "follow" our friends anywhere, clicking "like" on someone's photo is no substitute for real connection. We can take inspiration from Elisabeth Foley who said, "The most beautiful discovery true friends make is that they can grow separately without growing apart."

When it comes to close friends, it is the quality of relationships that matters most. Khalil Gibran writes beautifully of friendship in his book *The Prophet*:

A friend is your needs answered

He is your field which you sow with love and reap with thanksgiving...

...And let your best be for your friend

If he must know the ebb of your tide, let him know it's flood also

For what is your friend that you should seek him with hours to kill?

Seek him always with your hours to kill.

Both my wife and I have been blessed with many close friends, many of whom we have known from our teenage years. Despite moving across countries and continents, many have been a core part of our lives through the thick and thin of it over the last thirty-plus years. In my case, I moved from Delhi and Mumbai, India to Chicago, and then to Boulder. Of my twelve closest friends, I have known two since middle school (thirty-plus years), three since university (twenty-five-plus years), and four since my

MBA days (twenty-plus years). No matter how busy we are, not a month has gone by without checking in (either phone or text) to see how things are going. Our friendships have been witness to marriages, divorces, the birth of our children, new jobs, getting fired from jobs, and deaths of our loved ones.

My life has really been enriched by my friends, and it is so comforting to know that I have their unconditional love and support. However, it has required all of us to prioritize our friendships in order to continue this legacy of connection. Technology has been a big help. We like to play online games together, compete on Apple health/Strava, discuss in virtual book clubs, and play in virtual sports leagues. Nothing replaces being together in person, of course, and so we also make it a point to visit with each other at least once a year. My consulting job often took me cross-country, and I would intentionally plan my calendar in a way that allowed me to spend one-on-one time with these friends when I traveled near their hometowns.

Here are some tips based on what has worked for me in creating a rich community of friends who have stayed with me over the years.

1. **Step back, choose, and commit to the set of friends you want:** The number doesn't matter, whether it is one, or twelve, or more. What matters is that you are choosing and making a commitment to prioritize these relationships. If you are worried about rekindling lost friendships, don't worry. Friendship is like good wine: age makes it better. According to a study published in 2018 by Jeffrey Hall in the *Journal of Social and Personal Relationships*,[110] on average, it takes about thirty hours of time for someone to be considered a casual friend, fifty hours before they become real friends, and about one hundred and forty hours to become close friends.

2. **Keep the interactions meaningful, rich, and frequent:**
Calendar connection time together and use that to truly share
and listen to what is unfolding in both of your lives. We all have
a battle we are fighting inside, and often we don't want to share
that with others, thinking they won't be interested. Make the
time to truly listen and create space for that unfolding to occur.
Find a hobby or activity that you can do together. Remember,
staying in touch is 80 percent of the game.

3. **Don't let resentments and conflicts creep in:** Often most of
these arise from misunderstandings and our creating our own
stories about the other person's intent behind a behavior we
might not appreciate. By sharing your stories and perspectives
with your friend and inquiring into theirs, you can often resolve
the majority of these misunderstandings. For the remainder,
you can choose to forgive and move on with new commitments
to each other, in the spirit of preserving and deepening a
friendship.

4. **At least once a year, spend some meaningful time together
in person:** This could be a weekend activity or (if you can swing it)
a week-long getaway with your friends. You could choose to meet
somewhere new each time or visit the same place to spend time
together. Regardless, engage in an activity that allows you to
continue forming new memories, be with each other, and
strengthen your bonds.

5. **Be authentic and vulnerable with each other:** Nothing
deepens a friendship more over time than two individuals will-
ing to be vulnerable in order to build and preserve trust and
confidence. Being vulnerable in a relationship means allowing
your friends into your thoughts, feelings, fears, challenges, and

struggles. By being vulnerable yourself, you also give permission to your friends to be their imperfect self. In your close group of friends, you can practice shedding the armors we always carry around trying to fit into the world and let yourself relax into this circle of pure belonging. You can allow yourself to be seen as a beautiful, imperfect, flawed human being and truly be accepted unconditionally.

Socrates once said, "Be slow to fall into friendship; but when thou art in, continue firm and constant."

Community Exercise:
Creating Your *Hardwired for Happiness* Community

Forming a community of friends, colleagues, family members, and mentors to take the *Hardwired for Happiness* journey together can be a wonderful support mechanism to embed some or all of the practices from this book. I would encourage you to invite four to six people to participate in this journey with you. You can think of including your spouse, close friends, mentors, and others who could support you. Make sure everyone has a copy of the book and is willing to engage in undertaking this journey.

Conduct a kick-off session and work to jointly design the overall structure of the journey together, including:

1. How frequently will you meet (e.g., once every three weeks)?
2. How long will each meeting last (e.g., one hour or two hours)?
3. Will you meet in person or virtually? If in person, who hosts?

4. What is the expectation of prework (e.g., read one chapter of the book, or do personal work during sessions)?

5. How do you want to handle facilitation of your time together? Do you want to rotate that role depending on the topic and interest of individuals, or have the same person (e.g., you) organize and facilitate these?

6. What are some ground rules of engagement for your community meeting? For example, you could include some or all of the following ground rules: confidentiality, openness, respect, constructive participation, staying away from judgment, curiosity, etc.

7. How would you like others to support you in keeping you accountable and supporting deeper work you might want?

8. Do you want to invite any experts or external coaches to support you in your journeys and act as facilitators?

Once you go through the kick-off meeting, start meeting regularly and support each other in your journeys through this community.

Invest in a Broad Network of Acquaintances

High quality professional networks play a huge role in providing more opportunities, giving access to more information, and improving creativity and innovation. Remember, these so-called "weak ties" are actually your strongest professional allies! Individuals with rich networks progress faster in their careers and enjoy higher authority and recognition among their peers. However, there is more to networks than just the number of connections: the nature of these connections matters even more.

There are three golden rules to keep in mind as you build your acquaintances around you. First, successful networks are built on generosity and genuine interest in giving and helping others. Second, invest early and often into relationships that matter the most so that they will be there when you need them the most. Finally, take an active role in creating and managing your network as an asset no different than managing your health or financial resources.

Here are a few tips that have made a difference in helping me build a rich network of friends and acquaintances over the years.

1. **Adopt a mindset of curiosity and wonder:** We are a lot like icebergs: what we can see and observe above the surface is just 10 percent of our personas and lives. Each of us has a unique story to offer filled with adventures, setbacks, passions, and interests to be discovered. If you approach each conversation with that curiosity to discover what lies underneath, you will be amazed that you often have a lot more in common with others than you might imagine.

2. **Tap into positive feelings you get by helping others:** Actively shift the focus of your networking to getting to know others and finding ways in which you can help them. If you are an introvert, this orientation might help you overcome a key driver of aversion you might have in feeling like you are taking advantage of others. Thinking *How can I help this person?* will help you feel more authentic and willing to reach out.

3. **Actively reserve time on your calendar:** We live incredibly busy lives. Unless you are explicit about how you will grow your network and connect to others, you will end up procrastinating

and deprioritizing it. Remember, with weak ties, it doesn't take a lot (for some, just once or twice a year) to water these seeds for them to become saplings and over time, fruit-bearing trees that will serve you well. So block time on the calendar weekly to reconnect with old colleagues and classmates. Participate in groups outside of work in your community or industry to further expand your network.

One of my clients, Rob, was a newly elected partner at a consulting company in Chicago and had just been given an exciting assignment to lead an expansion in the greater China region. Rob had spent the majority of his life in the Midwest, and the prospect of moving to a completely new country was daunting. Rob and I had met at a lecture on relationships at his business school where he was pursuing his MBA. Rob admired the quality of my network I had built over time and reached out to me to brainstorm ideas on how he could build relationships quickly with companies without coming across as too commercial. Together we developed a strategy that leveraged Rob's strengths and what he had to offer to maximize his chances of success with the move.

Rob started practicing basic Mandarin using Duolingo, a learning website and app. He also proactively reached out to alumni from his alma mater who had moved to China recently and made sure he approached each conversation with curiosity to find common interests and shared goals. He would diligently follow up after the initial conversation and send articles and whitepapers on topics they were interested in.

Once Rob moved to Shanghai, he became a member of the local industry association and offered to lead talks and help others who were interested in his knowledge about the US market. Rob also worked with his local consulting team to launch a series of executive roundtables to convene CFOs, CEOs and CMOs once a quarter. For each of these round-tables, he enrolled the help of two to three executives at existing clients of the firm and leveraged their social connections to enroll others in the community. In less than six months, Rob's overseas network had blossomed because he had established himself as a key "connector," known for bringing people together.

Building Your Community Practice

It is my sincere hope that you are inspired to create a rich community of family, friends, and acquaintances. Helen Keller said it best, "Alone, we can do so little; together, we can do so much." Having a diverse set of relationships in your network will increase your ability to connect with others who can support and encourage you. This is especially true if you are looking to change your job, or even your career completely. Your network can help you access others who are already in jobs you want to have and can share valuable perspectives not just on what they like versus not like about their professions, but more importantly how they got there. By being more intentional in building this community and tapping into its collective wisdom and resources, you can scale the highest mountain and survive the stormiest seas because you will not be alone in your journey.

KEY TAKEAWAYS

- The power of social connections helps us live longer, healthier, and happier lives.
- By taking stock of your relationships (family, friends, and acquaintances) periodically, you can intentionally find creative,

achievable ways to prioritize spending time with those who are most important to you.

- Prioritize and protect time with your family by setting hard boundaries and anchoring on the bigger "Why?" Families are the number-one priority for most individuals above work and anything else.

- Not spending enough time with friends is one of the top regrets of the dying. Make sure to keep your friendships alive so you can support each other through the thick and thin of life.

- Building and nurturing professional relationships and a higher quality network also improves the quality of your work and increases job satisfaction. Surprisingly those on the fringe can be the most beneficial.

Live with Intention

"Vision without action is merely a dream.
Action without vision just passes the time.
Vision with action can change the world."

—Joel A. Barker[111]

How many New Year's resolutions have you started with gusto but quickly got lost in the cycle of life? Fewer than 8 percent of people actually stick to their resolutions each year. Over the course of reading this book, it is my hope that you have decided to make some positive changes in your life to support you in your *Hardwired for Happiness* journey. You might have decided to pursue a new direction in your career, renew focus on mastering mindfulness, or incorporate more gratitude and compassion. Regardless of what you have chosen, setting meaningful goals both long term and near term is critical to achieving them.

The growth journey toward happiness and contentment is not a quick fix but a commitment to a lifelong pursuit of living intentionally—meaning, setting a North Star for ourselves aligned to our purpose and goals, and then deliberately, persistently, consistently, and consciously investing our time and energy to make progress on that path. While living more intentionally takes some effort to master, the benefits far outweigh the costs. If you have been practicing with journaling, meditation, or community exercises in the prior chapters, you are already well on your way. You have learned how to shed what doesn't serve you and focus instead on the things that help you grow. You've practiced daily habits that have invited in more happiness, love, and fulfillment. You've become more aware of your emotions, learned to regulate them, and break bad, reactive habits. You have elevated your consciousness and have begun to make better decisions that are aligned with your values to serve your bigger purpose.

Over the course of this chapter, I will share several practical tips and suggestions to live more intentionally that will allow you to travel further on your journey. In the first section, I will offer you a framework to take a balcony view of how your life is going so far and identify changes you want to make. The next section will help free up space in your day-to-day life and focus on activities that get you closer to your goals while eliminating the noise created by the nonessentials. Finally, recognizing that almost 40 percent of your daily tasks are done unconsciously, you'll learn to build habits that will support your new goals and help you replace others that are hindering your progress.

Setting Your North Star

Life can often feel like our own version of the movie *Groundhog Day*: wake up, get the kids ready, rush to work, run from meeting to meeting, eat lunch on the go, battle the evening commute, help kids with sports or homework, put them to bed, and then get some more work done before collapsing, exhausted. Our weekends are no respite, filled with sports practices, birthday parties, grocery shopping, yard work, and other chores. The routine repeats itself week after week until maybe we get a vacation—

but by the time we actually start to relax, it's time to pack up and get back to the grind.

Most people rush through life this way not on purpose but feeling like victims with little agency to do anything about it. Looking back, they regret working so much. They feel guilty for not having enough time to spend with their families. And forget about self-care!

In my coaching conversations with hundreds of professionals and senior executives, I always ask what the most important thing in their lives is, or what brings them the most joy? Almost universally, the answer is: friends and family. Yet, depending on their profession and seniority, they spend roughly twelve to fourteen hours working each day during the week, and often several hours over the weekend. Most struggle to carve out two to three hours daily during the week to spend with their spouses and kids, leaving almost no time to focus on their own needs. When I dig deep to get underneath what drives them to spend time working over everything else, what I often find is they haven't made their family and friends a priority. We just get so caught up in day-to-day living and taking on the expectations of others because we don't want to fail in their eyes, that we fail to step back and see the forest from the trees; we consistently neglect our own priorities. We have lost sight of our North Star—what really matters.

Meditation Exercise:
Visualize Your Future Self

Visualization is a powerful technique that helps you by building a picture in your mind of what you want to achieve as a source of extra motivation. Most professional athletes use visualization techniques in their training and prep to improve their skills. The idea behind visualization is that if you "see" your goal, you are more likely to achieve it. This exercise also helps to bring awareness to the resources you will need to succeed. It can be done anytime but I find it most helpful first thing in the morning.

Duration: ten minutes

1. Sit in a comfortable position which allows you to be relaxed but also alert. A good way to start is to just practice sitting in a chair with your back straight. Keep your shoulders relaxed, your chin facing slightly upward, and close your eyes. Keep your jaw relaxed with your lips slightly open. You can rest your arms on your legs with palms facing downward.

2. Take three deep breaths, feeling the air fill your lungs and your stomach, and then slowly exhale with an open mouth, letting all the air out and feeling your stomach contract. Let yourself relax completely.

3. Resume breathing at your normal pace keeping attention on each inhale and exhale, feeling your belly rise with each inhale and fall with each exhale. You don't need to manipulate it. Let the inhale take as long as it needs to—it might take three, four, or five seconds. You don't have to interfere with your breathing. If your inhale is short, allow it to be short. If your exhale is long, let it be long. Keep breathing at your normal pace for the rest of the meditation.

4. As you continue breathing, bring your attention and focus to one of the goals you want to accomplish in your life.

It could be related to your work (changing careers, getting a promotion), your relationships (reconnecting with friends, spending more time with a loved one), or something personal (losing weight, completing a marathon).

5. Think about why this goal is important to you and how achieving it will add value to your life.

6. Now visualize yourself in the future after you have achieved that goal. What do you look like? What are you doing? Who are you with? What does it feel like in your body? What does it feel like emotionally? What has become possible now after achieving this goal? Use the power of your mind to focus sharply on that image and let what it feels like to be successful fill your whole way of being.

7. Continue breathing at your normal pace, and then shift your attention to your current starting point while staying anchored on your future successful self. Can you feel the gap between the two states? As you imagine that gap, bring to mind the smallest action that you can take to move a step closer to your future self. It could be a decision you have made, an action you have taken, or a practice you are committed to doing.

8. Bring attention to your solar plexus chakra, located in the upper abdomen two inches above the navel. This forms your deepest connections with willpower, self-discipline, and self-esteem. It embodies your unlimited potential to transform thought or inertia into action. Breathe into your solar plexus chakra and visualize powering and activating it

with each inhale to support you in your journey to accomplish your goal.

9. As you continue breathing into your solar plexus region, imagine a yellow glow above your navel, slowly expanding to the bottom of your rib cage and making the whole area warm and relaxed.

10. Visualize yourself harnessing the power within you to overcome any obstacles and see yourself progress toward your end state. Let the feelings of success wash over your mind, heart, and body as you see yourself completing the journey and reaching your end goals.

11. When you are ready, take a deep breath. Relax. Smile. And open your eyes.

The Dashboard of Life

Based on both extensive literature reviews on what people value in life, as well as hundreds of hours of coaching conversations, I put together a framework I call "The Dashboard of Life." This framework brings together the core metrics that people typically use to assess how they are doing against their wants as well as how they optimize their time across different activities.

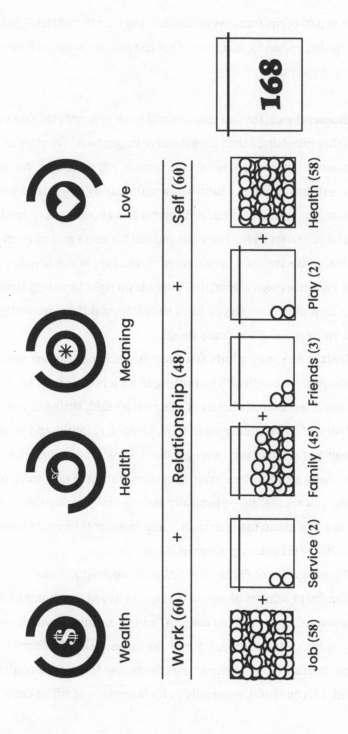

Figure 9.1: Dashboard of Life

The top part of the framework has four key output metrics—financial wealth, health, meaning, and love—that you can use to assess how things are going in your life.

- **Financial wealth:** Our income and bank accounts take up much higher mindshare than they deserve in our lives. We start to measure our worth based on our annual pay increases. We tackle uncertainty about the future by accumulating assets to ensure we will be well set for our retirement and allowing us to fund our kids' education. We justify our pursuit for more and more money because we are good providers who take care of our loved ones, and we give them a good life. There is no right or wrong answer for how much wealth you need to be happy. But do you really know how much *you* really need?

- **Health:** As young adults just starting out in our careers, we often suboptimize our health by putting in long hours at work, often getting less than six hours of sleep each night, sitting in our office chairs, and overindulging in food, alcohol, caffeine, and drugs to keep going. However, as we get older, it becomes apparent that our health should be a priority. It is important to take stock of how you are feeling—physically and mentally. No matter how old you are, you can make dramatic improvements in your overall health by prioritizing your wellbeing.

- **Meaning:** Viktor Frankl, the father of logotherapy, one of the prominent schools of psychotherapy, believed that humans are motivated by something called a "will to meaning," which corresponds to a desire to seek and make meaning in life. I have consistently found many of my clients over the years wrestling with this question, especially in their forties and fifties once they have reached a financially comfortable stage. Unlike wealth and health, which are measurable, meaning shows up in our hearts and our bodies in terms of flow and bliss when we work in coherence with our values. When meaning is missing, we experience a slow ache that never goes away and tugs on our heart saying, "There has to be more. Is this all life is meant to be?" We can take inspiration from the Cherokee saying: "Pay attention to the whispers so you don't have to listen to the screams."

- **Love:** More often than not, in the pursuit of professional success and financial wealth, we underinvest in relationships and often make withdrawals. Unfortunately, by the time we reach our thirties or forties, our accounts are overdrawn, and we may go through painful breakups, strained relationships with our kids, and lost connections with our friends. By keeping an eye on your "love" dial, you can course correct early before it is too late. Our quality of relationships with our family and friends determines how full we feel with love in our lives.

Start by assessing how you are doing in each of these domains and jot down two to three actions you might want to take that would allow you to close the gap between where you are and where you want to be. Remember, there is no right or wrong answer: everyone has a different optimal mix of these four outcomes. The starting and ending values that anchor the zero and one hundred points are highly individual as well. The actual number does not matter. What matters is your ideal point goal in that domain.

The bottom half of the dashboard focuses on where you spend your energies and time to achieve the outcomes that matter to you. Time is a precious commodity that does not differentiate between the rich and the poor. We all just have twenty-four hours in a day or 168 hours in a week.

We have to be intentional about how we choose to spend these hours and align them closely with our values. Otherwise someone else will dictate them for us.

- **Work (Paid, Unpaid):** The domain of work includes all activities that you do to create value in the world. It encompasses both your job (for which you get paid), but also other service endeavors like your involvement with boards, nonprofits, mentorship, and community service. This should also include the commute time to and from work.
- **Relationships (Family and Friends):** The domain of relationships includes all activities and time you spend with your family, friends, and acquaintances. It should also include time you spend formally or informally networking within your industry/function or local community with the intent to expand or deepen your relationships. We often unconsciously underinvest time in these relationships, losing touch with our friends, spending less and less time with family and, even if we are physically there, we are not fully present. Take stock of your relationships with your spouse, kids, parents, siblings, and friends, and set an intention of how you want to spend your time going forward to improve the quality of this domain.
- **Self (Health and Play):** I am sure you have heard the saying, "You can't pour from an empty cup." Yet so many of us give so much to our jobs and what is left to our families, and therefore we put ourselves last. We underinvest in our wellbeing and become numb to the normalized feelings of tiredness, exhaustion, and stress. We turn to food, alcohol, and other addictions which further wreak havoc on our bodies. Along the way, we have also

given up our passions and hobbies that used to fill our lives with joy. As you take stock of the time you invest in yourself, include the time you spend exercising, sleeping, meditating, or any other activity (hobbies, interests) that nourishes you. This bucket should also include time on maintenance activities like showering, grocery shopping, eating, etc.

I invite you to start by looking at your last month or quarter and take an inventory of how you spent your time. Define what your ideal set point was, or allocation of time across these different categories. Ask yourself: Is the time allocation in alignment with what matters to me and where I would like to spend it to get the most out of my life? Identify two to three actions that you might want to take or behaviors you want to change to reallocate that time from one category to another to support your journey.

Make Sustainable Behavior Shifts by Addressing Underlying Mindsets

Only 10 percent of an iceberg is visible above the surface of the water and over 90 percent stays hidden underneath. Humans are just like icebergs: what's visible to us externally is our behaviors, and what's hidden beneath the surface is a whole set of mindsets and beliefs that drive our behaviors. These mindsets and beliefs are made up of our thoughts, our emotions/moods, our values and priorities, our deepest needs, and our fears. Making a sustainable behavior change (e.g., practicing letting go or giving up our need to control) requires us to identify the underlying mindsets and beliefs that drive our behavior today and work on shifting these to a different set of mindsets/beliefs that will support the new set of behaviors.

The iceberg model (see Figure 9.2: Humans are like Icebergs) was first proposed by anthropologist Edward T. Hall in the 1970s as an analogy for the cultural codes that prevail in any society. It's a model that is extensively used by many coaches to help people make successful behavior changes.

HUMAN ICEBERG

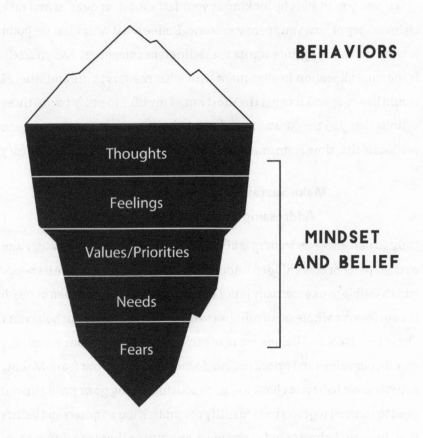

BEHAVIORS

Thoughts

Feelings

Values/Priorities

MINDSET
AND BELIEF

Needs

Fears

Internal Self-Awareness

Figure 9.2: Humans are like Icebergs

Community Practice:
Using Iceberg Coaching to Make
Sustainable Behavior Shifts

Choose a partner to engage with using the following coaching script[112] to help you dive deeper into each other's Icebergs. As you read through the questions, give 100 percent of your attention to your partner, not only listening to the words but also the emotions and other nonverbal cues. Your job is to ask the questions and invite reflection, not to problem solve or offer guidance. If you do have an insight you feel compelled to share, ask for permission first: "Do I have your permission to share...". Remember to keep the conversation confidential.

If you are the coach, ask your partner: What is the overall goal you want to achieve? What are the behaviors you want to shift?

Now, ask these questions to clarify how your partner can get FROM an unwanted behavior TO a positive shift.

Diving down the FROM:

1. What behaviors do you find yourself doing that are not serving you well?
2. What about this behavior shift is important to you? What would happen if you didn't make the behavior shift?
3. What are the thoughts running through your mind? What is the uncensored talk?
4. What are the feelings/emotions present?
5. What values seem to be at play here for you? Is there conflict in priorities between your different values?

6. What need or fear of yours does the current FROM behavior fulfill or take care of?
7. As you look at your thoughts, feelings, and values, can you identify the limiting belief that is at play here?
8. How is this belief serving you or not serving you?
9. Can you identify when this belief first showed up in your life? Any childhood or early-life experiences that you can point to?

Rising back up toward the TO:

1. What would become possible if you could put this belief aside? What are you willing to let go of?
2. What is a more empowering belief that would support you in meeting your "TO" goal?
3. Which (new) value would support you in living into this belief?
4. What thoughts do you have now as you think back to tackling your original challenge (old behavior) with this new belief?
5. What feelings and bodily sensations are present for you?
6. What emotions are present now?
7. What is the new "observer" who emerges from this shift in your thoughts, values, emotions, and feelings in your body?
8. What behaviors will now naturally show up? What would be the result of those behaviors?
9. How can you anchor the insights from this session in your body?
10. How will you know you are making progress in this behavior shift?

Setting Goals and Intentions

Completing the Dashboard of Life exercise should have highlighted a set of goals that you want to achieve to close the gaps between how life is going for you and where you want it to go over the next four to five years. American poet, writer, and historian Bill Copeland captured the importance of goal setting well: "The trouble with not having a goal is that you can spend your life running up and down the field and never score."[113] Goal setting allows you to establish and align what you are trying to achieve, ensure that the activities you pursue are in line with your purpose, assess your progress along the way, and more efficiently manage your time. Unfortunately, many people fail before they start by getting this wrong. Some set goals that are so big and far into the future that day-to-day decisions to focus on other urgent things and procrastinate feel justified. Others set them too vaguely, resulting in it being hard to measure the progress that they are making. There has been extensive research done by psychologists on both goal setting and implementation that you can harness to increase your odds of success.

Make Your Goals as Specific as Possible[114]

One of the ways to set specific goals is to use the SMART (Specific, Measurable, Achievable, Relevant, and Timebound) methodology, attributed to George Doran.[115] To ensure **S**pecificity, outline what you are trying to do, why this is important, who else will be involved, and resources you might need. Making them **M**easurable will enable you to track your progress easily and make course corrections as needed. It is critical to make the goal **A**chievable so as not to lose motivation along the way. Resources, skills, and assets you need and have all go into ensuring achievability of your goals. Goals also need to be **R**elevant and coherent with what you are trying to achieve overall in your life. In other words, they need to fit into your overall journey at this moment. Finally, make sure to make them **T**imebound by setting a deadline. For longer-term goals, it is especially important to break it down into smaller chunks and set guideposts at the weekly, monthly, quarterly, and yearly levels to ensure you are making progress.

Emphasize Positive Outcomes versus Preventing Negative Outcomes [116]

Research is clear in showing that you can significantly increase your odds at following through on the change you want when your personal vision of an ideal self is based on the positive outcomes that result versus avoiding the negative effects from status quo. So for example, if you are looking to lose weight, it would be a lot more powerful to anchor the benefits side of the equation in terms of being able to play with younger children and live longer to enjoy grandchildren, versus avoiding the negative effects of having a heart attack, needing more medical care, or dying sooner.

Set Learning Goals versus Performance Goals, Especially When Starting Out in a New Field [117]

When setting goals, it is important to draw a distinction between learning goals versus performance goals. Learning goals focus on acquiring knowledge or skill. For example, if you wanted to speak French, a learning goal would be to practice fifteen minutes daily using Duolingo or Babbel. Performance goals are those outcome-oriented goals that focus on getting a desired end result, or using the same example, wanting to be able to hold an informal conversation at a Parisian café for your upcoming vacation. When starting something new, setting a performance goal can have a negative impact on your performance. Stick with learning goals until you are ready to achieve something bigger.

Use the Practice of Daily Intentions to Stay on the Path

Each of our individual *Hardwired for Happiness* journeys is fundamentally about transforming our way of being in the world. Adopting a daily intention practice can provide the needed focus, discipline, and self-control we need to pick ourselves up every time we fall and keep moving toward our goals. Setting daily intentions allows us to persevere in our battle between choices that provide instant gratification versus those that allow us to reap long-term benefits by achieving our goals. Equally important to setting intentions about what we want to *do* is about how we want to *be*, how we create the space we want to hold for others, and how we contribute to the world.

> ### Journaling Exercise:
> ### Keep a Visual Record of Progress
>
> Journaling is a powerful tool that can help with goal setting and tracking. Based on research, even spending ten minutes a day to review and write about your goals can help increase focus and motivation. Keeping a journal is a visual record of your progress, whether you prefer a hard copy or digital format.
>
> I've researched over twenty different published journals and my top pick is the "Habit Journal" by James Clear, the author of *Atomic Habits*, which is available on Amazon.com. The journal includes a helpful "Habit Toolkit" which has step-by-step guides for tracking your habits, making better decisions, and improving productivity and time management.
>
> When it comes to digital apps, one of my favorites is called Momentum, which is available for iOS operating systems.

Momentum helps you set your goals and creates smaller, daily habits to work toward achieving them. Momentum also allows you to set weekly targets and take notes so you can easily take control of your habits. If you are an Android user, try Habitica, which has a unique, video-game-inspired design that makes keeping track of habits and goals fun. Each completed task levels up your customized avatar, giving you an extra incentive to stay motivated.

In addition to setting up a regular tracking mechanism, I would also invest in finding an accountability buddy, or someone who is committed to helping you reach your goals, which has been proven to increase your chances of achieving your goals. According to research conducted by the American Society of Training and Development, people are 65 percent more likely to meet a goal after committing to another person. Their chances of success increase to 95 percent when they build in ongoing meetings with their partners to check in on their progress.[118]

Schedule a recurring appointment, at least once every other week to meet with your accountability buddy. Be honest about what you have achieved and also what hindered your progress. Use your partner to brainstorm ideas on how to get past the obstacles that you might have encountered. Discuss ways to avoid future setbacks and how you're going to recommit to your goals.

The following is a step-by-step approach to goal setting that has worked very effectively for my clients and myself:

1. Start with the two to three goals you want to achieve in your journey and the time horizon over which you want to achieve them.

2. For each of the goals, clearly identify the benefit and the reason why you are interested in pursuing these goals. The more clearly you can visualize yourself receiving the benefits at the end and how they will improve your life, the greater the chances you can achieve them.

3. Clearly identify what you will need in terms of resources to achieve the goals and any obstacles and hurdles that can get in your way. It might be time, skills, a new degree, or money. Make a plan for how you will remove these obstacles. If they are not something that you can control, go back, and revisit the goal and reframe it.

4. Identify the specific activities you will need to do in order to achieve your goals. Ideally, you can identify these as a daily, weekly, and in some cases, monthly goal.

5. Identify people who can help you in achieving these goals and the roles they can play from being a source of inspiration, being an accountability partner, mentor, or connector to others.

6. Use the "SMART" goal-setting process to screen your goals and plan to achieve them to see if they can benefit from refinement.

7. Now that you have the goals and the supporting activities refined, it is time to hardwire them in your calendar. Use Figure 9.3: Urgent versus Important matrix to optimize your calendar and block time to focus on the important activities that will help you achieve your goals.

8. Finally, once every month, block one hour to review your progress, take stock of what is working, and what is not working, identify the interventions that can help you accelerate, or close the gap on the progress against your strategic goals.

Draining the Shallows to Focus on What Matters

Setting goals and intentions are not enough by themselves in helping you actually achieve them. You will also have to hack your calendar to ensure that you are focusing your days on what matters to you and free up space by eliminating others that are not essential to your goals. We have to learn the art and discipline of being able to say no gracefully to protect against the constant demands on our time. You will have to set boundaries and create buffers to ensure that the day-to-day chaos doesn't distract you from what you have prioritized. Finally, you have to create space and distance to step back and analyze what's working versus not, and be able to adjust continuously. The words of Greg McKeown, the author and founder of the *Essentialism* movement, ring true: "If you don't prioritize your life, someone else will."

One of the most effective tools toward living an intentional life is the Urgent-Important matrix. This matrix was originally created by former President Eisenhower but widely popularized by Steven Covey in *The 7 Habits of Highly Effective People*. It consists of four quadrants defined using two core axes of importance and urgency that you can use to segment your daily activities. The Urgency dimension is defined based on how quickly we need to act to respond to them, often taking attention away from others that we might be focused on. Important activities are those that are critical toward achieving our goals.

The basic idea is to increase the time we spend in Quadrant 2, which is the Important but Not Urgent quadrant. Actively blocking out time on the calendar for these activities will ensure that you are making progress toward your goals, whether it be focusing on your wellbeing, practicing mindfulness, or learning a new skill. I encourage my clients to start on Quadrant 2 and calendar those activities that are really important so as to protect them first.

URGENT vs IMPORTANT MATRIX

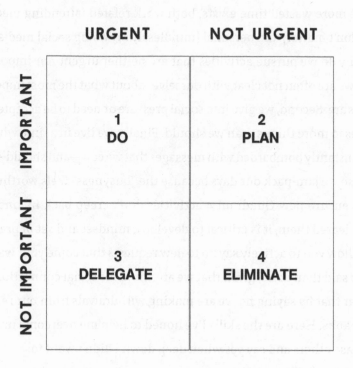

Figure 9.3: Urgent versus Important matrix

Think about filling a jar with large stones, smaller pebbles, and sand. The trick to fitting it all is the order in which you fill the jar. The large stones are your most important goals—these go in first. Next the pebbles, or "must do" activities that are important but not directly linked to your goals. They fill in the gaps between the stones. Finally, add the sand, or everything else, which flows around the other rocks and pebbles and fits wherever it can.

Equally important to prioritizing the activities that matter and hard wiring them into your calendar is to eliminate the nonessential Quadrant 4 activities. These activities are neither urgent nor important. In my coaching practice with clients, I consistently find that the busier one's life is, the more wasted time exists, both work-related (attending meetings that don't matter) and personal (mindlessly browsing social media).

Why do we pursue activities that are neither urgent nor important? First, we are often not clear with ourselves about what the most important things are. Second, we give into social pressure or need to be accepted and say yes to more things than we should. Finally, we live in a time when we are constantly bombarded with messages that we can—and should—have it all, so we jam-pack our days because the "busyness" feels worthwhile.

To ensure new Quadrant 4 activities don't creep back in, once you have cleared them, it is critical to develop a mindset and set of practices that allow you to actively say no to new requests that come your way. It is easier said than done, given that we are wired for social connection, and we fear that by saying no we are making withdrawals from our relationship banks. Here are the skills I've honed to help me overcome my need to please others and say yes when deep down I didn't want to:

Take a pause when a new request comes in before responding: My favorite phrase became: "Thank you for thinking of me. Let me get back to you after checking my capacity/calendar." This really helped me overcome my habitual responses.

Evaluate all requests against your core practices and boundaries: Think about how you are allocating your time between work, health, family, and community. Check the implications of saying yes to this request against your top priorities. What would you be saying no to if you said yes to this? Anchoring on the "why you are saying no" will give you the grounding and justification you need to stand on when declining to engage.

Think of who else could really use this opportunity and get them engaged: Bringing others into the equation allows you to go back to the requestor, not just with a no but also a name(s) who might be delighted to help them.

Quadrant 3 activities are those which are urgent and not important to us but important to someone else. I have found a three-pronged approach can be quite effective in ensuring that Quadrant 3 doesn't blow up and throw you off your path despite your best intentions. First, make sure you create a buffer for yourself in your daily schedule for the uncertainties of life. In my case, I typically keep at least a two-hour buffer every day in my calendar to allow me to cater to those urgent requests that come up from my clients or team members. Second, I typically delegate these activities which don't necessarily need my specific skills to others who might benefit from it. Finally, I try to batch the urgent requests that only I can handle and schedule them during periods when I am not at my peak. Peak times are reserved for the top priorities that are truly important to me.

You are then left finally with Quadrant 1 activities, which are both urgent *and* important. My experience has been that if we actively shrink the time that Quadrant 4 and 3 activities take up and focus on increasing the time we spend on Quadrant 2 activities, Quadrant 1 often automatically shrinks as you address the important activities in a timelier fashion so they don't become urgent.

Here are the steps I have followed with tremendous success in draining the shallows. This approach will help make space in your calendar to focus on what matters:

1. Take a detailed inventory of where you are actually spending your time. I would encourage documenting and categorizing every major activity in fifteen-minute chunks in your day over a period of two weeks from waking up to going to bed. You can invest in a

tool like Timeluar (https://timeular.com/product/tracker), which is an eight-sided device that you can label and use to track, or just use a simple spreadsheet.

2. At the end of two weeks, categorize every activity into which quadrant they fit into. Flag all those that are not core to achieving the goals (Quadrant 4: not urgent and not important; and Quadrant 3: urgent but not important) you have set for yourself.

3. Tackle the Quadrant 4 and 3 activities and actively develop strategies to eliminate or minimize them. For example, if there is a project or set of projects that you are spending time on that are not core toward your goals, you can choose to uncommit from them by either delegating them to someone else on your team, or identifying someone else who can take them on, or simply having a conversation with the person who assigned that task explaining your rationale.

4. Now start from a clean sheet of paper and first pencil into your calendar the big stones (activities that help you achieve the goals you have identified for yourself). Next, pencil in the activities that represent the little pebbles that are important to you and that you want to fit into your day schedule. Make sure that as you are calendaring these activities, you are allocating them across the three domains and making sure one domain is not overflowing into the other.

5. Only after scheduling in your Quadrant 1 and 2 activities, should you move on to putting in Quadrant 4 and 3 activities. For Quadrant 3 activities that remain, estimate the time those activities that only you can handle typically consume in your day and create a buffer zone on your calendar to tackle them. Schedule this buffer zone in times when you are not at your

creative best. For example, it might be activities you might do mid-morning or late afternoon.

Forming Actionable Habits and Routines

According to research published in 2006 at Duke University, almost 40–50 percent of our daily activities are driven by habits, or involuntary behaviors, versus through conscious actions that we take.[119] Octavia Butler, a famous American author, captures the importance of habits in supporting change beautifully: "First forget inspiration. Habit is more dependable. Habit will sustain you whether you're inspired or not."[120] Notice whether you follow the same sequence within any activity: how much toothpaste you put on your brush, which shoelace you tie first, and where you turn when you enter a grocery store. If you can understand how habits are formed, you can leverage those insights to automate the behaviors that enable you to achieve your goals along the way.

Personally, I struggled with dropping habits that were not serving me (like indulging in salty Indian snacks called *Bhujia*) and forming new habits that could serve me well (like a daily workout). I knew, when I began four years ago on my own *Hardwired for Happiness* journey, that forming new habits and dropping or changing existing ones would be critical. So I immersed myself in the science and practices behind habit formation and experimented on myself and my clients using the scientific advice. Some of my favorite books on this topic are: *The Power of Habits* by Charles Duhigg, *Tiny Habits* by BJ Fogg, *Atomic Habits* by James Clear, *The Kindness Method* by Shahroo Izadi, *Kaizen* by Sarah Harvey, and *Rewire* by Richard O'Connor.

In his book *The Power of Habit*, Charles Duhigg demystified how habits are formed based on research conducted at MIT.[121] When we first engage in a new activity, our thinking brain, the prefrontal cortex, is heavily involved in processing the information, learning through trial and error, and helping us complete it. This process is highly energy intensive and the big driver behind the almost 20 percent energy consumption by our brain (despite being only 5 percent of our body weight). Our brains are continuously looking to optimize their energy usage. One way the brain accomplishes this is by translating a set of actions that we frequently do into automatic routines and transferring them from the prefrontal cortex to the basal ganglia, a neurological structure situated deep in the brain. The more often we perform an action or behave a certain way, the more it gets hardwired into our brain. This property of the brain is called neuro-plasticity and understanding how it works can come in very handy to us.

Researchers at MIT broke down the anatomy of habits into three key steps that are the foundation of all habits: cue, routine, and reward.

Cues are the stimulus from the external environment received through sensory inputs that trigger the brain to take certain actions. Often the routines that we follow, whether physical, emotional, or mental (thoughts), are automatic, and we usually do these without needing to think. At the end of completing these actions, we usually get a reward in the form of a dopamine hit that tells the brain that this action is worth repeating. The more often we follow this loop, the deeper this pattern is engraved in our brain. In fact, over time the cues create a high degree of both mental and physical craving, as any cigarette, alcohol, or drug addict can attest to, so that we end up falling into the pattern of behavior despite our best intentions.

You can use these insights on the habit loop to your advantage, whether you want to create new habits or break old ones. Let's say you want to develop upper body strength. This would require you to repeat a set of actions (doing thirty pushups after waking up) over a period of time in response to a trigger or cue (alarm clock ringing in the morning) and then giving yourself a reward (enjoying pizza at the end of the week). If only it was that simple! We all start out strong but usually within a couple of days or weeks, our motivation vanishes, and we give up the new routine and fall back into old ways of doing things.

HABIT LOOP

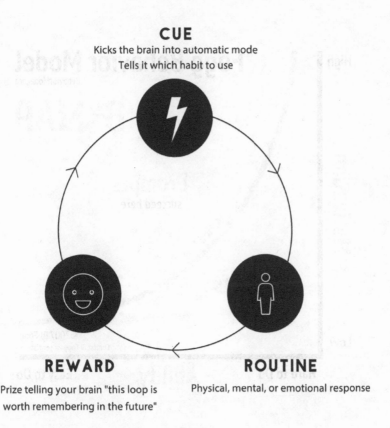

CUE
Kicks the brain into automatic mode
Tells it which habit to use

REWARD
Prize telling your brain "this loop is
worth remembering in the future"

ROUTINE
Physical, mental, or emotional response

Figure 9.4: Habit Loop as described by Charles Duhigg, *The Power of Habit*

I was in the same predicament when I discovered the work of BJ Fogg,[122] who used twenty years of his research studying human behavior to develop a method that he shared in his book, *Tiny Habits*. His method builds on a valuable insight of his on the role of Motivation, Ability, and Prompts (cues) in determining which behaviors individuals are more likely to repeat. His insight was that when our combination of Motivation and Ability is above a threshold, and we receive the prompt or cue, we are more likely to do the behavior.

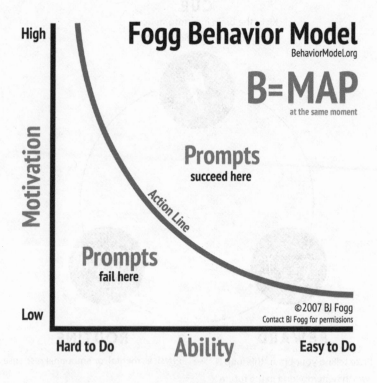

Figure 9.5: Fogg Behavior Model

This insight is brilliant because you no longer have to rely on motivation or willpower alone to be able to repeat a behavior until it becomes a habit. You can work on the "Ability" axis making the behavior so easy to do and designing the right prompts (cues), that you would be predisposed to completing the behavior, regardless of motivation level, thus sowing the seeds for the habit to form. In addition, by celebrating every time you complete a behavior, the dopamine hit you receive will start creating a powerful feedback loop, making it easier and more automatic the next time. You can follow his simple three-part "ABC" model to very effectively create new habits:

- Find an **A**nchor Moment that acts as the cue for you to initiate the new behavior.
- Design a tiny new **B**ehavior: This should be the easiest version of the behavior you want to convert into a habit.
- **C**elebrate right away: You celebrate immediately after doing the new behavior, to use positive emotions to lock in the behavior as a new habit.

Let's go back to the example above of developing upper body strength. If you are trying to develop a habit of daily pushups, start by committing to doing just two wall pushups (tiny behavior with a low ability needed) the moment your feet touch the ground in the morning (clear prompt) and celebrating this small win with a big smile and "*Yes!*" fist pump (reward). This way, you are setting yourself up for success even on days when you did not get enough sleep or are rushed in the morning and can't commit to your larger workout. Over time, as your abilities grow and upper body strength increases, the new cue-pattern-reward pathways are hardwired, and you will naturally increase the number of pushups. A positive new habit is formed.

Use Small Hacks to Create Big Habit Changes

You can also hack your environment to reinforce certain behaviors you want and create friction that make other behaviors you want to stop doing harder to do. I wanted to create a new habit to wake up early and exercise before work started. You see, I have hypothyroidism and so need to take a pill in the morning on an empty stomach. I used to keep the pill box right next to my bed so that when I woke up in the morning, I could take it right away and not forget. But more often than not, I would go back to sleep despite my best intentions of working out. I decided to hack my environment by moving my pill box to the kitchen. Now, when I wake up and go downstairs to get my medicine, I'm already more motivated to put on my workout gear and get on my Peloton bike.

Here are some other examples of how I've used environment hacking successfully to introduce new habits and change others that were not serving me:

- **Not checking emails first thing when I wake up:** I keep my electronic devices in the kitchen at night and put them in airplane mode, so no lights are blinking, ensuring I get a better, less interrupted sleep.
- **Eating healthier snacks:** I moved most sugary, salty snacks to a separate pantry and kept fresh fruit available in the kitchen where I can see it, encouraging myself to make healthier choices.
- **Prepping meals ahead of time:** I chop and store all the ingredients I need for my weekly salads over the weekend so preparing healthy, delicious meals is easier during busy workdays.

Lindsey is a senior director at a large software development company and reached out to me for guidance to help her find more balance. Lindsey had joined her current company eight years ago after graduating from business school, and since then, had gotten married and had two kids. She was promoted three times faster than any of her peers and the company had also grown, doubling its revenue almost every year.

Lindsey loved her job, but it seemed like her job was all she had time for. She struggled to find time with her family and felt like a "bad" mother and wife, constantly checking messages when they were together. Her sleep habits were terrible and she rarely exercised. Professionally, she felt irritable and began to lose her temper in front of her colleagues, who avoided her. Lindsey seriously considered quitting her job to find something else that would not make her feel like a total failure in every aspect.

I asked Lindsey to use the Life Dashboard to diagnose her current starting point and identify three priorities. While her wealth and meaning meters were full, she was running on fumes in health and love. She said family was the most important thing to her, and when I asked her to reflect on where she was actually spending time, she broke down as she realized how incoherent her life had become to what mattered to her. Together we set three goals: First, she wanted to spend more quality time with her family. Second, she wanted to create the space for self-care. Third, to make any of this happen, she needed to free up space in her daily schedule.

Recognizing perfection is the enemy of progress, we identified one meaningful activity that Lindsey could do with her family with undivided attention. She chose eating dinner together twice per week as a clear target. To make this happen, they decided to order in to ensure that dinner hour was spent enjoying each other's company rather than rushing to get the meal ready. Second, she decided to bring mindfulness into three meaningful moments every day by transforming what she was doing: brushing her teeth every morning and night, eating the first minute of her lunch mindfully, and incorporating mindfulness as a check-in practice for her daily team huddle. Finally, she engaged her entire team to use the Urgent-Importance matrix to identify a set of "not urgent, not important" activities that they could eliminate. She also delegated a set of "urgent, not important" requests to her team leader to free up one to two hours on her calendar each day.

Within a month, the seeds Lindsey had planted started to take root. Her new schedule felt so good it created a positive reinforcing cycle for her to continue making small, impactful changes. Pretty soon, Lindsey found the time to go to a yoga class on weekends, expanded her family dinner to every night, and started meditating every morning for ten minutes. Her team continued to optimize their calendar, continued to eliminate the nonessentials, and created the right boundaries for every team member to thrive and flourish.

Building Your Intention Practice

There is a Zen story in which a man walking down the road sees another man galloping down the road at breakneck speed on his horse. He shouts to the horse rider, "Where are you heading in such a rush?" The man on horseback replies, "I don't know. Ask the horse!"

Our lives are filled with frantic activities and driven by established habits and routines because that is what we have gotten used to. This habit energy pulls us here and there, running all over the place, driven by our surroundings and the demands of other people. We rarely step back to look at our intentions and use those to decide what we need to focus on. Become the boss of the horse versus making the horse the boss of you. Our actions shape who we become and the mark we leave on the world. As Aristotle said, "We are what we repeatedly do. Excellence is not an act, but a habit."

KEY TAKEAWAYS

- Living intentionally (setting a North Star) allows us to align our choices with our purpose and goals, and then deliberately and consistently invest time and energy to make progress on that path.
- We can take stock of how we feel we are doing using four metrics: financial wealth, health, meaning, and love.
- Time is a precious commodity—we can never get it back—and so we must be intentional about how we choose to spend it, whether on work (paid or unpaid), relationships (friends and family), and self (health and play).
- Successful goal setting allows you to establish and align with what you are trying to achieve, ensure that the activities you pursue are in line with your purpose, assess your progress along the way, and more efficiently manage your time.
- "Drain the shallows" by freeing up space, learning to say no, and setting boundaries to increase the time you can spend doing things that bring you joy.
- Form positive new habits to make bigger, sustainable behavior shifts to get you closer to your goals and desires.

Appendix

Further Reading

The following is a list of some of my favorite books, organized by category, that can help support you in your *Hardwired for Happiness* journey.

Spirituality and Mindfulness	Psychology and Happiness	Neurosciences/Science
Inner Engineering: A Yogi's Guide to Joy by Sadhguru	*Man's Search for Meaning* by Viktor Frankl	*Your Brain, Explained: What Neuroscience Reveals about Your Brain and Its Quirks* by Marc Dingman
You Are Here: Discovering the Magic of the Present Moment by Thich Nhat Hahn	*Winning from Within: A Breakthrough Method for Leading, Living, and Lasting Change* by Erica Ariel Fox	*Seven and a Half Lessons About the Brain* by Lisa Feldman Barrett
The Book of Forgiveness: The Fourfold Path for Healing Ourselves and Our World by Desmond Tutu and Mpho Tutu	*The Gifts of Imperfection: Let Go of Who You Think You're Supposed to Be and Embrace Who You Are* by Brené Brown	*Being You: A New Science of Consciousness* by Anil Seth

Spirituality and Mindfulness	Psychology and Happiness	Neurosciences/Science
Start Where You Are: A Guide to Compassionate Living by Pema Chödrön	Self-Compassion: The Proven Power of Being Kind to Yourself by Kristin Neff	How Emotions Are Made: The Secret Life of the Brain by Lisa Feldman Barrett
The Untethered Soul: The Journey Beyond Yourself by Michael Singer	Flourish: A Visionary New Understanding of Happiness and Well-being by Martin Seligman	Mindsight: The New Science of Personal Transformation by Daniel Siegel
The Prophet by Khalil Gibran	Happier, No Matter What: Cultivating Hope, Resilience, and Purpose in Hard Times by Tal Ben-Shahar	Livewired: The Inside Story of the Ever-Changing Brain by David Eagleman
The Book of Joy: Lasting Happiness in a Changing World by Dalai Lama and Desmond Tutu	Unlocking Leadership Mindtraps: How to Thrive in Complexity by Jennifer Garvey Berger	The Tao of Physics: An Exploration of the Parallels Between Modern Physics and Eastern Mysticism by Fritjof Capra
The Power of Now: A Guide to Spiritual Enlightenment by Eckhart Tolle	Stumbling on Happiness by Daniel Gilbert	Letting Go: The Pathway of Surrender by David Hawkins
Siddhartha by Hermann Hesse	The How of Happiness: A New Approach to Getting the Life You Want by Sonja Lyubomirsky	The Universe in a Single Atom: The Convergence of Science and Spirituality by Dalai Lama
Tao Te Ching by Lao Tzu	Happiness: Unlocking the Mysteries of Psychological Wealth by Ed Diener and Robert Biswas-Diener	The Biology of Belief: Unleashing the Power of Consciousness, Matter & Miracles by Bruce Lipton

The Srimad-Bhagavad Gita by Swami Paramananda	*The Happiness Track: How to Apply the Science of Happiness to Accelerate Your Success* by Emma Seppala	*Morphic Resonance: The Nature of Formative Causation* by Rupert Sheldrake
Yoga Sutras of Patanjali trans. by Sri Swami Satchidananda	*Daring Greatly: How the Courage to Be Vulnerable Transforms the Way We Live, Love, Parent, and Lead* by Brené Brown	
Lovingkindness Meditation: Learning to Love Through Insight Meditation by Sharon Salzberg	*Mindset: The New Psychology of Success* by Carol Dweck	
The Heart of the Buddha's Teaching: Transforming Suffering into Peace, Joy, and Liberation by Thich Nhat Hahn	*The Essentials of Theory U: Core Principles and Applications* by Otto Scharmer	

Mindfulness	Purpose	Other
How to Meditate: A Practical Guide to Making Friends with Your Mind by Pema Chödrön	How Will You Measure Your Life? by Clayton Christensen, James Allworth & Karen Dillon	Essentialism: The Disciplined Pursuit of Less by Greg McKeown
Full Catastrophe Living: Using the Wisdom of Your Body and Mind to Face Stress, Pain, and Illness by Jon Kabat-Zinn	The Second Mountain: The Quest for a Moral Life by David Brooks	Atomic Habits: An Easy & Proven Way to Build Good Habits & Break Bad Ones by James Clear
Jonathan Livingston Seagull by Richard Bach	Designing Your Life: How to Build a Well-Lived, Joyful Life by Bill Burnett and Dave Evans	Tiny Habits: The Small Changes That Change Everything by BJ Fogg
Search Inside Yourself: The Unexpected Path to Achieving Success, Happiness (and World Peace) by Chade-Meng Tan	Discover Your True North by Bill George	Why We Sleep: Unlocking the Power of Sleep and Dreams by Matthew Walker
Total Mediation: Practices in Living the Awakened Life by Deepak Chopra	Claiming Your Place at the Fire: Living the Second Half of Your Life on Purpose by Richard J. Leider and David A. Shapiro	The Core. Better Life, Better Performance by Saari Oskari and Aki Hintsa
Breathe, You Are Alive: The Sutra on the Full Awareness of Breathing by Thich Nhat Hanh	The Power of Purpose: Find Meaning, Live Longer, Better by Richard Leider	Language and the Pursuit of Leadership Excellence: How Extraordinary Leaders Build Relationships, Shape Culture and Drive Breakthrough Results by Chalmer Brothers and Vinay Kumar

		Centered Leadership: Leading with Purpose, Clarity, and Impact by Johanne Lavoie and Joanna Barsh
		Born to Win: Find Your Success by Zig Ziglar and Tom Ziglar

Measure Your Progress

The following are some of my favorite scales to measure the maturity of the nine core practices and help you assess where you are on your *Hardwired for Happiness* journey and where you may need to refocus your energies.

Practice	Scale details	Website
Self-Awareness	Adult development stage—The Maturity Assessment Profile (MAP) is the most well-researched and statistically sophisticated tool available for assessing a person's stage of development	https://www.adult-development.com/map
	Big 4 Profile Survey developed by Erica Fox allows you to discover more about your Inner Negotiators	https://www.erica arielfox.com/resources /big-four-profile/
	Leadership circle profile	https://leadershipcircle .com/en/products /leadership-circle -profile/
Purpose	CliftonStrengths assessment to understand your talents and maximize your potential	https://store.gallup .com/p/en-us/10003 /cliftonstrengths-34

Practice	Scale details	Website
Gratitude	Gratitude assessment developed by Drs. McCullough, Emmons, and Tsang to measure your disposition to experience gratitude	https://ppc.sas.upenn .edu/resources/ questionnaires -researchers/gratitude -questionnaire
	Gratitude quiz based on a scale developed by psychologists Mitchel Adler and Nancy Fagley	https://greatergood .berkeley.edu/quizzes /take_quiz/gratitude
Mindfulness	Mindfulness attention awareness scale is a fifteen-item scale designed to assess a core characteristic of mindfulness, namely, a receptive state of mind in which attention, informed by a sensitive awareness of what is occurring in the present, simply observes what is taking place	https://ggsc.berkeley .edu/images/uploads /The_Mindful_ Attention_Awareness _Scale_-_Trait_(1).pdf
	Mindfulness assessment developed by Jacqueline Carter, Rasmus Hougaard, and Rob Stembridge at Potential Project conducting mindfulness training for thousands of individuals in organizations around the globe	https://hbr.org/2017 /03/assessment-how -mindful-are-you
Compassion	Self-compassion assessment scale developed by Dr. Kristin Neff to measure your level of self-compassion	https://self-compassion .org/wp-content/ uploads/2021/03/SCS -information.pdf
	Compassion assessment scale developed by Dr. Kristin Neff to measure your compassion for others	https://self-compassion .org/wp-content /uploads/2021/03 /CS-information.pdf

Moods and Emotions	Anger assessment test will see how you react in stressful situations using a method developed in Novaco Anger Inventory	https://www.psycholo gistworld.com/stress /anger-test
	Anxiety self-assessment test provided by Mental Health America provides your level of anxiety	https://screening .mhanational.org /screening-tools /anxiety/
Wellbeing	The Maslach Burnout inventory measures burnout as defined by the World Health Organization (WHO) and in the ICD-11.	https://www.mind garden.com/117 -maslach-burnout -inventory-mbi
Community	The Gottman Relationship Checkup automatically scores a relationship's strengths and challenges and provides specific recommendations for intervention	https://checkup .gottman.com/
	This quiz provided by The Gottman Institute highlights elements of the "Love Map" of your partner. The Gottman Institute is the leading authority in the field of couple relationships and dedicated to combining wisdom from research and practice to support and strengthen marriages, families, and relationships.	https://www.gottman .com/how-well-do-you -know-your-partner /quiz/

Acknowledgments

I am deeply grateful to Johanne Lavoie and Amy Fox for introducing me to the field of leadership development and the ability to unlock human potential through becoming more aware of who you are and evolving your human consciousness to a higher level. Johanne is a fellow partner at McKinsey and the dean for our LMP program that has supported over 400 partners and senior partners like myself in evolving their leadership. Amy Elizabeth Fox is the founder and chief executive officer of Mobius Executive Leadership, a premier leadership firm dedicated to transformational leadership development and sustainable organizational culture change. Together, both of you helped me discover my purpose and supported me through your advice and mentorship on my journey to live it in my every day. Going through the leadership program with both of you was one of the three most transformative events in my adult life.

I am also deeply grateful to Julio Olalla and Veronica Love and coaches at Newfield Network for introducing me to the field of ontological coaching. Julio is a master coach and founder of the Newfield Network, that has provided transformational training for the last thirty years to coaches, leaders, and organizations—empowering them to authentically lead and design a new world. You helped me see our complex world with a new set of eyes and shift into new ways of being and overcome challenges. You taught me the art and science of ontological coaching to help others become better observers of themselves and discover for themselves a new set of possibilities that were not possible before.

I am grateful for my lovely wife Lizzie and my son Ashwin for supporting me in my life journey and particularly putting up with me for the last year as I put my heart and soul into researching and writing this book. Lizzie, you are my soulmate and a grounding force in my life who has always believed in me and given my dreams wings through your never-faltering support. Thank you my darling Ashwin for all your love, for blessing us with your joyous and beautiful presence, and for being a guru to me. You both are my deepest source of joy, meaning, and my teachers every day.

I am grateful to my parents who have been such wonderful role models for me from an early age on living a simple life dedicated to serving others, driving for excellence in whatever you did, showing respect, generosity, and kindness to all. You made so many sacrifices when we were growing up and gave us a solid foundation of education, stability, and a base of solid values, without which I would not have achieved the success in my life. You supported all my life choices unconditionally and stood by me with your love and blessings all my life.

Grateful to all my spiritual teachers including Sadhguru, Thich Nhat Hahn, Pema Chödrön, Sri Sri Ravishankar, Dalia Lama, Sharon Salzberg, and others for sharing your timeless wisdom over the years. In particular, I want to call out Sadhguru, who initiated me several years ago into the Shambhavi Kriya. Sadhguru is a yogi, mystic, internationally renowned speaker, and author who has dedicated his life to uplifting the physical, mental, and spiritual wellbeing of humanity. Sadhguru founded the Isha Foundation, which is dedicated to raising human consciousness, and fosters global harmony through individual transformation. Supported by eleven million volunteers in 300 centers worldwide, Isha Foundation's activities address all aspects of human wellbeing, from powerful yoga programs for inner transformation to its inspiring projects for society, environment, and education. I also wanted to thank several academics and thought leaders.

I also want to express my gratitude to the numerous academics, psychologists, neuroscientists, and authors who helped me learn so much about the human condition and how we can raise human consciousness to alleviate suffering and be happier and more effective as individuals, teams, and organizations. In particular, I would call out Martin Seligman, Brené Brown, Viktor Frankl, Clay Christensen, Lisa Feldman Barrett, Jennifer Garvey Berger, Daniel Goleman, Kristin Neff, Carol Dweck, Erica Fox, Sonja Lyubomirsky, Emma Seppala, Barbara Fredrickson, and Shawn Achor.

I am grateful to all my friends, fellow coaches, and clients over the years for all your support and love over the years. My life is richer because of all of you in it, and I am privileged to walk in this world in your fellowship.

Finally, I am so grateful to all my mentors and colleagues at McKinsey for teaching me so much about leadership, client counseling, and the art and science of individual, team, and enterprise transformations. It has been a real privilege growing and learning together over the last sixteen years. These years I spent at the firm have helped me become a better human being. I am convinced that there are very few places in the world that offer the opportunity for personal and professional growth like McKinsey.

Endnotes

1   Megan Brenan, "Americans' Mental Health Ratings Sink to New Low," Gallup, December 7, 2020, https://news.gallup.com/poll/327311/americans-mental-health-ratings-sink-new-low.aspx.

2   Marilyn J. Field and Christine K. Cassel, eds., *Approaching Death: Improving Care at the End of Life* (Washington, DC: National Academies Press, 1997), https://www.ncbi.nlm.nih.gov/books/NBK233601/.

3   "Supporting Older Patients with Chronic Conditions," National Institute on Aging (NIH), last reviewed May 27, 2017, https://www.nia.nih.gov/health/supporting-older-patients-chronic-conditions#:~:text=Approximately%2085%25%20of%20older%20adults,conditions%20is%20a%20real%20challenge.

4   Ipsos, *Loneliness and the Workplace: 2020 U.S. Report* (Edelman and Cigna, January 2020), https://www.cigna.com/static/www-cigna-com/docs/about-us/newsroom/studies-and-reports/combatting-loneliness/cigna-2020-loneliness-report.pdf.

5   Paul J. Silvia and Maureen E. O'Brien, "Self-Awareness and Constructive Functioning: Revisiting 'the Human Dilemma,'" *Journal of Social and Clinical Psychology* 23, no. 4 (August 2004): 475–489, https://doi.org/10.1521/jscp.23.4.475.40307.

6   Natalie L. Trent et al., "Improvements in Psychological and Occupational Wellbeing in a Pragmatic Controlled Trial of a Yoga-Based Program for Professionals," *The Journal of Alternative and Complementary Medicine* 25, no. 6 (June 2019): 593–605, https://doi.org/10.1089/acm.2018.0526.

7   Richard Gregory Cowden and Anna Meyer-Weitz, "Self-Reflection and Self-Insight Predict Resilience and Stress in Competitive Tennis," *Social Behavior and Personality* 44, no. 7 (2016): 1133–1149, https://doi.org/10.2224/sbp.2016.44.7.1133.

8   Christopher S. Howard and Justin A. Irving, "The Impact of Obstacles and Developmental Experiences on Resilience in Leadership Formation," *Proceedings of the American Society of Business and Behavioral Sciences* 20, no. 1 (February 2013): 679–687, http://asbbs.org/files/ASBBS2013/PDF/H/Howard_Irving(679-687).pdf.

9   Ron Carucci, "The Better You Know Yourself, the More Resilient You'll Be," *Harvard Business Review*, September 4, 2017, https://hbr.org/2017/09/the-better-you-know-yourself-the-more-resilient-youll-be.

10   Adam D. Galinsky et al., "Power and Perspectives Not Taken," *Psychological Science* 17, no. 12 (December 2006): 1068–1074, https://doi.org/10.1111/j.1467-9280.2006 .01824.x.

11   Paramahansa Yogananda, "The Eternal Nature of the Soul," Yogananda.com.au, accessed June 13, 2022, http://yogananda.com.au/gita/gita0223-25.html.

12   Tasha Eurich, "What Self-Awareness Really Is (and How to Cultivate It)," *Harvard Business Review*, January 4, 2018, https://hbr.org/2018/01/what-self-awareness -really-is-and-how-to-cultivate-it.

13   "The Frontline Leader Project," Development Dimensions International, accessed June 13, 2022, https://lp.ddiworld.com/eg/fllp.

14   "The Universal Model of Leadership," Leadership Circle, accessed June 13, 2022, https://leadershipcircle.com/en/why-leadership-circle/our-model/.

15   Natalie L. Trent et al., "Improvements in Psychological and Occupational Wellbeing in a Pragmatic Controlled Trial of a Yoga-Based Program for Professionals," *The Journal of Alternative and Complementary Medicine* 25, no. 6 (June 2019): 593–605, https://doi .org/10.1089/acm.2018.0526.

16   Richard Gregory Cowden and Anna Meyer-Weitz, "Self-Reflection and Self-Insight Predict Resilience and Stress in Competitive Tennis," *Social Behavior and Personality* 44, no. 7 (2016): 1133–1149, https://doi.org/10.2224/sbp.2016.44.7.1133.

17   Christopher S. Howard and Justin A. Irving, "The Impact of Obstacles and Develop- mental Experiences on Resilience in Leadership Formation," *Proceedings of the American Society of Business and Behavioral Sciences* 20, no. 1 (February 2013): 679–687, http://asbbs.org/files/ASBBS2013/PDF/H/Howard_Irving(679-687).pdf.

18   Monica Bigler, Greg J. Neimeyer, and Elliott Brown, "The Divided Self Revisited: Effects of Self-Concept Clarity and Self-Concept Differentiation on Psychological Adjustment," *Journal of Social and Clinical Psychology* 20, no. 3 (September 2001): 396–415, https://doi.org/10.1521/jscp.20.3.396.22302; Shelley A. Fahlman et al., "Does a Lack of Life Meaning Cause Boredom? Results from Psychometric, Longitud- inal, and Experimental Analyses," *Journal of Social and Clinical Psychology* 28, no. 3 (March 2009): 307–340, https://doi.org/10.1521/jscp.2009.28.3.307.

19   "Economic News Release: Job Openings and Labor Turnover Summary—April 2022," economic news release, U.S. Bureau of Labor Statistics, last modified June 1, 2022, https://www.bls.gov/news.release/jolts.nr0.htm.

20   Viktor E. Frankl, *Man's Search for Ultimate Meaning* (New York: Basic Books, 2000).

21   Kozo Tanno et al., "Associations of Ikigai as a Positive Psychological Factor with All-Cause Mortality and Cause-Specific Mortality among Middle-aged and Elderly

Japanese People: Findings from the Japan Collaborative Cohort Study," *Journal of Psychosomatic Research* 67, no. 1 (July 2009): 67–75, doi: 10.1016/j.jpsychores .2008.10.018.

22   Patrick L. Hill and Nicholas A. Turiano, "Purpose in Life as a Predictor of Mortality across Adulthood," *Psychological Science* 25, no. 7 (July 2014): 1482–1486, https:// doi.org/10.1177/0956797614531799.

23   Patricia A. Boyle, Aron S. Buchman, Lisa L. Barnes, and David A. Bennett, "Effect of a Purpose in Life on Risk of Incident Alzheimer Disease and Mild Cognitive Impairment in Community-Dwelling Older Persons," *Archives of General Psychiatry* 67, no 3 (March 2010): 304–310, doi: 10.1001/archgenpsychiatry.2009.208.

24   Nancy DiFiore, "Purpose in Life May Help Aging Brain," *Rush Stories* (blog), Rush University, accessed June 13, 2022, https://www.rush.edu/news/purpose-life-may -help-aging-brain.

25   Valéria M. Almeida, Cátia Carvalho, and M. Graça Pereira, (2019). "The Contribution of Purpose in Life to Psychological Morbidity and Quality of Life in Chronic Pain Patients," *Psychology, Health & Medicine.* 25, no 3 (February 2020): 1–11, doi: 10.1080/13548506.2019.1665189.

26   Monica Bigler, Greg J. Neimeyer, and Elliott Brown, "The Divided Self Revisited: Effects of Self-Concept Clarity and Self-Concept Differentiation on Psychological Adjustment," *Journal of Social and Clinical Psychology* 20, no. 3 (September 2001): 396–415, https://doi.org/10.1521/jscp.20.3.396.22302.

27   Patrick L. Hill et al., "The Value of a Purposeful Life: Sense of Purpose Predicts Greater Income and Net Worth," *Journal of Research in Personality* 65 (December 2016): 38–42, https://doi.org/10.1016/j.jrp.2016.07.003.

28   Ken Mogi, *The Little Book of Ikigai* (London: Quercus Publishing, 2017), 1–10.

29   Naina Dhingra et al., "Help Your Employees Find Purpose—or Watch Them Leave," *McKinsey Quarterly*, April 5, 2021, https://www.mckinsey.com/business-functions /organization/our-insights/help-your-employees-find-purpose-or-watch-them -leave.

30   Bill Burnett and Dave Evans, "Designing Your Life: How to Build a Well-Lived, Joyful Life," Creative Live, accessed June 13, 2022, https://www.creativelive.com /class/designing-your-life-how-to-build-a-well-lived-joyful-life-bill-burnett -dave-evans.

31   Matthew A. Killingsworth and Daniel T. Gilbert, "A Wandering Mind Is an Unhappy Mind," *Science* 330, no. 6006 (November 12, 2010): 932, https://doi.org/10.1126 /science.1192439.

32   "More Adults and Children Are Using Yoga and Meditation," National Center for Complementary and Integrative Health, November 8, 2018, https://www.nccih.nih .gov/news/press-releases/more-adults-and-children-are-using-yoga-and -meditation.

33   Richard J. Davidson et al., "Alterations in Brain and Immune Function Produced by Mindfulness Meditation," *Psychosomatic Medicine* 65, no. 4 (July 2003): 564–570, https://doi.org/10.1097/01.PSY.0000077505.67574.E3.

34   Kieran C. R. Fox et al., "Is Meditation Associated with Altered Brain Structure? A Systematic Review and Meta-Analysis of Morphometric Neuroimaging in Mediation Practitioners," *Neuroscience and Biobehavioral Reviews* 43 (June 2014): 48–73, https://doi.org/10.1016/j.neubiorev.2014.03.016.

35   Sara W. Lazar et al., "Meditation Experience Is Associated with Increased Cortical Thickness," *NeuroReport* 16, no. 17 (November 2005): 1893–1897, https://doi.org/10 .1097/01.wnr.0000186598.66243.19.

36   Steven W. Kennerley et al., "Optimal Decision Making and the Anterior Cingulate Cortex," *Nature Neuroscience* 9, no. 7 (July 2006): 940–947, https://doi.org/10.1038 /nn1724.

37   Britta K. Hölzel et al., "Differential Engagement of Anterior Cingulate and Adjacent Medial Frontal Cortex in Adept Mediators and Non-Meditators," *Neuroscience Letters* 421, no. 1 (June 2007): 16–21, https://doi.org/10.1016/j.neulet.2007.04.074.

38   Adrienne A. Taren et al., "Mindfulness Meditation Training Alters Stress-Related Amygdala Resting State Functional Connectivity," *Social Cognitive and Affective Neuroscience* 10, no. 12 (December 2015): 1758–1768, https://doi.org/10.1093/scan /nsv066; Adrienne A. Taren, J. David Creswell, and Peter J. Gianaros, "Dispositional Mindfulness Co-Varies with Smaller Amygdala and Caudate Volumes in Community Adults," *PLoS One* 8, no. 5 (May 2013): e64574, https://doi.org/10.1371/journal.pone .0064574.

39   Britta K. Hölzel et al., "Mindfulness Practice Leads to Increases in Regional Brain Gray Matter Density," *Psychiatry Research: Neuroimaging* 191, no. 1 (January 2011): 36–43, https://doi.org/10.1016/j.pscychresns.2010.08.006.

40   F. Zeidan et al., "Mindfulness Meditation-Related Pain Relief: Evidence for Unique Brain Mechanisms in the Regulations of Pain," *Neuroscience Letters* 520, no. 2 (June 2012): 165–173, https://doi.org/10.1016/j.neulet.2012.03.082.

41   Christian Greiser and Jan-Philipp Martini, "How Companies Can Instill Mindfulness," *Knowledge at Wharton*, April 19, 2018, https://knowledge.wharton.upenn.edu/article /how-companies-can-instill-mindfulness/.

42　Alice Gomstyn, "Tips from Successful Executives on How to Practice Mindfulness at Work," *Aetna* (blog), accessed June 13, 2022, https://www.aetna.com/health-guide /yes-can-stop-multi-tasking-successful-executives-share-mindfulness-secrets.html.

43　Jon Kabat-Zinn, *Full Catastrophe Living: How to Cope with Stress, Pain and Illness Using Mindfulness Meditation* (London: Piatkus, 2004), 32.

44　Julie Tseng and Jordan Poppenk, "Brain Meta-State Transitions Demarcate Thoughts across Task Contexts Exposing the Mental Noise of Trait Neuroticism," *Nature Communications* 11, no. 1 (July 2020): 3480, https://doi.org/10.1038/s41467-020 -17255-9.

45　Trevor Wheelwright, "2022 Cell Phone Usage Statistics: How Obsessed Are We?" Reviews.org, January 24, 2022, https://www.reviews.org/mobile/cell-phone -addiction/#2021_Cell_Phone_Behavior.

46　Casey Yzquierdo, "The Physiology of Art: The Effect of Coloring on Blood Pressure and Heart Rate as Measures of Stress," (Unpublished thesis, Texas State University, San Marcos, Texas, 2019).

47　Carol H. DeLue, "Physiological Effects of Creating Mandalas," in *Medical Art Therapy with Children*, ed. Cathy A. Malchiodi (London: Jessica Kingsley Publishers, 1999), 33–49.

48　Thich Nhat Hanh, *Peace Is Every Step: The Path of Mindfulness in Everyday Life*, ed. Arnold Kotler (New York: Bantam Books, 1991), 28.

49　Bob Stahl and Elisha Goldstein, *A Mindfulness-Based Stress Reduction Workbook* (Oakland: New Harbinger Publications, 2010), 60–61.

50　Robert Emmons, "Why Gratitude Is Good," *Greater Good Magazine*, November 16, 2010, https://greatergood.berkeley.edu/article/item/why_gratitude_is_good.

51　Emmons, "Why Gratitude Is Good."

52　Joel Wong and Joshua Brown in 2017 at Indiana University studied how gratitude affects us mentally and physically. They assigned students to three groups, each of which was also receiving counseling. Group 1 wrote a gratitude letter to another person every day for three weeks. Group 2 wrote about their thoughts and feelings about negative experiences. Group 3 was not asked to write anything. They found members from Group 1 reported significantly better mental health four and twelve weeks after the writing intervention ended. Y. Joel Wong et al., "Does Gratitude Writing Improve the Mental Health of Psychotherapy Clients? Evidence from a Randomized Controlled Trial," *Psychotherapy Research* 28, no. 2 (March 2018): 192–202, https://doi.org/10.1080/10503307.2016.1169332. Another 2006 study in behavior research and therapy found war veterans with high levels of gratitude experienced lower rates of PTSD. Todd B. Kashdan, Gitendra Uswatte, and Terri Julian, "Gratitude and Hedonic and Eudaimonic Wellbeing in Vietnam War Veterans," *Behaviour Research and Therapy* 44, no. 2 (February 2006): 177–199, https://doi.org/10.1016/j.brat.2005.01.005.

53 Bartlett and DeSteano found in 2006 a positive relationship between prosocial behavior (willingness to help others and kindness) and gratitude. Monica Y. Bartlett and David DeSteno, "Gratitude and Prosocial Behavior: Helping When It Costs You," *Psychological Science* 17, no. 4 (May 2006): 319–325, https://doi.org/10.1111/j.1467 -9280.2006.01705.x. This is not just limited to humans, but also across all species including primates. Research done by Dickens and DeStefano in 2018 found an association between self-control and gratitude. Leah Dickens and David DeSteno, "The Grateful Are Patient: Heightened Daily Gratitude Is Associated with Attenuated Temporal Discounting," *Emotion* 16, no. 4 (June 2016): 421–425, https://doi. org/10.1037/emo0000176.

54 Charles Darwin, *The Expression of the Emotions in Man and Animals* (London: John Murray, Albemarle Street, 1872).

55 Brittany Cohen-Brown, "Do Chimpanzees Know How to Say or Show 'Thank You'?" *Jane Goodall's Good for All News*, November 25, 2018, https://news.janegoodall .org/2018/11/25/chimpanzees-know-say-show-thank/.

56 Adam Hoffman, "What Does a Grateful Brain Look Like?" *Greater Good Magazine*, November 16, 2015, https://greatergood.berkeley.edu/article/item/what_does_a _grateful_brain_look_like; Glenn R. Fox et al., "Neural Correlates of Gratitude," *Frontiers in Psychology* 6, no. 1491 (September 2015), https://doi.org/10.3389/fpsyg .2015.01491.

57 Joseph Chamie, "As Cities Grow, So Do the Numbers of Homeless," *YaleGlobal Online*, July 13, 2017, https://archive-yaleglobal.yale.edu/content/cities-grow-so-do -numbers-homeless.

58 Helen Keller, "Three Days to See," *The Atlantic Monthly* 151, no. 1 (January 1933): 35–42, https://www.theatlantic.com/past/docs/issues/33jan/keller.htm.

59 Martin E. P. Seligman et al., "Positive Psychology Progress: Empirical Validation of Interventions," *American Psychologist* 60, no. 5 (July–August 2005): 410–421, https://doi.org/10.1037/0003-066X.60.5.410.

60 Regina F. Lark, "Are There 300,000 Things in a Home?" *A Clear Path* (blog), accessed June 21, 2022, https://aclearpath.net/are-there-300000-things-in-a-home/.

61 Joshua Becker, "Why We Buy More Than We Need," *Forbes*, November 27, 2018, https://www.forbes.com/sites/joshuabecker/2018/11/27/why-we-buy-more-than -we-need/?sh=30abd2af6417.

62 Joseph Chancellor and Sonja Lyubomirsky, "Money for Happiness: The Hedonic Benefits of Thrift," in *Consumption and Wellbeing in the Material World*, ed. Miriam Tatzel (Dordrecht: Springer, 2014), 13–47, https://doi.org/10.1007/978-94-007-7368-4_2.

63 Daniel Kahneman and Angus Deaton, "High Income Improves Evaluation of Life but Not Emotional Wellbeing," *Proceedings of the National Academy of Sciences* 107, no. 38 (September 2010): 16489–16493, https://doi.org/10.1073/pnas.1011492107.

64 Jeffrey J. Froh et al., "Interpersonal Relationships and Irrationality as Predictors of Life Satisfaction," *The Journal of Positive Psychology* 2, no. 1 (2007): 29–39, https://doi.org/10.1080/17439760601069051.

65 Sonja Lyubomirsky, "Hedonic Adaptation to Positive and Negative Experiences," in *The Oxford Handbook of Stress, Health, and Coping*, ed. Susan Folkman (New York: Oxford University Press, 2011), 200–224.

66 Jon Simpson, "Finding Brand Success in the Digital World," *Forbes*, August 25, 2017, https://www.forbes.com/sites/forbesagencycouncil/2017/08/25/finding-brand-success-in-the-digital-world/?sh=5ec2266b626e.

67 Barbara Jacquelyn Sahakian, Christelle Langley, and Muzaffer Kaser, "How Chronic Stress Changes the Brain—and What You Can Do to Reverse the Damage," The Conversation, March 11, 2020, https://theconversation.com/how-chronic-stress-changes-the-brain-and-what-you-can-do-to-reverse-the-damage-133194.

68 Baljinder Kaur Sahdra, Phillip R. Shaver, and Kirk Warren Brown, "A Scale to Measure Nonattachment: A Buddhist Complement to Western Research on Attachment and Adaptive Functioning," *Journal of Personality Assessment* 92, no. 2 (March 2010): 116–127, https://doi.org/10.1080/00223890903425960.

69 Baljinder K. Sahdra et al., "Empathy and Nonattachment Independently Predict Peer Nominations of Prosocial Behavior of Adolescents," *Frontiers in Psychology* 6, no. 263 (March 2015), https://doi.org/10.3389/fpsyg.2015.00263; Richard Whitehead et al., "Nonattachment Mediates the Relationship between Mindfulness and Psychological Wellbeing, Subjective Wellbeing, and Depression, Anxiety and Stress," *Journal of Happiness Studies* 20, no. 1 (October 2019): 2141–2158, https://doi.org/10.1007/s10902-018-0041-9.

70 Yoichi Chida and Andrew Steptoe, "The Association of Anger and Hostility with Future Coronary Heart Disease: A Meta-Analytic Review of Prospective Evidence," *Journal of the American College of Cardiology* 53, no. 11 (March 2009): 936–946, https://doi.org/10.1016/j.jacc.2008.11.044.

71 Loren L. Toussaint, Everett L. Worthington Jr., and David R. Williams, eds., *Forgiveness and Health: Scientific Evidence and Theories Relating Forgiveness to Better Health* (Dordrecht: Springer, 2015).

72 Sarah N. Garfinkel et al., "Anger in Brain and Body: The Neural and Physiological Perturbation of Decision-Making by Emotion," *Social Cognitive and Affective Neuroscience* 11, no. 1 (January 2016): 150–158, https://doi.org/10.1093/scan/nsv099; Relly Nadler, "Where Did My IQ Points Go," *Psychology Today*, April 29, 2011, https://www.psychologytoday.com/us/blog/leading-emotional-intelligence /201104/where-did-my-iq-points-go.

73 David H. Barlow, *Anxiety and Its Disorders, Second Edition: The Nature and Treatment of Anxiety and Panic* (New York: The Guilford Press, 2002), 6–7.

74 "Facts and Statistics," Anxiety and Depression Association of America (ADAA), accessed June 21, 2022, https://adaa.org/understanding-anxiety/facts-statistics.

75 "Physical Activity Reduces Stress," ADAA, accessed July 21, 2022, https://adaa.org/understanding-anxiety/related-illnesses/other-related-conditions /stress/physical-activity-reduces-st.

76 Inspired by Edmund J. Bourne, *The Anxiety and Phobia Workbook* (Oakland: New Harbinger Publications, 1990), 70–74.

77 Felix Warneken and Michael Tomasello, "Varieties of Altruism in Children and Chimpanzees," *Trends in Cognitive Sciences* 13, no. 9 (September 2009): 397–402, https://doi.org/10.1016/j.tics.2009.06.008.

78 Inbal Ben-Ami Bartal, Jean Decety, and Peggy Mason, "Empathy and Pro-Social Behavior in Rats," *Science* 334, no. 6061 (December 2011): 1427–1430, https://doi.org/10.1126/science.1210789.

79 Helen Y. Weng et al., "Visual Attention to Suffering after Compassion Training Is Associated with Decreased Amygdala Responses," *Frontiers in Psychology* 9, no. 771 (May 2018), https://doi.org/10.3389/fpsyg.2018.00771.

80 Emma Seppala, "Compassionate Mind, Healthy Body," *Greater Good Magazine*, July 24, 2013, https://greatergood.berkeley.edu/article/item/compassionate _mind_healthy_body.

81 Michael J. Poulin et al., "Giving to Others and the Association between Stress and Mortality," *American Journal of Public Health* 103, no. 9 (September 2013): 1649–1655, https://doi.org/10.2105/AJPH.2012.300876.

82 David C. McClelland and Carol Kirshnit, "The Effect of Motivational Arousal through Films on Salivary Immunoglobulin A," *Psychology and Health* 2, no. 1 (1988): 31–52, https://doi.org/10.1080/08870448808400343.

83 Haesung Jung et al., "Prosocial Modeling: A Meta-Analytic Review and Synthesis," *Psychological Bulletin* 146, no. 8 (May 2020): 635–663, https://doi.org/10.1037 /bul0000235.

84 Lara B. Aknin et al., "Prosocial Spending and Wellbeing: Cross-Cultural Evidence for a Psychological Universal," *Journal of Personality and Social Psychology* 104, no. 4 (April 2013): 635–652, https://doi.org/10.1037/a0031578.

85 Lee Rowland and Oliver Scott Curry, "A Range of Kindness Activities Boost Happiness," *The Journal of Social Psychology* 159, no. 3 (2019): 340–343, https://doi.org/10.1080/00224545.2018.1469461.

86 Kathryn E. Buchanan and Anat Bardi, "Acts of Kindness and Acts of Novelty Affect Life Satisfaction," *The Journal of Social Psychology* 150, no. 3 (2010): 235–237, https://doi.org/10.1080/00224540903365554.

87 Jill Suttie, "How Kindness Fits into a Happy Life," *Greater Good Magazine*, February 17, 2021, https://greatergood.berkeley.edu/article/item/how_kindness_fits_into_a _happy_life.

88 Mental Health America (MHA), *Spotlight 2021: COVID-19 and Mental Health* (2021).

89 The term *ayurveda* is derived from the Sanskrit words of "ayur" (life) and "veda" (science).

90 Dan Buettner and Sam Skemp, "Blue Zones: Lessons from the World's Longest Lived," *American Journal of Lifestyle Medicine* 10, no. 5 (September 2016): 318–321, https://doi.org/10.1177/1559827616637066.

91 Emily N. Ussery et al., "Joint Prevalence of Sitting Time and Leisure-Time Physical Activity among US Adults, 2015–2016," *JAMA* 320, no. 19 (2018): 2036–2038, https://doi.org/10.1001/jama.2018.17797.

92 E. G. Wilmot et al., "Sedentary Time in Adults and the Association with Diabetes, Cardiovascular Disease and Death: Systematic Review and Meta-Analysis," *Diabetologia* 55, no. 11 (November 2012): 2895–2905, https://doi.org/10.1007/s00125-012-2677-z.

93 "About Chronic Diseases," National Center for Chronic Disease Prevention and Health Promotion (NCCDPHP), U.S. Centers for Disease Control and Prevention, last modified May 6, 2022, https://www.cdc.gov/chronicdisease/about/index.htm.

94 Esther Molina-Montes et al., "The Impact of Plant-Based Dietary Patterns on Cancer-Related Outcomes: A Rapid Review and Meta-Analysis," *Nutrients*, no 12 (7) (July 6, 2020), https://doi.org/10.3390/nu12072010.

95 Hyunju Kim et al., "Plant-Based Diets Are Associated with a Lower Risk of Incident Cardiovascular Disease, Cardiovascular Disease Mortality, and All-Cause Mortality in a General Population of Middle-Aged Adults," *Journal of the American Heart Association* 8, no. 16 (August 2019): e012865, https://doi.org/10.1161/JAHA.119.012865.

96 Jeffrey M. Jones, "In U.S., 40% Get Less Than Recommended Amount of Sleep," Gallup, December 19, 2013, https://news.gallup.com/poll/166553/less-recommended-amount-sleep.aspx.

97 Yasmin Anwar, "Poor Sleep Linked to Toxic Buildup of Alzheimer's Protein, Memory Loss," Berkeley News, June 1, 2015, https://news.berkeley.edu/2015/06/01/alzheimers-protein-memory-loss/.

98 Trevor Wheelwright, "2022 Cell Phone Usage Statistics: How Obsessed Are We?" Reviews.org, January 24, 2022, https://www.reviews.org/mobile/cell-phone-addiction/#2021_Cell_Phone_Behavior.

99 "The Brain Cannot Multitask," Brain Rules, March 16, 2008, http://brainrules.blogspot.com/2008/03/brain-cannot-multitask_16.html.

100 John Naish, "Is Multi-Tasking Bad for Your Brain? Experts Reveal the Hidden Perils of Juggling Too Many Jobs," *Daily Mail*, August 11, 2009, https://www.dailymail.co.uk/health/article-1205669/Is-multi-tasking-bad-brain-Experts-reveal-hidden-perils-juggling-jobs.html; Peter Bregman, "How (and Why) to Stop Multitasking," *Harvard Business Review*, May 20, 2010, https://hbr.org/2010/05/how-and-why-to-stop-multitaski.

101 Jacques Launay and Eiluned Pearce, "Choir Singing Improves Health, Happiness—And Is the Perfect Icebreaker," *The Conversation*, October 28, 2015, https://theconversation.com/choir-singing-improves-health-happiness-and-is-the-perfect-icebreaker-47619.

102 Daniel A. Cox, "The State of American Friendship: Change, Challenges, and Loss," Survey Center on American Life, American Enterprise Institute, June 8, 2021, https://www.americansurveycenter.org/research/the-state-of-american-friendship-change-challenges-and-loss/.

103 Robert Waldinger, "What Makes a Good Life? Lessons from the Longest Study on Happiness," presented at TEDxBeaconStreet, December 2015, TED video, 12:38, https://www.ted.com/talks/robert_waldinger_what_makes_a_good_life_lessons_from_the_longest_study_on_happiness?language=en.

104 Julianne Holt-Lunstad et al., "Loneliness and Social Isolation as Risk Factors for Mortality: A Meta-Analytic Review," *Perspectives on Psychological Science* 10, no. 2 (March 2015): 227–237, https://doi.org/10.1177/1745691614568352.

105 Mark S. Granovetter, "The Strength of Weak Ties," *American Journal of Sociology* 78, no. 6 (May 1973): 1360–1380, https://doi.org/10.1086/225469.

106 Ronald S. Burt, Martin Kilduff, and Stefano Tasselli, "Social Network Analysis: Foundations and Frontiers on Advantage," *Annual Review of Psychology* 64, no. 1 (January 2013): 527–547, https://doi.org/10.1146/annurev-psych-113011-143828.

107 Dennis Lynn, "Six Traits of Strong Families," *Synergies*, Oregon State University, November 20, 2018, https://synergies.oregonstate.edu/2018/six-qualities -of-strong-families-2/.

108 John Gottman, *Why Marriages Succeed or Fail* (New York: Simon and Schuster, 1994), 29.

109 Gottman, *Why Marriages Succeed or Fail*, 72–93.

110 Jeffrey A Hall, "How Many Hours Does It Take to Make a Friend?" *Journal of Social and Personal Relationships* 36, no. 4 (April 2019): 1278–1296, https://doi.org/10.1177 /0265407518761225.

111 *Oxford Essential Quotations*, 6th ed., ed. Susan Ratcliffe (Oxford: Oxford University Press, 2018), s.v. "Joel Arthur Barker," https://www.oxfordreference.com/view /10.1093/acref/9780191866692.001.0001/q-oro-ed6-00011987?rskey=c9uXeS& result=252.

112 Inspired by the iceberg coaching model used by Aberkyn, the coaching arm of McKinsey.

113 Reader's Digest Association, *Quotable Quotes: Wit and Wisdom for Every Occasion* (New York: Reader's Digest, 1997).

114 Albert Bandura and Dale H. Schunk, "Cultivating Competence, Self-Efficacy and Intrinsic Interest through Proximal Self-Motivation," *Journal of Personality and Social Psychology* 41, no. 3 (1981): 586–598, https://doi.org/10.1037/0022-3514.41.3.586.

115 George T. Doran, "There's A S.M.A.R.T. Way to Write Management's Goals and Objectives," *Management Review* 70, no. 11 (November 1981): 35–36.

116 E. Tory Higgins, "Beyond Pleasure and Pain," *American Psychologist* 52, no. 12 (January 1998): 1280–1300, https://doi.org/10.1037/0003-066X.52.12.1280; Richard E. Boyatzis, Kylie Rochford, and Scott N. Taylor, "The Role of the Positive Emotional Attractor in Vision and Shared Vision: Toward Effective Leadership, Relationships, and Engagement," *Frontiers in Psychology* 6, no. 670 (2015), https://doi.org/10.3389/fpsyg.2015.00670.

117 Carol S. Dweck, *Self-Theories: Their Role in Motivation, Personality, and Development* (New York: Psychology Press, 2000), 15–19.

118 Barrett Wissman, "An Accountability Partner Makes You Vastly More Likely to Succeed," *Entrepreneur*, March 20, 2018, https://www.entrepreneur.com/article /310062.

119 David T. Neal, Wendy Wood, and Jeffrey M. Quinn, "Habits—A Repeat Performance," *Current Directions in Psychological Science* 15, no. 4 (August 2006), https://doi.org /10.1111/j.1467-8721.2006.00435.x.

120   Octavia E. Butler, "Furor Scribendi," in *Bloodchild and Other Stories: Second Edition* (New York: Seven Stories Press, 2005), 141.

121   Charles Duhigg, *The Power of Habit: Why We Do What We Do in Life and Business* (New York: Random House Trade Paperbacks, 2014).

122   B. J. Fogg, *Tiny Habits: The Small Changes That Change Everything* (New York: Mariner Books, 2020).

Index

Note: Page numbers followed by f represents figure.